Mirth Making

Studies in Rhetoric/Communication

Thomas W. Benson, Series Editor

Mirth Making

The Rhetorical
Discourse on
Jesting in Early
Modern England

―――――

Chris Holcomb

University of South Carolina Press

UNIVERSITY OF SOUTH CAROLINA *BICENTENNIAL*

© 2001 University of South Carolina

Published in Columbia, South Carolina, by the
University of South Carolina Press

Manufactured in the United States of America

05 04 03 02 01   5 4 3 2 1

Library of Congress Cataloging-in-Publication Data

Holcomb, Chris.
   Mirth making : the rhetorical discourse on jesting in early modern England /
Chris Holcomb.
     p. cm. — (Studies in rhetoric/communication)
   Includes bibliographical references (p.) and index.
   ISBN 1-57003-397-8 (alk. paper)
   1. English wit and humor—History and criticism. 2. Oral communication—
England—History—16th century. 3. Oral communication—England—History—
17th century. 4. English language—Early modern, 1500–1700—Rhetoric.
5. Courtesy books—England—History—16th century. 6. Courtesy books—
England—History—17th century. 7. Jestbooks, English—History and criticism.
8. Courts and courtiers in literature. 9. Rhetoric, Renaissance—England. 10. Fools
and jesters in literature. I. Title. II. Series.
   PR933 .H65 2001
   808.7—dc21   00-012175

Portions of "A Man in a Painted Garment: The Social Functions of Jesting
in Elizabethan Rhetoric and Courtesy Manuals," *Humor* 13 (2000): 429–55,
appear in slightly different form in this study.

Contents

Contents

Series Editor's Preface

In *Mirth Making: The Rhetorical Discourse of Jesting in Early Modern England,* Chris Holcomb tells the story of English courtesy and rhetoric manuals as complex cultural balancing acts tuned to a changing historical context. Jesting was seen as an essential persuasive tool for communicating across differences of culture, class, and status, but a tool whose effects were difficult to predict and control and whose misuse might prompt rhetorical failure and social disorder. Social difference, argues Professor Holcomb, may be seen as the circumstance giving rise to jesting, as the subject matter of jests, and as the problem that jesting may regulate. The authors of rhetorical manuals described jesting as arising from situations to which a speaker must adapt, but they also proposed that jesting could manage or even change situations. Whereas ancient rhetorics understood jesting as a means to ridicule a rival of equal rank and status, the manuals of early modern England also described jesting that regulated the relations of preachers and their lay audiences or courtiers and their princes—relations that produced new purposes, new risks, and a new decorum.

At a time when the rhetoric of jesting was being rewritten, the early modern rhetoricians—who differed among themselves on the propriety of jesting—implicitly agreed that the choice of whether to jest depended on situation (church, court) and on social identity (of the speaker, the audience, and the target of the jest). Hence the stability of the situation and of the subject, which are often explicitly affirmed, are implicitly revealed in Professor Holcomb's reading to be contingent on the judgments and words of others. The affirmation of stability that is so often the point of a jest depends, Holcomb demonstrates, on the simultaneous acknowledgment of ambiguity, instability, and potential disorder.

In adapting the classical rhetorical models to their own ends, early modern manual writers developed a topical guide to the invention of jests, training in which would give rise to a seemingly spontaneous command of appropriate jests. The tension between the spontaneous and the planned is paralleled by a tension between serious argument (for which the topical system was developed) and the advice given about jesting, which came to include not only a system of topics but also figures of speech and thought as well as "disruptive conversational gambits," thus straining the structure of rhetorical theory itself and again revealing the transfiguring potential of mirth.

In defending the use of jests, the manual writers acknowledged that others questioned its propriety. Holcomb finds in the manuals a complex defense of jesting that also explores its risks of failure through the selection of inappropriate targets, obscurity, or inadequate performance. All of these risks reflect the changing social conditions of the period and thus acknowledge the historically contingent quality of jesting and of the manuals themselves.

Holcomb finds in the manuals of rhetoric a complex and nuanced understanding of the social identity of the speaker, the audience, and the subject of jesting. The orator or courtier engaging in jesting was at risk of seeming to be a mere buffoon—a recognized social and theatrical type. Speakers and their audiences were understood to be in conflict, with the speaker bearing an inherent obligation and a theoretical potential to sway the audience's mind and body. But the audience was capable of resisting, either through the inattention and stupidity of a dull public or through the unwillingness of a superior to be moved to laughter by an inferior courtier. And yet even here there were additional risks, since the unresponsive public might declare its superiority by resisting, just as an unresponsive prince might declare his dullness by failing to get the joke.

Chris Holcomb's *Mirth Making* is a scrupulous and compelling analysis of the social and cultural ambiguities of the rhetoric of jesting in a time of rapid historical change.

Thomas W. Benson

Acknowledgments

Writing a book, like telling a joke, is a social event: the completion of both depends greatly on the responses of others, whether in the form of appreciative laughter or in the thoughtful and constructive feedback of readers. In its earlier stages, this book benefited enormously from the contributions of Richard Cherwitz, Linda Fierra-Buckley, James L. Kinneavy, Frank Whigham, and especially Wayne A. Rebhorn, who was untiring in his support of my work. I also owe many thanks to my colleagues at Texas A&M University: Valerie Balester, Marian Eide, Craig Kallendorf, Howard Marchitello, J. Lawrence Mitchell, Mary Ann O'Farrell, Christopher Renshaw, James Rosenheim, and Susan Stabile. I owe particular thanks to Anne Lake Prescott for her invaluable reading of the manuscript; Thomas W. Benson, editor of the series in which the book appears; and Barry Blose at the University of South Carolina Press. James Butrica was very generous in sharing portions of his working translation of *Ecclesiastae,* which will appear in the University of Toronto Press's ongoing series Collected Works of Erasmus. Above all, I would like to thank my good friend and colleague M. Jimmie Killingsworth, who encouraged me to pursue this project and helped me carry it through to its completion. I am also grateful to Jimmie's daughter, Myrth, who inspired the book's title.

Introduction

Jesting is a neglected subject in historical studies of rhetoric. Its neglect, however, cannot be attributed to a lack of discussions in the rhetorical treatises themselves. From antiquity into the nineteenth century, many rhetoricians viewed jesting as part, oftentimes an important part, of rhetoric. It would take a lifetime, and perhaps then some, to chase down every rhetoric manual from antiquity forward that includes a discussion of jesting, but the subject is addressed by writers whose works have come to constitute the canon of historical rhetoric, including Aristotle, Cicero, Quintilian, Robert of Basevorn, Thomas Wilson, George Puttenham, Francis Bacon, George Campbell, and Richard Whately.[1] Given this partial but impressive list, why have historians of rhetoric all but ignored jesting?[2] This is a difficult question to answer, but perhaps its neglect results, at least in part, from a belief that jesting is a trivial matter not worthy of scholarly attention. This notion has become something of a commonplace in our own time, and the titles of several recent studies of humor—such as John Morreal's *Taking Laughter Seriously* and Jerry Palmer's *Taking Humor Seriously*—allude to it while trying to reverse its valence. Or perhaps jesting has been largely overlooked because the idea of an art of jesting (that is, something that can be reduced to a set of teachable prescriptions) seems strange to those who think it is a spontaneous, natural talent that cannot be cultivated by formal instruction. Cicero and several of his imitators raise this objection. Apparently, though, they were little troubled by it, for after raising the question of whether or not jesting could be taught, they go on to offer what amounts to an art of jesting.[3] Another possible and closely related reason for its neglect might be the fact that interest in humor has disappeared from modern rhetoric curricula. When the rhetorical tradition was resuscitated in the 1960s and 1970s, and arguments were advanced for its relevance to the modern classroom, it seems that humor was left for dead, unlike invention, arrangement, and style, which receive wide coverage in both contemporary handbooks and histories of rhetoric.[4] Even in the 1980s and 1990s, when calls were going out for rethinking and revising histories of rhetoric, jesting was still overlooked.[5] Whatever the reasons for its neglect, one thing remains clear: a discrepancy exists between the subject's absence in histories of rhetoric and its persistence in the treatises about which those histories are written.[6]

This study takes a step toward restoring this important and vital communicative strategy to historical studies of rhetoric. Focusing on the English Renaissance—a brief but crucial phase in the history of the rhetorical discourse on jesting—I examine the complex and often contradictory ways in which early modern writers of rhetoric and courtesy manuals characterize the operation of jesting in specific situations. Moreover, I show how these characterizations point to and participate in broader cultural issues and debates that were central to early modern England. In its most general formulation, the discourse on jesting in the period is about communication between different kinds of people—between preachers and their lay congregations, ambassadors and foreign dignitaries, masters and servants, nobles and tradesmen, courtiers and kings. This formulation distinguishes such discourse from its classical and medieval sources and locates it squarely within its own historical context. It also sums up one of the principal challenges early modern writers confronted while trying to capture, explain, and teach a rhetorical strategy that is both powerful and chaotic, elusive and ubiquitous, highly economical in form and potentially unpredictable in effect. The manuals celebrate jesting as a powerful strategy for communicating across social difference, but they also fear that, precisely because of its power, jesting may go out of control and release energies not only damaging to a speaker's immediate persuasive aims, but also disruptive of the boundaries and distinctions that ought to be preserved when different kinds of people occupy the same social space. To ensure that it remains under control and within bounds, the manuals deploy a number of recuperative strategies to regulate a speaker's jesting and rein in its potentially volatile and chaotic energies. While many of these strategies are pragmatic in intent and seek to govern the rhetorical dynamics of a local jesting exchange, they nevertheless embody a conservative ideology and require speakers to jest only in ways that maintain the status quo—that is, preserve social relations already in place prior to a jesting exchange. As the manuals themselves reveal, however, jesting secures its effects through ambiguity, contradiction, duplicity, and other linguistic and rhetorical strategies that upset the conventions and proprieties normally governing serious, nonjesting communicative exchanges. Moreover, situations in which different kinds of people interact are primed for inversions and reversals of all sorts. In many instances, the humor in such interaction depends on these inversions and reversals; without them, there would be no jest to speak of. For these reasons, jesting often eludes or exceeds prescription and thus resists the manuals' efforts to restrict and limit its use. Jesting, in short, is always a flirtation with disorder.

The Early Modern Jest
A Paradigm for Rhetorical and Courtly Communication

Early modern rhetoric and courtesy manuals are obsessed with jesting. Not only do many of them include discussions of the practice and claim jesting as an essential component of an orator's or courtier's repertoire of rhetorical strategies, but they also frequently resort to jests and humorous anecdotes to serve other purposes as well. In addition to its lengthy treatment of wit and laughter, Castiglione's *Book of the Courtier* (1528, 1561) is peppered with jests and witty sayings used to illustrate more general points about good courtiership—often through negative examples. While warning against the dangers of self-praise, for instance, one of Castiglione's interlocutors, Count Lodovico, tells of a braggart who refused to own a mirror "because in hys rage he was so terrible to beholde, that in lookynge upon his owne countenaunce he should put himself into much fear" (51). George Puttenham's *Arte of English Poesie* (1589) also employs many funny stories in its treatment of decorum to distinguish appropriate from inappropriate forms of speech and behavior at court. In one of these, an ambassador delivers a long and tedious report to a king who, after enduring the hearing of it and then being asked for his comment, says, "The first part of your tale was so long, that I remember it not, which made that the second I understoode not, and as for the third part I doe nothing well allow of."[7] According to Stefano Guazzo's *Civile Conversation* (1574, 1581), "a certaine wittie and readie pleasantnesse" is "verie necessary in Conversation."[8] In keeping with this dictum, the two interlocutors of Guazzo's treatise often swap jests and humorous anecdotes as they discuss other conversational proprieties to be observed in diverse company. While censoring those who claim credit for the achievements of others, for instance, one of the interlocutors, Annibale, tells the story of a moth, "who sitting on the horne of an Oxe that was tilling the grounde, beeing askte what hee did there, answered, that he went to plough" (1:153). Equally fond of jests is Thomas Wilson, whose *Art of Rhetoric* (1560), in addition to including a theoretical discussion of the practice, is full of funny stories and one-liners. Many of these are used to illustrate rhetorical prescriptions and principles, although on occasion it seems as if Wilson cannot resist chatting with his reader by way of comic aside. At one point, Wilson goes so far as to play the fool: while discouraging his reader from using "inkhorn terms," he presents a fictional letter from a provincial scholar to an attendant of the lord chancellor, a letter rife with pseudo-Latinate diction and syntax. In presenting this parody of business correspondence, Wilson claims he is following the pattern of Will Summers, famous court jester of Henry VIII.[9]

Why this preoccupation with jesting—one that often exceeds the manuals' designated discussions of the subject? Part of the answer resides in early modern writers' reverence for all things classical and more specifically, all things Ciceronian. Discussions of jesting or examples of wit appear in the works of many authors from antiquity (including the dialogues of Plato, Aristotle's *Nicomachean Ethics,* Plutarch's *Moralia,* Martial's epigrams, and Macrobius's *Saturnalia*), and early modern writers often cite these and other ancient authors as precedents or models for their present endeavors. Moreover, Cicero was revered in the period not only as an orator, statesman, and philosopher but also as a man particularly adept at (although one tradition has it that he was overly addicted to) humor and flashes of wit. His discussion of jesting in *De oratore* had a profound influence on early modern treatments of the subject, but so did the many jests attributed to him. These jests were transmitted to early modern writings through the works of Quintilian, Plutarch, and Macrobius, and they are featured in such early modern texts as Erasmus's *Apophthegmata* (1531), Wilson's *Art of Rhetoric,* and the anonymous *Schoolemaster or Teacher of Table Phylosophie* (1583).

A more compelling explanation for the handbooks' keen interest in wit and laughter is that, for them, the jest serves as a paradigm for rhetorical and courtly communication. It encapsulates, in a highly economical and entertaining form, the kinds of situations the handbook writers thought orators and courtiers would face on a daily basis. These situations typically involve interaction between different kinds of people, and the sample jests the handbooks use to illustrate their prescriptions, although they can be adopted by a speaker and recited on their own, can also be seen as a collection of scripts or cautionary tales to be followed or avoided in the arenas of the orator's or courtier's professional activity. To understand how and why the jest served as a paradigm for communication, we need to begin with a relatively simple observation about the early modern jest itself—the kinds of situations it typically dramatizes, the functions it might serve, and its connection to changing social relations in early modern England. As we shall see, there are striking similarities between the early modern jest and rhetoric and courtesy manuals of the period, similarities that help account for the prominent place jesting often assumes in discussions of oratory and courtly conduct. But in assuming this place of prominence, jesting often undermines the very pre-scriptions it is meant to illustrate.

Jests of the period typically dramatize encounters between people of divergent social origins or occupations, and in doing so, they play on the ten-sions and anxieties that almost invariably occur when different kinds of peo-ple find themselves in one another's company. Like the "comedy of the London Stage," says Keith Thomas, early modern jests "reveal the social tensions of the time, particularly those arising from the meeting of divergent customs and unequal knowledge, as town dweller collided with peasant, noble with plebeian, clerk with layman."[10] Michael Mangan makes a similar observation, claiming that the situations dramatized in these jests usually involve encounters "between country-folk and townsfolk; between English people and foreigners; between ordinary honest folk and the learned scholar or clergyman; between men and women."[11] A cursory glance at almost any jest book of the period (including those from the continent) will bear out these claims. There are numerous jests about servants and masters, farmers and friars, foreigners and indigenous folk, wives and husbands, carters and courtiers, bumpkins and kings.

Although this observation about early modern jests is relatively easy to come by, it is highly suggestive. Thomas develops it further to establish connections between the dramatic structure of jests and their contexts of production. Using Tudor and Stuart jest books as his primary sources, Thomas argues that jests of the period point to "joking situations, areas of structural ambiguity in society itself."[12] As such, they not only "reveal the social tensions of the time," but are strategies for dealing with them. Jests about husbands and their supposedly unruly wives, for instance, "were a means of confronting the anomalies of insubordinate female behaviour which constantly threatened the working of what was supposed to be a male-dominated marital system."[13] Thomas goes on to establish other connections between the subject matter of early modern jests and the broader social scene. What he fails to note, however, is that the jest book is, in many ways, a Renaissance phenomenon and that its appearance coincides with drastic social changes occurring not only in England, but all across Europe: namely, widespread increases in social and geographic mobility.[14] In other words, encounters similar to those portrayed in jests of the period were happening with greater frequency in everyday life. Nobles and the baseborn increasingly found themselves in one another's company owing to the upward mobility of the latter, the downward mobility of the former, or some combination of these two processes. In addition, migration of members from all strata of society was on the rise: those who chose (or were forced) to relocate typically gravitated to towns and cities where they hoped either to escape unlivable conditions in the country or to protect (or even further) their social, economic, or political interests.[15] Viewed in this expanded context, jests dramatizing meetings between people of divergent social and geographic origins can be seen as a response to these oftentimes seismic changes in social relations, a way to manage (or exploit) the anxieties, ambiguities, and contradictions resulting from different kinds of people living in relatively close proximity.

Pushing Thomas's and Mangan's observations even further, can we say that if jests of the period typically dramatize encounters between different kinds of people, then any meeting between people of different orders of being is inherently or at least potentially funny, that such an encounter is a jest waiting to happen? As many have claimed, humor issues from the perception of some form of incongruity, ambiguity, or interpretive disjunction.[16] If this is so, then a meeting between people of divergent social or geographic origins, which is in many ways an incongruous encounter, has all the ingredients of a jest, even if no jesting takes place. Or if we place ourselves inside a jest, within the situation dramatized, can we say that jesting is not only an available strategy for communicating across social boundaries, but also a particularly powerful one? Some forms of jesting, especially jesting that is derisive in nature, can be used to maintain distinctions that may be blurred or elided when different kinds of people find themselves together. Speakers who deride (that is, laugh *down* and *at*) certain individuals or groups assert both their difference from and their superiority to the objects of their laughter.

Derision, however, need not flow from the top down or from the inside out. When an inferior speaker, for instance, derides his superior, jesting may have a leveling or inversionary effect. As Wilson says, even a "common jester" skilled in jesting is "able to match with the best" and "abash a right worthy man" (164). There is yet another set of possibilities. Some forms of jesting may be used not to preserve or challenge social difference but to transcend it. In addition to putting people down, derision may be used as a tool of socialization, a way to nudge delinquents back into line or to indoctrinate newcomers in appropriate modes of behavior before they are fully admitted within the fold. The many jests and anecdotes in Puttenham's discussion of decorum, for instance, are intended to instruct the would-be courtly poet in the manners of the court. Or reciprocally, the social outsider or inferior may, with a well-placed jest, cause the insider or superior to laugh—that is, to share, if only temporarily, the same comic perspective. In modern parlance we call this "getting the joke," and its desired effect we call "breaking the ice." A final possibility is that jesting may transcend and preserve social distinctions simultaneously. Castiglione's Count Lodovico praises the Cardinal of Ferrara, saying "in company with menne and women of all degrees, in sportynge, in laughynge, and in jestynge he hath in hym a certayne sweetenesse, and so comely demeanours, that whoso speaketh with hym or yet beholdeth hym, muste nedes beare hym an affeccion for ever" (45). The sweetness and comeliness the Cardinal displays in sporting, laughing, and jesting cut across hierarchical distinctions and affect people "of all degrees," yet they also set him apart from the crowd, making him wonderful to converse with or simply to behold.

Jests involving encounters between different kinds of people, however, are not unique to the early modern period; similar encounters appear in both ancient and medieval comic texts. Greek and Roman comedy, for instance, is full of masters and their crafty servants, courtesans and braggart soldiers, grumpy old men and love-struck youth. In addition, medieval collections of *exempla,* which preachers used to flavor their sermons and keep their listeners awake and attentive, often feature humorous tales involving interaction between wives and husbands, laymen and clergymen, and foolish rustics and town dwellers.[17] These representations of comic interaction may also be responses to various kinds of mobility resulting from, say, increased trade and commerce in Greece and some loosening of the social hierarchy in Rome (Cicero was himself a *novus homo,* and Horace was the son of a slave). As

Christie Davies suggests, jokes dramatizing interaction across social and geographic difference will surface whenever and wherever "transitional or wavering people" appear on the scene, which is as much to say that only the most homogenous cultures will be without such jokes.[18] But there does seem to be a shift, at least in emphasis, in early modern England, for the typical jest book of the period shows a greater range and diversity in its cast of characters than its classical and medieval predecessors. In *A Hundred Merry Tales* (1526), for instance, we find not only crafty servants, but also quick-witted carters and colliers; not only foolish rustics, but also literal-minded millers, cobblers, and Welshmen; not only braggart soldiers and courtesans, but also pedantic scholars, absentminded astronomers, haughty courtiers, clergymen of all degrees, and maids, widows, hostesses, and gentlewomen; not only grumpy old men but also miserly merchants, incompetent physicians, godless Irishmen, and hoodwinked nobles and knights. Stage plays of the period are even more preoccupied with mobility: Marlowe's Dr. Faustus and Gaveston (Edward II's "night grown mushroom" of a lover); Shakespeare's Malvolio and Don Armado; Dekker's protagonist in *The Shoemaker's Holiday;* and Jonson's Sir Politic Would-be and Sogliardo. The greater diversity of social types in the jest books and the social grasping dramatized on the stage suggest that the possibilities and anxieties associated with mobility, if not greater than in previous periods (which I believe they were), are at least given greater expression in early modern representations of comic and noncomic interaction.

These possibilities and pressures are also given greater expression in rhetoric and courtesy manuals of early modern England where the incorporation of jests dramatizing meetings between different kinds of people distinguishes these manuals' discussions of jesting from their classical sources. As we shall see in chapter 1, the treatments of jesting in classical rhetorics (their prescriptions and sample jests) are primarily concerned with interaction, not between different kinds of people, but between people of roughly the same status and occupation—that is, two rival orators of equestrian or senatorial rank engaged in a contest of wit in either a deliberative or (more likely) a forensic setting.[19] Early modern handbooks, by contrast, feature interaction between people of divergent social and geographic origins and are thus closely affiliated with the jest books of the period—with respect to their contexts of production, the situations they feature, and (as we shall see in the next section) their authors and intended uses.

Like the early modern jest, rhetoric and courtesy manuals of the period must be viewed, at least in part, as responses to widespread increases in geographic and, especially, social mobility, although the nature of each kind of manual's response differs considerably. The rhetorics were, in effect, handbooks on social mobility. They were typically written by men of ignoble origins who aspired to rise above their lowly status and occupy positions of power and privilege. Wayne A. Rebhorn calls their authors "men on the make" who, although baseborn, were driven by a fervent desire for social preferment. Their social aspirations, according to Rebhorn, led many of these authors to write into their rhetorical theory the possibility of their own (and their readers') social advancement.[20] In his *Arte of English Poesie,* for instance, George Puttenham is very explicit about the perceived connection between rhetorical skill and social mobility, for he promises to pull his reader "first from the carte to the schoole, and from thence to the Court, and . . . [prefer] him to your Majesties service" (304), that is, from the geographic margins to the center, from the bottom of the social scale to its top. Thomas Wilson's life actually follows this trajectory. The son of a yeomen, Wilson was born around 1523 in the provincial region of Lincolnshire. After receiving his education at Eton College and then Cambridge, Wilson established himself as a humanist, two of his more famous scholarly achievements being *The Rule of Reason* (1551) and *The Art of Rhetoric.* When Edward VI died and Mary assumed the throne, Wilson left England and settled in Italy where he was eventually tried and imprisoned by the Roman Inquisition for the Protestant (and hence heretical) sentiments expressed in his treatises on logic and rhetoric. Through a strange turn of events, which he recounts in the prologue to the 1560 edition of his *Rhetoric,* Wilson escaped prison and eventually returned to England where he became a servant of the crown and launched what was to be a very successful career. In 1563, he was appointed Master of St. Katherine's Hospital in the Tower of London; between 1574 and 1577, he served as a royal ambassador to the Low Countries; and from 1577 to his death in 1581, he advanced to the position of principal secretariat of the Privy Council.[21] Wilson's personal history was indeed "from the carte . . . to the Court," from being the son of a provincial yeomen to being part of Elizabeth's inner circle.

Handbooks on courtly conduct were also written in response to increases in social and geographic mobility. Unlike the rhetorics, however, which tried to facilitate mobility, the courtesy manuals, at least initially, sought to suppress it. Writing about changing standards of behavior in Renaissance Europe, Norbert Elias argues that mobility had a profound impact on the "affective life" of early modern Europe, particularly that of the nobleman. After the disintegration of the feudal system and before the complete consolidation of absolutist states in the seventeenth century, there occurred a temporary loosening of social hierarchies, and social mobility increased dramatically. As a consequence, people "of different social origins . . . [were] thrown together," and because they were "forced to live with one another in a new way . . . [they became] more sensitive to the impulses of others." It is in this context of changing social relations that "the writings on manners of Erasmus, Castiglione, Della Casa, and others are produced."[22] Arguing along similar lines, Frank Whigham says that the "corpus of Renaissance courtesy theory began to develop at a time when an exclusive sense of aristocratic identity . . . was being stolen, or at least encroached upon, by a horde of young men not born to it." As part of their effort to repulse this "horde" of newcomers and upstarts, members of the elite composed handbooks on courtly conduct "in a gesture of exclusion," a gesture meant to reinforce and fortify boundaries between ruling and subject classes.[23] This seems to be precisely what Castiglione has in mind when he has one of his interlocutors propose that he and the others discuss the ideal courtier in order to "disgrace therefore many untowardly asseheades, that through malepertness thinke to purchase the name of good Courtyer" (41). Ironically, however, courtesy manuals were then "read, rewritten, and reemployed by mobile base readers to serve their own social aggressions."[24] Once the modes of behavior and speech supposedly (and exclusively) characteristic of aristocratic identity had been made explicit and codified, they became available for imitation by gentry and baseborn alike. In this way, the early courtesy manuals undermined their own attempts to stifle the ambitions of this "mobile base" readership. Instead, they unwittingly fueled such ambitions.

The handbooks' preoccupation with social and geographic mobility, with the possibilities and hazards of different kinds of people occupying the same social space, leads to an even more striking similarity between jests of the period and what the manuals present as the near paradigmatic situation an orator or courtier will face. Throughout these manuals, orators and courtiers are frequently, but not exclusively, portrayed communicating with people whose social origins or occupations differ from their own. In other words, the near paradigmatic situation found in the handbooks is structured like an early modern jest. The rhetorics often place orators in situations in which they speak down to a baseborn populace, persuading them this way or that. Or they give accounts of orators addressing princes and kings, offering them counsel and advising them on important matters of state. These diverse communicative settings are summed up by Richard Rainolde in his *Foundacion of Rhetorike* (1563) when he says orators "drawe unto theim the hartes of a multitude . . . and speake before Princes and rulers."[25] Even in the more mundane world of the professional letter writer or secretary, communication across social difference is presented as the norm. In *The English Secretary* (1599), an Elizabethan *ars dictaminis,* Angel Day advises his readers to consider "the reputation of the partie with whom we write" when composing a letter, for the secretary will have occasion to address diverse audiences, and the form and content of the letter should be adapted accordingly: "In one sort we frame them [letters] to old men, in another sort to young men, one way to sad and grave persons, another to light and young fellowes: one platforme to Courtiers, another to Philosophers. To great and notable personages, with dutie speciall, appropriate to their calling: To our betters, always with submission: To our inferiors benignly and favorably."[26] This list of the range of rhetorical situations the secretary is likely to confront suggests the complexities of writing business letters in the period—how the secretary's discourse must embody not only the character or disposition but also the relative status of the person he addresses. This list, however, also reads like a catalog of "joking situations" found in the jest books. A situation, for instance, in which a secretary addresses "great and notable personages" is structurally ambiguous, and although Day's prescription to address such people "with dutie speciall, appropriate to their calling" is intended to manage that ambiguity and lessen its impact, the situation is nevertheless fraught with incongruities and the potential for interpretive disjunctions that may be drawn upon or result in the production of jests.

Courtesy manuals of the period are also concerned with communication across social boundaries. The title page of Simon Robson's *Courte of Civill Courtesie* (1582) announces the manual's primary aim: to teach "younge Gentlemen, and others, that are desirous to frame their behaviour according to their states, at all time, and in all companies: Thereby to purchase worthy praise, of their inferiours: and estimation and credite among theyr betters."[27]

As the rest of the manual suggests, these "younge Gentlemen" will purchase this praise and estimation if they can shift effortlessly between two modes of interaction, "curtesy" and "curiositie": that is, between showing respect and deferring to their social betters, on the one hand; and maintaining a certain distance and standoffishness when in the company of their inferiors, on the other. Della Casa's *Galateo* (1558, 1576) is for the reader "who so disposeth himselfe to live, not in solitarie and deserte places, as Heremites, but in fellowship with men, and in populous cities" where he will presumably come in contact with and thus have to behave accordingly to a range of people from divergent social and geographic origins (15). The second book of Stefano Guazzo's *Civile Conversation* is all about communication between different kinds of people. Its argument promises to discuss "first of the manner of conversation, meete for all persons, which shal come in any companie, out of their owne houses, and then the particular points, which ought to bee observed in companie betweene yong men, and old, gentlemen, and yomen, Princes and private persons, learned, and unlearned, citizens, and straungers, religious, and secular, men, and women" (1:109). Again this reads like a catalog of potential joking situations. In fact, Guazzo makes extensive use of jests and funny anecdotes in this book as he presents those forms of conversation "meete for all persons, which shal come in any companie." For Guazzo, not only is jesting an essential ingredient of any civil conversation (1:158–59), but it is also a vehicle for modeling situations in which different kinds of people interact.

The handbooks' interest in jests, then, is central to one of their primary concerns—that is, communication between different kinds of people. The jest serves as a paradigm for such communication. Puttenham even suggests that if one were to collect enough anecdotes (comic or otherwise), then one would be able "to skan the trueth of every case that shall happen in the affaires of man" (271). But as a paradigm for communication, the jest proves somewhat troubling. For the most part, the handbooks use jests to illustrate how the relative ranks, positions, and identities of participants should be preserved in any rhetorical or courtly exchange. But they also reveal (often unwittingly) that jesting can just as easily blur or even invert hierarchical distinctions. Take, for instance, an anecdote that Peacham uses to explain how jesting in some forms "mitigateth hard matters with pleasant words." A "certaine man" was "apprehended, and brought before Alexander the Great king of Macedonia, for rayling against him." When Alexander demanded of this man why "he and his companie had so done," the man replied, "Had not the wine fayled . . . [we would have] spoken much worse." Peacham then interprets this anecdote, trying to nail down the ambiguity upon which it hangs and gauge its effect. He says, "By which answer he [the man] signified, that those words proceeded rather from wine than malice," and as a result of this "free and pleasant confession," the man "asswaged Alexanders great displeasure, and obtained forgiveness" (36–37). This interpretation seeks to neutralize the man's irreverent act and reinstate each participant in his proper social place—that is, the man showing deference through his confession, and Alexander dispensing forgiveness from on high. Moreover, the anecdote, together with Peacham's interpretation of it, offers a model of communication between different kinds of people, suggesting that an inferior speaker can, in general, use jesting as a strategy for mollifying the anger of his superior. But things are not as straightforward as Peacham would have them. Elsewhere, Peacham explicitly forbids social inferiors from deriding their betters (36). Here, however, he presents an example of a man not only "rayling against" the emperor, but also getting away with it—and his doing so may encourage some of Peacham's readers to attempt the same. More important, the man's witty answer to Alexander is both an excuse (and thus a sign of deference) and a threat: had the wine held out, the man and his "companie" would have said "much worse." Readers need to keep both possibilities in view to recognize and appreciate the humor in the man's "pleasant confession," which is, in itself, a curious and double-valenced expression, acknowledging the transgression as it seeks to disarm or mitigate it.

This jest from Peacham does more than suggest the problems with using jesting as a paradigm for communication. It also illustrates a broader movement characteristic of the handbooks' discussions of jesting in general. As Peacham does with his claim that a jest sometimes "mitigateth hard matters," the handbooks repeatedly advertise the power of jesting and promote its use in handling diverse social situations. Having made such claims, however, the handbooks (like Peacham's interpretation of the man's "pleasant confession") then try to rein in the power of jesting and channel its energies into socially conservative uses: servants shouldn't ridicule their masters, for instance, nor should noblemen banter with peasants. But jesting eludes these attempts to limit and restrain it. It secures its effects through ambiguities, verbal feints, equivocations, saying one thing and meaning another—strategies, in short, that resist or circumvent measures of control.

FROM JEST BOOKS TO THE
DISCOURSE ON JESTING

Thus far, I have moved almost without concession or qualification from handbooks on oratory to courtesy manuals to jest books and back again. Although scholars traditionally regard these texts as generically distinct, their shared concern with social and geographic mobility and their representations of interaction between different kinds of people have made such interpretive movements relatively easy. In this section, I will examine relationships among these texts more carefully. My main purpose here is to survey those works that will serve as my primary sources and to discuss the methods and strategies I will use to analyze them. In the process, I also offer a brief (and thus necessarily tentative) history of the early modern discourse on jesting—a history beginning with collections of *facetiae* (or funny stories) compiled by continental humanists early in the period through discussions of jesting in sixteenth-century rhetoric and courtesy manuals, either native to England or domesticated through English translation.[28] These manuals are the principal object of this study, but in order to understand them more fully, we need to examine from where they came and (as will be suggested below) where they ultimately went.

Although deeply indebted to classical discussions of wit and humor, the discourse on jesting in early modern England has more immediate sources in collections of *facetiae* gathered by continental humanists in the fifteenth and early sixteenth centuries. According to Joanna Brizdale Lipking, these collections were the "first growth of a more self-conscious and formal tradition . . . that confirmed the place of jokes in public life and encouraged their use in literature."[29] This "tradition" culminated in theoretical discussions of jesting found in the handbooks, but it began with the humanists' collections of *facetiae*. The earliest and perhaps most influential of these was the *Facetiae* compiled between 1438 and 1452 by Poggio Bracciolini, a humanist and apostolic secretary who recovered, among other manuscripts, a complete version of Quintilian's *Institutio oratoria*. Poggio's collection is a fusion of classical authority and medieval comic form.[30] It comes with no theoretical apparatus, but Poggio does include a brief introduction where he refers to ancient precedents in defense of his present work: "I have read that our ancestors, men of the greatest prudence and learning, took delight in jests, pleasantries, and anecdotes, and that they received praise rather than blame for this."[31] He goes on to assure his readers that "his is not an indecorous work," but the tales he does include are more akin to the oftentimes bawdy and scatological humor of the medieval *exemplum* and *novella* than to the more restrained jests found in Cicero, Quintilian, and their sixteenth-century imitators.[32] At the end of his collection, Poggio also includes a brief postscript where he describes the setting in which the tales of his *Facetiae* were supposedly first told before he wrote them down: "Before closing the series of these little stories of ours, it is my intention to mention also the locale where the majority of them were told. This was our *Bugiale,* a sort of workshop of lies, which was founded by the secretaries in order that they might have an occasional laugh. Since the days of Pope Martin [Martin V (1419–31)] we had the custom of choosing an out-of-the-way place where we exchanged news, and where we would talk of various things, both in earnest, and to distract our minds. Here, we spared no one, and we spoke evil of everything that vexed us. Often the Pope himself was the subject of our criticisms, and for this reason many came to that place for fear of being the first one harassed."[33] Although this passage offers no explicit theory of jesting, it does address several issues that are central to both ancient and early modern discussions of wit and humor. In addressing these issues, however, it also reveals how differently Poggio handles them in comparison to earlier and later writers on jesting. For one, the setting in which the *facetiae* were told is removed and clearly demarcated from the arenas of the secretaries' professional activities: the *Bugiale* is located in an "out-of-the-way place" where the purpose of jesting is geared primarily toward relaxation, amusement, and letting off steam. While Cicero, Quintilian, and their sixteenth-century imitators all recognize the value of jesting as a form of recreation, their orientation is clearly more pragmatic: the settings these writers feature actually *coincide* with the professional arenas of the orator and (later) the courtier—the law courts and public assemblies, the pulpit and the royal court where the power of jesting is directed toward gaining some practical rhetorical advantage. For another, and as I have already suggested, Poggio seems less bounded by classical standards of decorum, which later writers revived, if not in practice, at least in theory. Poggio's boast that he and his companions "spared no one" from their ridicule (not even the Pope) agrees well, not with characterizations of the witty orator or courtier, but with the lower-class buffoon or *scurra.* Indeed, Poggio's boast recalls Aristotle's influential formulation of the buffoon as one who "will not keep his tongue off himself or any one else, if he can raise a laugh" (*Ethics,* 4.8.10). So while Poggio and his companions may have limited their jesting to the place of the *Bugiale,* the license they enjoyed there is clearly at odds with what earlier and later writers would have deemed decorous.

In spite of its many scurrilous jests (or, more likely, because of them), Poggio's *Facetiae* was immensely popular. As F. P. Wilson says, "Poggio earned more reputation by his collection of *Facetiae* than by his zeal in combing the monasteries of Europe for classical manuscripts." Even before the *Facetiae* was published in 1470, his "collection was known throughout Italy, France, Spain, Germany, and England, and was read by all who understood Latin."[34] Not only was Poggio's collection read by many, it was also imitated by some of the more renowned humanists and scholars of the period. In her survey of authors of these imitations, Lipking lists Ludovico Carbone, professor of rhetoric at Ferrara; Angelo Poliziano, philologist and poet at the academy of Florence; Ottmar Nachtigall (Luscinus), a member of the *sodalitas literaria* of Strassburg; and Heinrich Bebel, poet laureate and professor of rhetoric at Tubingen.[35] "There were many others," says Lipking, but one worthy of special note is Erasmus whose monumental *Apophthegmata* (1531), although participating in the humanist tradition of jest collections, constitutes a departure from its immediate predecessors. According to Lipking, "Erasmus's great work may be seen, at least in part, as a reaction against the kind of diversion offered to public men and young students by earlier humanists, an attempt to substitute something more authoritatively classical, more moral, more educational" (149). In the preface to his *Apophthegmata,* Erasmus does not mention Poggio or his imitators by name, but he does contrast the stories and sayings he is about to offer with tales that would have been at home in the earlier collections—that is, he prefers "honest myrth and jestying," eschewing "fables voide of honestie, voide of learning, and full of rebaudrie."[36] While Erasmus, on several occasions, claims that jests are valuable for sheer amusement and recreation, his orientation is more practical. Citing classical custom as his authority, Erasmus states that "feacte saiyngs and honeste bourding" are instruments of moral instruction, "either to the commendacion and praise of honestee and vertue, or els to the rebukyng of vice." They should also be used in teaching more academic subjects, for "the joyly auncie[n]te wyse mene of old tyme" would often "spiece and powther Cosmographie, Astrologie, Musike & philosophie aswel natural as morall with fables and tales preatly and wittyly feigned" in order to make these subjects more palatable to students. With Erasmus, then, the jest moves from the informal gatherings of the *Bugiale* to the classroom where it becomes a rhetorical resource to humanists in at least one of their self-professed roles—that is, as educator. Moreover, Erasmus is more concerned than Poggio with decorum, and he repeatedly forbids the use of humor that exceeds the bounds of "honest myrth."

The practice of compiling collections of jests migrated to England in the closing decades of the fifteenth century. English translations of nine of Poggio's 274 *facetiae* appeared at the end of William Caxton's *Fables of Aesop* (1484). Later, in 1526, Thomas More's brother-in-law John Rastell published *A Hundred Merry Tales,* the book from which Shakespeare's Benedick "accused Beatrice of stealing her wit."[37] Around 1532, king's printer Thomas Berthelet published *Tales and Quick Answers* (1532), which according to Lipking, is squarely within the tradition of the humanists' collections.[38] According to Anne Lake Prescott, many of the jests appearing in these two English collections can be seen as vehicles for exploring, demonstrating, even parodying "matters of keen interest" to humanists in general, including issues of interpretation, the relationship between context and meaning, and sophistic reasoning.[39] In 1542 Nicholas Udall provided an English translation of two books from Erasmus's *Apophthegmata,* and nearly a century later Francis Bacon came out with his own collection of jests and witty sayings, *Apophthegms New and Old* (1625). During the intervening years, over two dozen collections of detached jests, jest biographies, and collections of comic *novelle* are noted in F. P. Wilson's bibliography, although (in the case of many of these texts) their relation to the humanists' collections is tenuous at best.[40] All told, the early modern period saw a flourishing of jest collections, and the people chiefly responsible for the "first growth" of this flourishing were among those humanists who insisted upon the educational, political, and cultural significance of rhetoric in general.

The first sustained discussion of jesting in the early modern period was Gioviano Pontano's *De Sermone* (1509). Although Pontano expands upon classical theories of decorum and jesting, his work seems meant "to disseminate classical precepts rather than to teach practical lessons."[41] It was not until Castiglione's *Book of the Courtier* that we find a discussion of jesting that combines classical standards of decorum with the more practical orientation found in Cicero and Quintilian. Castiglione offers a full-scale imitation of Cicero's discussion of wit in *De oratore,* although Castiglione replaces Cicero's central figure (the orator) with the courtier, a substitution that helps account for Castiglione's frequent departures from his classical source. Several treatments of jesting appearing in subsequent courtesy manuals (those of Della Casa, Guazzo, and Robson, and Puttenham's lengthy section on decorum) are less directly influenced by Cicero, yet they all conceive of jesting as a rhetorical strategy to be used, not in some "out-of-the-way place," but in the courtier's daily conversations and negotiations in the royal court.

Thomas Wilson's discussion of jesting in his *Art of Rhetoric* offers another full-scale imitation of Cicero, and it thus serves as a counterpart to Castiglione's treatment of the same subject. In addition to the orator, Wilson includes the preacher as one of his central figures. As with Castiglione, Wilson's addition helps account for his frequent departures from Cicero—most notable is his emphasis on jesting from the pulpit (rather than in the forum), where preachers use funny stories and witty sayings to gain and then hold the attention of parishioners. Wilson's addition also invites us to consider conceptions of jesting found in preaching manuals of the period, including Erasmus's *Ecclesiastae* (1535) and Leonard Wright's *Patterne for Pastors* (1596), although, as we shall see in chapter 1, not every preaching manual sanctions pulpit jesting. As is the case with several courtesy manuals, some of the English rhetorics do not take their cue from Cicero. Writers of manuals on style, including Richard Sherry, Peacham, Puttenham, and Day, all present (in their oftentimes staggering catalogs of stylistic devices) seven or sometimes only six figures of speech designed primarily to serve humorous purposes. This group of figures (hereafter called the "jesting figures") attempt to register the tone of a particular kind of jesting or its degree of aggressiveness or directness, and all are to be included among the orator's, courtier's, and poet's repertoire of rhetorical strategies.

Although discussions of jesting in sixteenth-century rhetoric and courtesy manuals are in many ways the culmination of collections of *facetiae* compiled by humanists early in the period, jest books continued to be published alongside the handbooks, and several of these conceived of jesting in distinctly rhetorical terms. In the introduction to *Jests to Make You Merry* (1607), authored by George Wilkins and "T. D." (most likely Thomas Dekker), the jest is defined as a "weapon wherewith a fool does oftentimes fight and a wise man defends himself by" (Zall, *Nest of Ninnies,* 75). This characterization of the jest has analogues in the handbooks' discussions of jesting—in the nips, scoffs, and other verbal body blows Wilson catalogs for making a speaker's opponent "believe that he is no wiser than a goose" (165), and in the bitter taunts, broad flouts, and the fleering frumps listed in Puttenham (200–201). Other jest books assign to jesting more pacific and ingratiating functions—functions that again have analogues in the handbooks. The introduction to *Howelglas* (?1528), the English rendition of *Til Eulenspiegel,* rehearses a commonplace about laughter and jesting that is at least as old as Aristotle's *Nicomachean Ethics.*[42] This introduction promises that the story of Howelglas will "renew the minds of men and women of all degrees from the use of sadness, to pass the time with laughter and mirth" (Zall, *Hundred Merry Tales,* 156). Variations of this commonplace are ubiquitous in the period, and they crop up almost every time recreation and jesting are subjects of discussion. The author of *The Mirror of Mirth* even casts it in the form of an anecdote, and in doing so, he transforms it into a recipe for persuasion. There was a philosopher who, whenever "he perceived the people to wax weary by his long and tedious orations, and to drop out of doors ere he had done," would pick up his harp (an instrument of pleasure related here to a jest) and begin to play. Upon hearing the "sweet and pleasant sound" of the philosopher's music, the "people . . . [would] come running faster than before they went forth—whose dulled spirits being revived with that pleasant melody and their minds (before cloyed with over-many circumstances of gravity) being by this means marvelously delighted—did the better and with greater ease continue the time of his conclusion" (Zall, *Hundred Merry Tales,* 353). As we shall see in chapter 4, the situation dramatized here—one in which a speaker is in danger of losing his audience owing to the tediousness of his speech—is a preoccupation of Wilson who repeatedly offers jesting as its remedy. A similar situation and dynamic can be found in Castiglione's quasi-historical account of the origins of recreation where kings and rulers use various forms of amusement not only to provide their subjects with a time of temporary release but also to secure their willing compliance.

In addition to occasionally participating in the discourse on wit and laughter, the jest books offered orators, courtiers, preachers, poets, and other public figures repositories of humor that they could draw upon and incorporate into their daily conversations, public speeches, sermons, and literary compositions.[43] A number of Thomas More's epigrams, for instance, are verse renderings of tales and witticisms found in the jest books, and preacher Hugh Latimer was not above borrowing from *A Hundred Merry Tales* in order to cheer his congregation.[44] John Harington, godson of the Queen and court wag, also turned to the printed collections on occasion for materials for his epigrams—literary efforts that he hoped would further his career and reputation at court.[45] There must have been many others who recycled funny stories and witticisms from the jest books in attempts to win friends and influence people through facetious conversation. William Cornwallis claims he encountered a few of these would-be wits but complained that they "never utter any thing of their owne, but get Jestes by heart, and robbe bookes, and men of prettie tales, and yet hope for this to have roome above the Salt."[46] Having one's wit exposed as secondhand must have been degrading, and that is part of the point of Benedick's accusation against Beatrice— that is, to put her down. But the pressures to secure a more prestigious place at the table (that is, "above the Salt") and at court for that matter were extremely intense during the period, and as F. P. Wilson speculates, for "men of lesser parts the jest-books were a godsend."[47] Francis Bacon, unlike Cornwallis, was less troubled by people who lifted jests from collections. In the preface to his *Apophthegms New and Old,* Bacon invites his readers to borrow freely from his offering of "pointed speeches," as he calls them: "They serve to be interlaced in continued speech. They serve to be recited on their own. They serve if you take the kernel out of them, and make them your own" (7:123). For Bacon, *apophthegms* are not only "for pleasure and ornament"; they are also for "use and action."[48]

In addition to examining rhetoric and courtesy manuals and jest books of the period, I will make the occasional foray into dramatic comedy and into accounts of the jesting of several real-life courtiers of sixteenth-century England. For representations of the comic behaviors of fictitious or historical characters often participate in the early modern discourse of jesting. As Rebhorn argues about the relationship between Renaissance rhetoric and literature in general, literature "presents a direct modeling of rhetorical situations. . . . That modeling allows authors to scrutinize the discourse of rhetoric even as they repeat it; it enables them to analyze and evaluate its assumptions, assertions, and judgments about human beings and the social and political world in which they live."[49] The same might be said about biographical accounts of historical figures engaged in rhetorical action, accounts that almost invariably evaluate and comment upon the actions they report. In the case of comic actions (whether dramatized on the stage or reported in prose), they also "scrutinize" the discourse on jesting found in rhetoric and courtesy manuals of the period, repeating, testing, even challenging its prescriptions. Chapter 1, for instance, shows how the jests that Latimer incorporates into his sermons agree with at least some writers' prescriptions concerning pulpit jesting. Chapter 3 explores how Shakespeare's characterization of Falstaff and contemporary representations of the jests of John Skelton, Thomas More, and Harington complicate several key features the handbooks rely on to distinguish orators and courtiers from buffoons.

As a whole, the discourse on jesting in early modern England is relatively vast, and in addition to the handbooks' discussions of jesting, bits and pieces of it can be found in a wide variety of texts. Accordingly, my approach to this discourse will be somewhat eclectic, drawing upon theoretical contributions of humor studies (a vaguely defined field, but roughly, one that consists of interdisciplinary studies of humor primarily by social scientists but also by scholars in communication, linguistics, American studies, and American and British literature). It seems (and this claim will not be argued explicitly, but suggested throughout this study) that the rhetoric of humor migrated to the social sciences in the late nineteenth and early twentieth centuries—at a time, that is, when the importance of rhetoric as an academic discipline diminished considerably and the presence of the emerging social sciences was increasingly felt. In this way, the rhetoric of jesting and humor seems to have followed the same trajectory Kenneth Burke uses to chart the history of rhetoric in general: "When rhetoric as a term fell into disuse . . . other specialized disciplines such as esthetics, anthropology, psychoanalysis, and sociology came to the fore (so that esthetics sought to outlaw rhetoric, while the other sciences we have mentioned took over, each in its own terms, the rich rhetorical elements that esthetics would ban."[50] Similarly, Winifred Bryan Horner and Kerri Morris argue that although scholars "speak of the 'decline' of rhetoric," rhetoric "as the study of human communication survived under other names, and as the basic concepts changed focus the terminology changed as well." An effect of these changes was that "rhetoric spread over a number of disciplines in the nineteenth- and twentieth-century academic communities."[51] My use of materials from the social sciences is not an attempt to reclaim what "properly" belongs to rhetoric. Rather, my study integrates rhetorical and social scientific approaches to laughter and jesting, importing back into rhetoric concepts enriched by social scientific research and suggesting, in turn, that social scientists have something to learn from rhetorical treatments of jesting.

Of all the secondary sources I draw upon, Bakhtin's influential account of medieval and Renaissance laughter is worthy of special note. Although Bakhtin informs this study throughout (especially with its emphasis on the disorderly properties of jesting), he only offers a partial explanation of how laughter and jesting were conceived of during the period. Bakhtin views laughter and jesting from the bottom up—from the perspective of the populace—and celebrates the disruptive energies of laughter and its opposition to the "official world." According to Bakhtin, these disruptive and oppositional energies are most freely and potently expressed during times of carnival, although they eventually found their way into Renaissance literature: "As opposed to the official feast, one might say that carnival celebrated temporary liberation from the prevailing truth and from the established order; it marked a suspension of all hierarchical rank, privileges, norms, and prohibitions. Carnival was the true feast of time, the feast of becoming, change, renewal. It was hostile to all that was immortalized and completed."[52] The laughter of carnival levels hierarchical distinctions. It "degrades and materializes," bringing "all that is high, spiritual, ideal, abstract" to the "material level, to the sphere of the earth and body."[53] This process of "degradation" is by no means solely destructive or negative in character; rather, it is profoundly ambivalent. While the laughter of carnival "degrades and materializes," it also rejuvenates and renews: "To degrade is to bury, to sow, and to kill simultaneously, in order to bring forth something more and better."[54] Images used to express the nature and spirit of carnival laughter are also deeply ambivalent. Its most potent and fundamental image is the body, particularly its topography and boundaries. In the aesthetic of carnival, or what Bakhtin calls "grotesque realism," there is a downward shift in focus from the head and face to the "genital organs, the belly, and the buttocks."[55] Grotesque realism also represents the body as transgressing and exceeding its own boundaries, emphasizing the body's apertures and appendices: "the open mouth, the genital organs, the breasts, the phallus, the potbelly, and the nose."[56] In the seventeenth century, however, a gradual shift began from grotesque realism to a new aesthetic, the "classical." Central to this new aesthetic, says Bakhtin, was an image of the body that was essentially the opposite of that found in grotesque realism. Contrasting sharply with the grotesque body, the classical body was "a strictly completed, finished product." Any feature suggesting openness or incompleteness was eliminated: "its protuberances and offshoots were removed, its convexities (signs of new sprouts and buds) smoothed out, its apertures closed."[57] Not only did images of the body lose their rich ambivalence; so too did the nature and spirit of laughter. Stripped off were its rejuvenating powers so that by the eighteenth century, it "was cut down to cold humor, irony, sarcasm."[58]

As original and suggestive as his work is, Bakhtin fails to account for representations of jesting and laughter found in handbooks on oratory and courtly conduct in the period.[59] As we shall see, these handbooks repeatedly express a range of conflicting, yet interconnected, perspectives toward laughter and jesting. Although the manuals acknowledge that laughter can come from below and release energies that are hostile to "all that is high," the perspective voiced most strongly in their discussions of jesting is one that views laughter not from the bottom up, but from the top down. According to this perspective, laughter is not a release from the constraints of the "official world"; rather, it is in the service of, and reinforces, the established order. It is conceived primarily as a socially conservative force, one that maintains and preserves the status quo in the face of pressures (e.g., those of social and geographic mobility) that seek to alter the existing order. This is not to say that laughter, as conceived by the handbook writers, lost its rich ambivalence as Bakhtin says it does later under the aesthetic of classicism. The ambivalence of jesting and laughter—its disorderly and unruly energies—is a continual preoccupation of the handbook writers, and one of their principal challenges is to rein those energies in and channel them toward socially conservative ends, even if these efforts ultimately fail. In other words, it seems that Bakhtin underestimates the rate of change from the aesthetic of grotesque realism to that of classicism. Over three-quarters of a century before Cervantes's *Don Quixote,* a work that Bakhtin claims constitutes an "initial stage" in the change from the one aesthetic to the other, we can find manuals that are deeply informed by classicism. Castiglione and Della Casa, for instance, both reject the grotesque body and the aesthetic it implies, favoring instead an image of the body that comes closer to the one that Bakhtin attributes to the classicism of the seventeenth and eighteenth centuries.[60] In short, the perspective offered by Bakhtin is incomplete and overlooks other, radically different conceptions of laughter and jesting in the period, and while some of these conceptions retain elements of grotesque realism, others are clear departures from such an aesthetic.

The principle that organizes this study is the jesting situation itself. The first chapter deals with this situation in general, and each of the remaining three chapters examines a particular element of a jesting exchange: the comic butt or subject matter of laughter, the speaker who delivers jests, and the listeners who receive them. As we shall see, this particular organization is invited by several of the manuals themselves, manuals that offer a tripartite model of a jesting exchange in which a speaker jests in order to create or reaffirm an alliance with his listeners at the expense and exclusion of the comic butt.

Chapter 1 examines several permutations of this model as they appear in the handbooks and explores one instance in which the manuals' enthusiasm over jesting is countered by their desire to keep jesting under control and within bounds. More specifically, the manuals view jesting as a powerful and highly economical strategy for managing particular rhetorical situations, but they also insist that speakers observe decorum and adapt their jesting to the immediate needs of those situations as well as to the more general social circumstances. In ancient treatments of jesting, particularly those of Cicero and Quintilian, the typical jesting situation consists of two rival orators of roughly the same social status engaged in a battle of wits in either a forensic or deliberative setting. The orator who jests in either of these settings seeks to distinguish himself from his rival by turning him into an object of laughter. In the early modern handbooks, by contrast, social differentiation is usually a precondition, and not a byproduct, of a jesting exchange. That is, in its most general formulation, the early modern jesting situation involves encounters between people of divergent social origins and occupations, and although the handbooks present many specific instances of this general formulation, two of these receive special attention: jesting from the pulpit and at the court of a prince. In pulpit oratory, the relationship of interest is not the one between speaker and opponent as in classical texts, but between speaker and audience where, in this case, a preacher uses jesting as a way to capture and hold the attention of his lay congregation in preparation for religious instruction. In the highly stratified and differentiated environment of the court, jesting is primarily seen as a way for a courtier to present a self, to preserve or enhance his own ethos in the hope of favor and promotion. If jesting confers power on speakers and increases their ability to manage diverse social situations, then decorum seeks to hold that power and ability in check. It is shorthand for the rhetorical situation and operates on both a pragmatic and social level, imposing limits on a speaker's jesting so that it accords with the exigencies of a particular situation and, in most cases, with the demands of the social order itself. However, what the handbooks often ignore in their invocations of decorum, but reveal nevertheless, is that jesting fuses the decorous and indecorous, the seemly and unseemly, in fittingly unfitting combinations. In this way, a single jest can simultaneously conform to and upset the dictates of decorum.

Chapter 2 focuses on one of the three components of a jesting exchange, the comic butt or subject matter of laughter, and it examines another way in which jesting dodges and evades the manuals' attempts to harness its energies. In their discussions of the subject matter of laughter, several of the manuals (both ancient and early modern) invoke the language of rhetorical invention, posit deformity as a general *topos* or "place" of jesting, and go on to offer a set of more specific *topoi* of jesting related to this general *topos* of deformity. In this way, it seems the manuals are trying not only to offer orators and courtiers a method of jest production analogous to topical invention, but also to stabilize the subject matter of the laughable and restrict its objects to bounded spaces—the "places" of jesting. However, as this method for jest production unfolds, it becomes clear that the subject matter of laughter is ultimately indeterminate and exceeds any boundaries meant to limit or comprehend it. Jests about foreigners and rustics, for instance, may be intended to clarify and reinforce boundaries between the social and geographical center and its margins; however, these same jests may also unleash the dangerous energies embodied by an outsider, energies that the joke teller cannot completely control or discredit. In many ways, the manuals' approach to the subject matter of laughter is similar to several modern models of joking that try to pinpoint a joke's butt and determine, once and for all, its function. What is needed, and what this chapter provides, is a more flexible model of jesting, one that does not abandon Elizabethan and modern approaches to jesting (the notion of *topoi* of jesting, for instance, is valuable in identifying recurrent objects of laughter in a given culture), but does nevertheless preserve the multiple and often contradictory interpretations to which a single jest is susceptible.

Chapter 3 picks up two threads from the first and second chapters (the power of jesting and deformity) and examines them in relation to the orator or courtier who jests. In particular, this chapter claims that despite their enthusiasm for jesting, the manuals betray a deep anxiety over a speaker losing control of his jesting and becoming identified with the deformed and unseemly persons and actions he ridicules—that is, becoming an object of laughter himself. While substantiating this claim, I chart thresholds of jesting found in the manuals, boundaries that mark the lines between success and failure, between the seemly and unseemly, and I argue that these thresholds coincide with, though they sometimes violate, what Elias calls in his *Civilizing Process* thresholds of shame and embarrassment. Because both kinds of thresholds were shifting and expanding during the early modern period, they serve as an important index of social change. A few of the courtesy manuals, for instance, exclude deformity from the realm of the laughable, an exclusion that not only constitutes a departure from the prevailing view of laughter during the period, but also suggests the emergence of a new sensibility and sensitivity toward others. In addition to charting thresholds of jesting, this chapter examines the manuals' anxiety over the lower-class buffoon who is a perpetual presence in their discussions of humor, but who embodies everything an orator or courtier must distance himself from in his jesting: the low, the deformed, the indecorous, and the disorderly. Although the buffoon appears frequently in the classical rhetorics, he is perceived as a greater threat to the Elizabethan orator and courtier whose social standing is precarious at best. Indeed, the greatest risk an Elizabethan orator or courtier takes while jesting is not to have a joke fall flat and fail to raise a laugh (although this too is serious), but to be taken for a common buffoon, for the consequence of such an identification is not only enduring the laughter of others but also suffering social degradation.

Chapter 4 examines perhaps the most important (and, as it turns out, the most unstable) relationship in a jesting situation: the one between speakers and listeners. My argument in this chapter derives from the manuals' repeated claims about the power of laughter over an audience: because laughter has an irresistible impact on the bodies and minds of those who laugh, jesting allows speakers to gain control over their listeners. However, what the manuals are reluctant to admit, but reveal nevertheless, is that in order to achieve this control, speakers must paradoxically submit to and become the servants of the audiences they are addressing. I situate this argument in the context of the ethical and medical lore on recreation from antiquity into the early modern period. This lore offers laughter and jesting as recipes for regulating an individual's emotional and bodily health. Orators and courtiers are to use these same recipes, the manuals insist, if they are to gain control over the minds and bodies of their listeners. Several of the manuals even go so far as to suggest that these same recipes can serve as a means of ruling an entire kingdom—that is, ruling the body politic. However, the need to control audiences presupposes their power, which they can express in relatively innocuous ways, such as falling asleep or wandering off out of earshot, or in the more fearful and aggressive acts of an unruly mob. To guard against these possibilities, speakers must continually accommodate their speech to the needs of their listeners and continually feed them merry tales and witty sayings. These dynamics become even more complicated when the relative statuses of speaker and audience are taken into consideration. The socially superior speaker still must submit to the needs of his listeners, but his social superiority does offer him a kind of buffer, which he can invoke should his jesting fail. The socially inferior speaker, by contrast, has virtually no buffer against failure: while he can use jesting to manage a socially superior audience, a failure on his part to make his betters laugh is compounded by his own social inferiority. Moreover, several of the manuals insist that gentlemen observe stricter regimens of bodily control and carefully regulate, among other things, the intensity and frequency of their laughter. Not only do these new regimens give evidence for the ever widening gap between aristocratic and popular culture, but they also suggest that listeners (or at least some listeners) can master powers that seek to master them, including the powers of jesting.

Keith Thomas claims that early modern jests are worthy of scholarly attention because "their subject matter can be a revealing guide to past tensions and anxieties."[61] Early modern rhetoric and courtesy manuals in England go one better. In addition to including sample jests that also reveal similar "tensions and anxieties," they embed those jests in oftentimes rich and highly complex discussions of the practice of jesting itself. In this way, these discussions give us some indication of what early modern writers thought of these jests and—what is more—how jesting in general fit into at least some aspects of early modern life. For the practicing orator or courtier, jesting is an available resource for navigating diverse social situations, particularly situations in which they come into contact with people whose social origins or occupations differ from their own. As the manuals repeatedly make clear, however, these situations are fraught with possibilities and dangers, and while the manuals recommend that orators and courtiers make the most of these possibilities, they also insist that they avoid the dangers of jesting, particularly those associated with its disruptive and chaotic energies. The problem, of course, with such a program is that jesting always involves such energies; it is always a flirtation with disorder.

I

Jesting Situations

Early modern rhetoric and courtesy manuals, like their classical sources, view jesting as a situational phenomenon: its significance and function are invariably linked to its context of production. From this perspective, they have much in common with the work of several modern social scientists who stress the importance of the immediate communicative situation and the larger social context in any humorous exchange. According to Gary Alan Fine, "Humor, like all interpersonal behavior, is socially situated. . . . For humor to work—that is, be funny—it must be responsive to the immediate situation and to be appropriate to the normative properties of the more general social circumstances."[1] The present chapter will examine how rhetoric and courtesy manuals view the relationship between jesting and both immediate situations and the larger social context. It will also qualify sociological and anthropological theories about such relationships in one important way, a qualification that the manuals themselves suggest. There is a tendency in the social scientific discourse on humor to posit a unidirectional determinism between context and humor: context determines and constrains all humorous activity.[2] The manuals, by contrast, see the relationship between context and jesting as a dialectical one: they view jesting as a powerful resource speakers can use to manage, even alter, specific situations, but they also recognize that the success of the speaker depends on his ability to observe decorum and adapt his jesting to the particular occasion as well as to the larger social context, even if that means refraining from jesting altogether.

Although jesting is invariably a situational phenomenon, the character of each situation is historically contingent, a historic variability that is implicit in the manuals' treatments of jesting. In ancient rhetorics, the typical jesting situation involves encounters between people who are more or less equals in terms of both status and profession. More specifically, these rhetorics present two rival orators of equestrian or senatorial rank verbally sparring in either a deliberative or forensic setting. There, although the rhetorics assign other functions to jesting, its principal use is to defeat an opponent by ridiculing his character, credibility, or any witnesses he might bring forward in support of his case.[3] While writers of early modern handbooks on oratory and courtly conduct also recognize the possibility of using jesting to combat a rival, the situations uppermost in their minds involve interaction, not between people of the same status or profession (that is, rival orators), but between people of divergent social origins or occupations. Two jesting situations in particular receive special attention in the early modern manuals: jesting from the pulpit and at the court of a prince. In pulpit oratory, jesting is viewed (at least by some) as an available strategy for keeping listeners attentive, refreshed, and under control. That is, the relationship of interest here is not the one between speakers and their rivals as in ancient texts, but between preachers and their lay congregations where jesting is to be used to overcome barriers to communication and prepare listeners for religious instruction. In the highly stratified and differentiated environment of the royal court, jesting is seen primarily as a means for the courtier to present a self, ideally one that is socially elevated and clearly distinguishable from his ambitious inferiors. Not every manual treats both of these situations, and, of course, these situations do not exhaust every possible setting in which jesting was thought to occur in the period. Many of the sample jests the manuals use to illustrate their prescriptions involve a wide variety of other, less formally structured settings. Even so, because jesting from the pulpit and at court are featured in the early modern discourse on jesting, they can be considered as special instances of situations in which different kinds of people interact.

If jesting enhances the power of orators and courtiers and their ability to manage specific social situations, then decorum seeks to hold that power and ability in check. It is a force that limits and constrains the jesting of speakers on both a practical and social level. In terms of its practical consequences, it requires a speaker to adapt and accommodate his jesting behaviors to every element and participant in a jesting exchange—to the time and place where he jests, to the people for whom he jests, to the subject matter or butts of his jests, and even to the character or self he hopes to project though jesting. All of these elements and participants impinge upon (or should impinge upon) the jesting practices of orators and courtiers, and speakers who ignore them risk undermining their more general persuasive aims. In terms of its social consequences, decorum often seeks to preserve a particular set of values and behaviors (usually those of the culturally dominant group) in the face of pressures that threaten, challenge, or even aim to displace those values and behaviors. Of all the issues related to decorum and jesting in classical discussions of wit, two oveerlapping concepts are relevant to this discussion: the character or social identity of the speaker and the place or arena in which he operates. Above all, classical writers insist that orators only jest in ways that befit a gentleman, and they by and large forbid them from engaging in antics associated with the lowly buffoon, stage comedian, and mime. These prescriptions entail a more general opposition between the professional arenas of orators and comic performers—that is, between the forum and theater, between the rostrum and the stage. Quintilian insists that these two arenas (and the behaviors associated with them) be kept separate, an insistence that participates in Quintilian's more general concerns about the decline of eloquence during the early Empire. While Cicero shares (and is actually the source for) Quintilian's views on the separation of these two arenas, he also confuses them on occasion, both in his theory of wit and in his actual practice as an orator. In doing so, he circumvents at least some of the strictures of decorum and gives freer rein to the unruly energies of jesting.

I focus on these two issues—the character of the speaker and the place in which he operates—because they are rehearsed in early modern discussions of decorum and jesting, although the terms and contexts in which they are replayed there differ in significant and remarkable ways. The tension between the rostrum and stage found in Cicero and Quintilian reappears in early modern discussions of preachers jesting as a rivalry between pulpit and playhouse. While some writers allow (if only grudgingly) preachers to take a lesson from the stage's success and incorporate theatrical fooling into sermons, others (particularly ultra-Protestants and Puritans) forbid the practice, claiming that mirth making of any kind in the pulpit is itself a violation of decorum. These competing views over pulpit jesting are related to several debates crucial to the Protestant Reformation in England, including efforts to eliminate all vestiges of Catholicism (with which jesting and theatrical performances are associated) from the Protestant liturgy. They also constitute an instance in which a socially marginal group (in this case, Puritans) use arguments based on decorum to change, and not to preserve, the status quo. As for the courtier in early modern England, he is to follow the example of the Roman orator and jest only in ways that befit a gentleman. Toward this end, he must fashion all of his jests in accordance with hierarchical relationships already in place before a jesting exchange commences—decorum here is shorthand for the social hierarchy itself. The problem with this project is that, owing to increases in social and geographic mobility, the signs and markers of a gentlemanly status were dislodged from any notion of a stable and absolute self and, instead, manifested themselves in stylized behaviors available to anyone with the talent and inclination to appropriate them. While jesting agrees well with the new ideal of courtly identity and provides courtiers opportunities for displaying effortlessness (Castglione's *sprezzatura* which should govern all of the courtier's behavior), it also encourages confusion between the decorous and indecorous, the gentlemanly and the baseborn, and, most important, the socially conservative and socially disruptive.

JESTING IN
THE ROMAN FORUM

Aristotle, Cicero, and Quintilian all view jesting as a powerful resource orators can use to manage deliberative and, especially, forensic settings. This is not to suggest that they think jesting is only useful in, or appropriate to, public assemblies and the law courts. Aristotle, for instance, notes the value, even the necessity, of jesting as a form of relaxation well suited to informal settings such as conversations among friends, perhaps over dinner (*Ethics,* 4.8.1). In his *De officiis,* Cicero offers a similar observation and says that jesting is particularly appropriate during times of rest and relaxation "when we have satisfied the claims of our earnest, serious tasks" (1.29.103). Quintilian also views jesting as suitable to informal gatherings and daily conversations (6.3.28), and when commenting on Cicero's wit, Quintilian claims this orator was remarkable for his jesting in multiple settings: "For his daily speech was full of humor, while in his disputes at court and in his examination of witnesses he produced more good jests than any other [orator]" (6.3.4). For all three of these writers, jesting is suited to times of relaxation and work (*otium* and *negotium*); however, the functions it might serve vary with the setting in which it is deployed.

Although jesting is useful and appropriate to multiple settings, its operation in the law courts attracts particular interest. In his *Rhetoric,* Aristotle

says that jests are "of some service in controversy." He then rehearses a statement he attributes to Gorgias: "you should kill your opponents' earnestness
with jesting and their jesting with earnestness" (1419b 3–5). The situation
implicit in this statement is one in which two (or more) orators are engaged
in a verbal contest, one trying to counter the other's rhetorical strategy with
its opposite. In a crucial passage from *De oratore,* Cicero provides a similar,
though more detailed, description of what he sees as the typical jesting situation and its dynamics. He prefaces this description by raising the question
of whether or not it is appropriate for an orator to jest and then goes on to
answer in the affirmative: "It clearly becomes an orator to raise laughter, and
this on various grounds; for instance, merriment naturally wins goodwill for
its author; and everyone admires acuteness, which is often concentrated in a
single word, uttered generally in repelling, though sometimes in delivering
an attack; and it shatters or obstructs or makes light of an opponent, or
alarms or repulses him; and it shows the orator himself to be a man of finish, accomplishment and taste; and best of all, it relieves dullness and tones
down austerity, and, by a jest or laugh, often dispels distasteful suggestions
not easily weakened by reasonings" (2.58.236). Here Cicero defends an orator's use of jesting by arguing for its pragmatic value. And the type of situation implicit in this defense is one with which Cicero himself is very familiar:
a speaker combats an opponent, in a forensic setting, over the adherence of
an audience.[4] In such a setting, jesting can affect every participant in a
rhetorical exchange. It can enhance the ethos of a speaker and show him to
be a man of "finish, accomplishment, and taste." It can win the admiration
and goodwill of his audience and ease tensions and relax his hearers. Finally,
and most important, it can shatter the ethos of an opponent or undermine or
attract attention away from his arguments.[5] Throughout this passage, Cicero
is not talking about the witty banter that takes place among friends in informal gatherings. Instead, he is primarily concerned with humor deployed in
the wrangle of the law courts where jesting, among other things, helps an
orator secure a victory over his rival.

If the situation implicit in Cicero's defense of jesting is a forensic one,
then we need to characterize this particular setting in greater detail in order
to understand more fully Cicero's treatment of jesting and what he sees as
the typical jesting situation. The most important location for litigation and
speech making in ancient Rome was the forum, which was also a central
place for business and social transactions. As such, it was characterized by a

"dense and incessant stream of traffic."[6] According to Richard Enos, the nature of this situation had a profound impact on the character of Roman oratory, especially forensic oratory. Because of its location in the forum, says Enos, Roman litigation was marked "increasingly by colorful oratory— particularly in cases of a violent or personal nature."[7] In such a "climate," Enos continues, orators recognized the importance of winning the approval of their listeners since those listeners "set the standard for successful rheto- ric"—that is, the surest avenue to success was for an orator to be popular with his audience. [8] This claim is substantiated by Cicero himself who says, "the very mark of a supreme orator [is] that the supreme orator is recognized by the people."[9] However, Enos's pragmatics of speech making in the forum is incomplete and ignores an important component of a forensic setting. He fails to account for how the presence of an opponent (*adversarius*) affects a forensic situation and its rhetorical dynamics. An orator did not speak before the judges and spectators unchallenged. Rather, he fought an opponent to gain the adherence of the audience. The listeners did, of course, make the final judgment, and emotional appeals and the public image of each speaker would presumably influence their decision. However, their decision must have also been influenced by how well each orator performed in the verbal fray. In other words, although winning the approval of listeners was the goal of every orator, an orator only won that approval by defeating his opponent.

This emphasis on defeating an opponent is implicit in the ways Cicero and Quintilian characterize orators and the situations in which they operate. Typically, these writers portray orators as soldiers or fighters who are "theo- retically equals," and they describe the arena in which they deliver speeches as if it were a battlefield.[10] In *De oratore,* Cicero speaks of the necessity of training and practice so that orators will know what to do in the "battle-line [*in acie*] . . . of the Courts" (1.32.147). The figures of speech are the orator's weapons or *arma,* and they are to be used "to threaten and to attack, or sim- ply brandished for show" (3.54.206). The culmination of all an orator's train- ing is, according to Cicero, verbal battle in the forum: "Then at last must our Oratory be conducted out of this sheltered training-ground at home, right into action, into the dust and uproar, into the camp and the fighting line of public debate [*aciem forensem*]" (1.34.157). Quintilian also imagines the ora- tor to be a soldier who fights in the "battle of the forum [*pugnam forensem*]" (5.12.17). His armament includes the common topics (*communes loci*) that he must have stored in his "armoury ready for immediate use" (2.1.12), and the figures of speech that he must wield like "flashing weapons [*fulgentibus armis*]" (8.3.2). Quintilian later uses an extended battle metaphor to illustrate the dangers of being "led by a desire to win applause" at the expense of the "actual case," especially when it is a difficult one. Like a general leading his troops across rugged terrain, an orator who is caught in a difficult spot "will not go prancing in front of the enemy's lines nor launch [his] shafts of quivering and passionate epigram . . . , but will wage war by means of sap and mine and ambush and all the tactics of secrecy" (12.9.3). Here the desire to win the audience's approval, which Enos claims was paramount, is subordinated to overcoming an opponent and winning the case.

If the forum is a field of combat where rival orators do battle, then jesting is a weapon with which they can fight. As we have already seen in Cicero's defense of humor, jesting "shatters an opponent [*frangit adversarium*]." Elsewhere, he refers to a joke as if it were a spear which "is hurled [*infligitur*]" at an adversary (*De oratore,* 2.63.256). Earlier, Cicero divides humor into two modes: humor expressed in short spontaneous quips (*dicacites*), and humor expressed in an extended or narrative form (*facetiae*). Praising Crassus for his use of humor against Brutus, Cicero says that Crassus "fought [*pugnavit*] in both modes" (*De oratore,* 2.55.222). In the *Orator,* Cicero says that with a shaft of wit, an orator "adversarios figet," a phrase suggesting that an orator pierces his opponents with wit as if fixing them on a spit (26.89). Quintilian also uses martial imagery to describe the effects of jesting. Concerned over the injuries jesting can inflict, he cautions the orator to be prudent when jesting in "social gatherings and the intercourse of everyday." In such a setting, a speaker's jest "should never be designed to wound [*laudere*]" (6.3.28). He also says, however, that the combative nature of a forensic setting actually sanctions hostile jesting: in a "forensic battle [*pugna forensi*] . . . it is permissible to speak harshly and abusively against our opponents [*adversarios*]" (6.3.28). Jesting is especially useful, says Quintilian, when cross-examining a witness or during the forensic debates (*altercationis*) that would typically follow the delivery of set speeches by the plaintiff and defense. In cross-examinations, Quintilian includes jesting among those "weapons" or *tela* that the orator must have ready at hand (*ad manum*) (5.7.8; 5.7.26), and in debates where the "advocate must speak at once and return the blow almost before it has been dealt by his opponent" (6.4.8), jesting is a powerful resource for refuting or making light of an opponent and any arguments he might advance in support of his position (6.4.10).

Not only do Cicero and Quintilian portray jesting as a weapon, but they also offer many examples of orators verbally sparing in the courts.[11] In one example, Cicero tells of the witty retort made by Catulus (a name which means "little dog") during a trial. When his adversary, Philippus, asks him, "What are you barking at, Master Puppy?" Catulus responds, "I see a thief" (*De oratore,* 2.54.220). Later, Cicero interprets the technique of this jest: "a word is snatched from . . . [Catulus's] antagonist and used to hurl a shaft at the assailant himself [Philippus]" (2.63.255).[12] Even this interpretation of the jest's operation suggests that this sort of aggressive banter was conceived as a skirmish between rivals. In another example, Gallus accuses Piso of extortion and of giving one of his lieutenants, Magius, a vast sum of money for his part in the crime. The advocate for the defense, Scauras, attempts to refute these allegations by claiming that this lieutenant had no money and was, in fact, living in "straitened circumstances." Gallus responds, "You are missing the point, Scaurus, for I do not assert that Magius still has the fund, but that he has tucked it away in his paunch, like a naked man who goes nutting" (2.66.265). A final example from Cicero: Servius Galba, the defendant, had just handed a list of prospective judges to the tribunal of the commons, when the prosecutor, Libo, asks sarcastically, "Galba, whenever will you go outside your own dining-room?" Galba immediately replies, "As soon as ever you come away from other people's bedrooms" (2.65.263). Apparently, Libo had a reputation for engaging in adulterous affairs. More to the point, Libo's initial jest constitutes a challenge to Galba and tries to define the situation as one in which Galba is stacking the odds in his own favor by proposing that his friends sit on the tribunal.[13] Galba does not deny this definition of the situation, but with his retort, he deflects the force of Libo's remark and counters with an even more damaging blow.

Quintilian offers even more jests that are set in the law courts. He is particularly fond of rehearsing jests delivered by Cicero. In one such example, he recites a jest that "Cicero levelled against Curio, who always began his speech by asking indulgence for his youth." On one occasion, when Curio asks for such indulgence, Cicero says to him (and presumably to the court), "You will find your exordium easier everyday" (6.3.76). Here Cicero's jest undermines Curio's ethos precisely at the moment when Curio is trying to establish it. Another example is taken from the sensational trial of fifty-two in which Cicero defended T. Annius Milo who was accused of murdering Publius Clodius, a longtime enemy of Cicero, who a few years earlier had

Cicero's house and villas destroyed. The prosecutor, who is trying to convince the court that Milo had lain in wait for Clodius, repeatedly asks, "Quo tempore Clodius occisus esset [When was Clodius killed]?" To this Cicero responds with a pun: "Sero," which can mean "at a late hour" or "too late." A final example, which also appears in *De oratore* and features one of its interlocutors, suggests how jests that amount to little more than ad hominem attacks are nevertheless prized for the devastating effects they may secure. During a legal trial, Helvius Mancia "kept clamouring" against C. Julius Caesar (who is not to be confused with Gaius Julius Caesar). Fed up with the racket his opponents was making, Caesar finally says to him, "I will show you what you are like!" He then points to a picture of a Gaul painted on a Cimbric shield hanging over one of the shops in the forum (Quintilian, 6.3.38). In the picture, the body of the Gaul is twisted, his "tongue protruding" and his "cheeks baggy" (*De oratore,* 2.66.266). Observing the striking resemblance between Mancia and the painting of the deformed Gaul, the listeners burst out laughing, a response that was presumably satisfying to Caesar and humiliating to his opponent.

For Cicero and Quintilian, jesting is a powerful and economical resource for managing situations in which two rival orators square off in the *pugnam forensem*. In such a setting, the successful jest affects every participant, realigning the audience on the side of the witty orator over and against that orator's opponent. But as Cicero and Quintilian also make clear, the orator who resorts to jesting in a forensic dispute must fashion all of his jests in accordance with the dictates of decorum, and in doing so, he must conform his behavior to the needs and requirements of the situation he hopes to manage through jesting. It is difficult to overestimate the importance of decorum in discussions of jesting or in classical and early modern rhetorical theory in general. Robert Hariman calls it an "architectonic concept," and while summarizing Cicero's views on the subject, he says that decorum provides "a means for thinking about how we coordinate words, thoughts, acts, and gestures to behave purposively in shifting social circumstances."[14] It embodies a theory of practice, and in mastering this difficult concept, the orator cultivates a certain flexibility that enables him to navigate diverse social settings. While making his way through these settings, however, the orator is also constrained by them, for decorum also requires that he conform his behavior to the character he hopes to project; to the tastes, values, and needs of his audience; to his subject matter; and to the time and place in which he speaks and acts. Respecting the bounds of and limitations imposed by decorum is especially challenging in the case of jesting. As we shall see throughout this study, the orator or courtier who jests often skirts, or even straddles, the line separating the decorous from the indecorous—that is, he momentarily breaks from serious forms of address, undermines or cheats the expectations of listeners, and points out something ridiculous in his opponent or some third party while trying not to appear ridiculous himself. Jesting is risky and potentially irreverent business. Decorum helps speakers minimize those risks and, more important, keeps the oftentimes volatile and aggressive impulses associated with jesting in check.

Invoking decorum in its most general and streamlined formulation and applying it specifically to jesting, Cicero says that "regard ought to be paid to personages, topics, and occasions, so that a jest should not detract from dignity" (*De oratore*, 2.56.229). Quintilian offers a similar formulation: "The first points to be taken in consideration [when jesting] are who the speaker is, what is the nature of the case, who is the judge, who is the victim, and what are the character of the remarks that are made" (6.3.28). In both of these passages, we find every element and participant in a jesting exchange, and as their discussions unfold, Cicero and Quintilian describe how each of these elements or participants restricts (or should restrict) the jesting practices of orators. Oftentimes, several elements or participants will constrain an orator's jesting simultaneously. With respect to "topics" or "victims," for instance, the character or condition of the comic butt, the tastes and values of the audience, and the self the orator hopes to project all require the orator to be circumspect about the kinds of people he singles out for ridicule. According to Cicero and Quintilian, three groups of people are inappropriate objects of laughter: the miserable or unfortunate, the wicked, and the "well-beloved" or those in positions of authority (*De oratore*, 2.58.237; Quintilian, 6.3.31–33). These three groups are off-limits because the orator who jests at their expense risks alienating his audience and, as a consequence, earning a reputation as one who offends against propriety and popular tastes. The unfortunate are unsuitable objects of laughter because it is the listeners who "dislike mockery of the wretched" (*De oratore*, 2.58.237) and will not endure "an advocate . . . who makes merry over [a case] . . . that calls for pity" (Quintilian, 6.3.31). Nor should an orator attack the wicked "for the public would have the villainous hurt by a weapon rather more formidable than ridicule" (*De oratore*, 2.58.237; see also Quintilian, 6.3.31). As for the well-beloved and those in positions of authority, the orator "must be tender of popular esteem" (*De oratore*, 2.58.237), for "any insolence shown them would only hurt the assailant" (Quintilian, 6.3.33). Listeners are clearly a force that constrains and limits the jesting of orators, and should a speaker ignore what they deem as inappropriate objects of laughter, then he risks undermining his own ethos and, more generally, impairing his chances for winning his case.

In addition to embodying a theory of practice (one that facilitates as it constrains possibilities for action), decorum also implies (and often seeks to naturalize) a particular social and cultural arrangement. Discussing the challenges ancient and early modern rhetoricians faced when trying to define decorum in general, Rebhorn says that the "typical procedure" was "to set up an opposition between the decorous and the indecorous that entails the juxtaposition of contrasting sets of value and behaviors as well as the distinct social groups linked to them." The opposition is usually "one between the values and behavior of the dominant social group and those of marginal or external ones, between the center and the periphery, in short, between 'us' and 'them.'"[15] The "procedure" Rebhorn describes here is generally followed by ancient rhetoricians in their treatments of wit, and the oppositions they "set up" to distinguish decorous from indecorous forms of jesting often correspond to oppositions used more generally to organize the social world, including young versus old, play versus work, city versus country, things versus words.[16] In addition to these, two oppositions are worthy of special note because they figure prominently in Cicero's and Quintilian's theories of wit: the first one is between the gentlemanly and the ignoble (or the *liberalis* and *illiberalis*); and the second, between oratory and comedy or, more concretely, the rostrum and the stage. There is considerable overlap between these two oppositions (stage performers in antiquity were almost exclusively of ignoble origins, and those who practiced oratory were typically of equestrian or senatorial rank), but they do allow Cicero and Quintilian to identify with greater clarity those forms of jesting that befit the orator and those that do not. More generally, these oppositions aim to preserve the orator's respectability and social preeminence, and to guard against any confusion between the professional arena of orators and those of comic performers. As we shall see, however, things are rarely this straightforward or clear-cut, and this is generally the case with jesting. Cicero and Quintilian are by and large in agreement over how the elevated social status of the orator ought to limit his jesting, but they diverge somewhat in their attitudes toward comic performers. Quintilian adamantly insists that orators avoid the antics of the stage (particularly the mime and Atellan farce), while Cicero allows for orators to borrow comic techniques from theatrical performances, provided that they do so discretely and without degenerating into excess.

Associations between social status and certain forms of jesting appear as early as the *Nicomachean Ethics,* where Aristotle classifies different modes of jesting according to three social types: the boor, the buffoon, and the witty man of tact.[17] Aristotle has little to say about boorish men except that they never say "anything funny themselves and take offense at those who do" (4.8.3). Instead, Aristotle dwells on differences between the buffoon and man of wit, and in differentiating these two social types, he associates indecorous jests with those of the lower-class buffoon and decorous ones with those of a gentleman. "Those who go to excess in ridicule are thought to be buffoons or vulgar fellows, who itch to have their joke at all costs, and are more concerned to raise a laugh than to keep within the bounds of decorum" (4.8.3). The buffoon often jests in a "servile" and often obscene fashion (4.8.5–6), he "cannot resist a joke," he will "not keep his tongue off himself or anyone else, if he can raise a laugh," and he "will say things which a man of refinement would never say" (4.8.10). Those "who jest with good taste," by contrast, will say "only the sort of things that are suitable to a virtuous man and a gentleman" (4.8.5). They prefer to jest by way of "innuendo, which marks a great advance in decorum," and they will never stoop so low in their jesting as to say anything "unbecoming to a gentleman" (4.8.6–7). The line Aristotle draws here is not simply one between the indecorous and decorous; it is also one between the lower and upper classes. And while Aristotle couches his distinctions in more or less descriptive (although elitist) terms, they do have prescriptive force. If a speaker is to show himself as a "man of refinement," he must limit his jesting behaviors and avoid the excesses of the buffoon.

Cicero and Quintilian adopt Aristotle's method of classifying decorous and indecorous jests along class lines, and they both use the buffoon and well-bred man of tact to define forms of jesting befitting an orator (the boor, as often happens in everyday life, is left out of their discussions of jesting). But they add to the ranks of the buffoon (or *scurra,* in Latin) a cast of characters familiar from the Roman stage, street performances, and entertainments provided at a gentleman's dinner party—characters including the mime (*mimus*), pantomime (*ethologus*), and clown (*sannio*).[18] Cicero says that "an orator must avoid each of two dangers: he must not let his jesting become buffoonery or mere mimicking [*scurrilis . . . aut mimicus*]" (2.58.239). Like Aristotle's buffoon, the Latin *scurra* violates proprieties of time. Cicero says he jests "from morning to night, and without any reason at all" (2.60.247). He also shows no restraint in his selection of objects of ridicule, and his jests, like a scattergun, will often strike "unintended victims" (2.60.245). He will even turn himself into an object of ridicule if he thinks he can raise a laugh (Quintilian, 6.3.82). Most important, the *scurra* is a member of the lower classes, a parasite who would often perform at a gentleman's dinner party for table scraps, and his antics almost always bespoke his lowly position.[19] For all of these reasons, especially the last, Cicero and Quintilian repeatedly insist that orators avoid all likeness to buffoons, and toward this end, they offer a set of strictures limiting the jesting practices of orators so that those practices accord with the orator's gentlemanly status. With respect to proprieties of time, Cicero says, "Regard then to occasions, control and restraint of our actual raillery, and economy in bon-mots, will distinguish an orator from a buffoon [*oratorem a scurra*]" (2.60.247). As we have seen, orators should also be careful in their selection of comic butts and avoid targeting the excessively wretched or wicked and the well-beloved. Moreover, they must never turn themselves into objects of laughter for, as Quintilian says, "To make jokes against oneself is scarcely fit for any save professed buffoons and is strongly to be disapproved in an orator" (6.3.82). Presumably, orators should keep the audience's laughter off themselves and direct it only at their opponents. Above all, the orator should only jest in ways that befit a gentleman or *liberalis*. He should avoid obscenities in his jesting, which are "not only degrading to a public speaker, but also hardly sufferable at a gentlemen's dinner party [*convivio liberorum*]" (*De oratore*, 2.61.252), and "scurrilous or brutal jests, although they may raise a laugh, are quite unworthy of a gentleman [*liberali*]" (Quintilian, 6.3.83). In an allusion to his famous formulation of the orator as a good man, or *vir bonus,* skilled in speaking, Quintilian sums up his attitudes toward buffoonery, a summation that will serve for Cicero's views on the subject as well: "A good man [*vir bonus*] will see that everything he says is consistent with his dignity and the respectability of his character [*dignitate ac verecundia*]; for we pay too dear for the laugh we raise if it is at the cost of our own integrity [*probitatis*]" (6.3.35).

Cicero's and Quintilian's attitudes toward the comic actor and especially the mime are more complex. While both of these rhetoricians occasionally turn to the actor as a model for eloquence—more specifically, as a model for delivery—they also fear that orators who go too far in imitating the actor or other performers will blur distinctions between oratory and theater to the detriment of the former. References to Quintus Roscius, the celebrated comic actor, appear in several of Cicero's rhetorical treatises, and he was a teacher, friend, and one-time client of Cicero.[20] So high is his regard for this comic actor that, at one point in his *De oratore,* he says, "In whatsoever craft a man excelled, the same was called a Roscius in his own line" (1.28.130; see also *Brutus,* 84.290). For all his admiration for Roscius, Cicero does insist on crucial differences between the orator and actor: each is judged by different standards (*De oratore,* 1.27.125 and 1.61.259); actors seek only to delight listeners, but orators must secure a wide range of effects (*De oratore,* 1.61.259); and acting is a "mean and trivial craft," while oratory is "admittedly the greatest" of arts (*De oratore,* 1.28.129). As for Quintilian, he recommends that young students learn pronunciation and the delivery of narratives from comic actors (1.11.1–14), and toward the end of his discussion of delivery in book 11, Quintilian considers at length the respective merits of Demetrius and Stratocles, whom he praises as "the greatest of comic actors" (11.3.178–80). These recommendations and praise, however, are framed within a series of qualifications warning students and public speakers against going too far in adopting the theatrical practices and methods of actors. After all, says Quintilian, "I am not trying to form a comic actor, but an orator [*non comoedum . . . sed oratorem*]" (11.3.181).

In his discussion of jesting, Quintilian's attitude toward the stage, particularly mime and Atellan farce, are decisively more negative: "It is most unbecoming for an orator to distort his features or use uncouth gestures, tricks that arouse such merriment in farce [*in mimis*]. No less unbecoming are ribald jests, and such as are employed upon the stage [*scenica*]" (6.3.29). Later, while considering suitable "topics" or *loci* for an orator's jests, Quintilian says that "*doubles entendres* and obscenity, such as is dear to the Atellan farce [*Atellani*], are to be avoided, as also are those coarse jibes so common on the lips of the rabble [*vulgo*]" (6.3.47). These are not idle rants, but constitute an attempt on Quintilian's part to shore up boundaries between orators and comic performers, boundaries that were increasingly blurred in ancient Rome. Of rural origins, then appended to stage comedies as "farcical tags," *Atellani* and mimes became immensely popular in the late Republic and early Empire—so popular, in fact, that they all but eclipsed dramatic comedy, becoming one of the central attractions during the festivals and games held at Rome.[21] The players who performed in these shows were typically slaves, and they were known for their "shocking behavior both onstage and off."[22] Moralists of the period "frequently lumped them together with other low-life denizens; whores, pimps, parasites, and the like."[23] The mimes did not wear masks, as comedic and tragic actors did, and "their grimacing, gesticulation, and general expressiveness"—to which Quintilian objects— "were an essential part of the performance."[24] Despite their seedy origins and reputations for seedy behavior, it was not uncommon for the politically powerful, including Sulla, Pompey, and Caesar, to sponsor a mime show in order to enhance their popularity with and influence over the masses.[25] Mark Antony even socialized with mimes, and Sulla had an affair with one "who specialized in some refinement of female impersonation."[26] In addition to being an instrument of power, the stage of the mimes often became a platform for political rhetoric, although a rhetoric whose messages were cloaked (in some instances, only barely) in the expressions of fictional characters set in imaginary settings. According to Richard C. Beacham, audiences at these performances were "quick . . . to recognize the frequent topical and satirical allusion, or veiled political comment."[27] In a letter to Atticus, Cicero asks his friend to give him "full details as to who were cheered by the people at the mimes" so that he might gather from their reactions the popular opinion over Caesar's recent death.[28] Quintilian even suggests, to his dismay, that orators were taking a lesson from the mime's tremendous success and incorporating some of its comic techniques into their public speeches. As if reacting to the practices of contemporary orators, Quintilian says, "There is . . . good reason for the condemnation on a delivery which entails the continual alteration of facial expression, annoying restlessness of gesture and gusty changes of tone" (11.3.183). Alterations of the face, body, and voice are the stock-in-trade of the mimes, and for this reason, Quintilian disapproves of their use in public speaking, saying that "oratory has a different flavor and objects to elaborate condiments, since it consists in serious pleading, not in mimicry" (11.3.182). Despite these strictures, says Quintilian, "a rather more violent form of delivery has come into fashion and is demanded of our orators" (11.3.184). Rather than cave in to popular tastes, Quintilian advises his orators to keep their manner of delivery "under control" so that "in our attempt to ape the elegances of the stage," we do not "lose the authority [*auctoritatem*] which should characterise the man of dignity and virtue [*viri boni et gravis*]"

(11.3.184). Quintilian's references to *auctoritas* (which can mean "tradition" as well as "power to command") and to the *vir bonus* are telling, for they suggest that Quintilian's complaints here are one instance of a more general lament that runs throughout his treatise, a lament over what he sees as the degenerate state into which contemporary oratory has fallen. His *Institutio* is not simply an effort to outline the education and career of the orator from cradle to retirement. It also aims to restore eloquence to its supposedly former glory—that is, to usher in a new age of Ciceronianism.[29]

Ironically, the namesake of this new age was himself more sympathetic to mimes and other comic performances. As we have already seen, Cicero names *mimicus* as one of the two dangers an orator ought to avoid, and in his *Orator,* he advises the orator to stay clear of obscenity so that he does "not seem to be acting a farce [*mimicum*]" (26.88).[30] In spite of these warnings, Cicero did attend the mimes, and as I have already noted, he considered audience reactions to these performances to be revealing indicators of public opinion. On occasion (and to his surprise), he even dined with them. At times in his discussion of jesting, and contrary to his warnings elsewhere, Cicero even permits, unlike Quintilian, the orator to engage in theatrics and mimicry, provided that he does not go to extremes. Among the forms of jesting available to an orator, Cicero includes funny stories and "vulgarized mimicry [*depravata imitatio*]." Elaborating on the former, he says, "Now the beauty of such jesting is, that you state your incidents in such a way, that the character, the manner of speaking and all the facial expressions of the hero of your tale, are so presented that those incidents seem to your audience to take place and to be transacted concurrently with your description of them" (*De oratore,* 2.59.241).[31] For Cicero, telling funny stories is not simply a matter of narration, of the orator recounting past events whether real or fabricated for comic effect.[32] It is also a matter of performance. The orator who follows Cicero's advice actually takes on the role of the person he is ridiculing. In doing so, however, he risks confusing his professional identity as an orator with that of an actor. More interesting, he collapses the distance between himself and the object of fun, between himself and, in the typical case, his opponent. For this reason, a performance of this kind raises interesting questions with regard to its practical consequences. How is the orator to keep the laughter off himself as he plays the part of someone who is laughable? Or phrased somewhat differently: Does the audience laugh *with* or *at* the speaker, or is it a mixture of both? For while the performative aspects of storytelling may lend this form of jesting its "beauty," they also confuse distinctions between orators and actors, between a speaker and his opponent, between laughing *with* and laughing *at*—in short, between the decorous and the indecorous.

In his remarks on "vulgarized mimicry," Cicero seems more cautious, adding an explicit warning against taking this comic technique too far. But this warning does little toward lessening the risks involved. Cicero begins his consideration of this form of jesting with two examples: the first is taken from an oratorical dispute, and the second from the stage. In the first example, Crassus mimics his adversary Domitus, who was presumably known for his arrogance: "By your rank, by your lineage!" Cicero comments on the technique of this jest and its effect upon the audience: "What else had the assembly to laugh at in this than that mimicry [*imitatio*] of facial expression and intonation?" And when Crassus "went on to say, 'By your statuary,' and lent a touch of action to the word by stretching out his arm," the audience "laughed quite consumedly" (2.59.242). The second example is Roscius's "famous" portrayal of an old man who "quavers out, 'For you, son Antipho, I'm planting these." This snippet of dialogue comes from a lost play, but its humor (whatever that may be) is not lost on Cicero, who says with appreciation, "I think I am listening to testy Eld [*Senium*] personified" (2.59.242). Both of these examples endorse the use of performance conventions associated with comic actors and mimes—that is, alterations in voice, expression, and gesture for comic effect. But Cicero is quick to add a caution: "This particular kind of laughing-matter is all such as to need extreme circumspection in the handling of it. For if the caricature is too extravagant, it becomes the work of buffoons in pantomime [*mimorum . . . ethologorum*]." Rather, the orator should "borrow merely a suspicion of mimicry, so that his hearers may imagine more than meets the eye" (2.59.242). Presumably the orator keeps the laughter off himself by not becoming too consumed by the part he plays and by allowing listeners to supply—almost enthymematically—what is missing. But such a performance (no matter how muted) is nevertheless a gamble, for what the orator is asking his listeners to do is separate in their minds whom they are laughing at (the person portrayed) from whom they are laughing with (the orator), despite the fact that they are looking at the same person.

As a practicing orator, Cicero himself often walked the thin line between oratory and theatrics, wit and buffoonery. In an interesting analysis of

Cicero's *Pro Caelio,* Katherine A. Geffcken examines the comic techniques Cicero used to defend his client against the charge of disturbing the peace with seditious intent. The last day of the trial, the day upon which Cicero addressed the court, coincided with the first day of the *Ludi Megalenses,* an arrangement that "meant that officials of the court and the *iudices* had to work when all the rest of Rome could be at the theater, at games, at the circus."[33] In an attempt to lessen any annoyance this conflict in scheduling might cause his audience, Cicero delivered a speech that attempted "to bring the holiday mood into the Forum, to turn the court into a comic theater, to play a variety of roles, to adopt the wily and shrewd machinations of the comic hero."[34] Geffcken praises Cicero for devising this "solution" to the problem of an ill-timed trial. But Cicero's reputation for humor did not always fare so well with those who were closer to being his contemporaries. Quintilian mentions "insipid" and "vulgar" jests that were attributed to Cicero in a jest book of sorts supposedly compiled by Tiro, his secretary and friend. In an attempt to preserve the good name of his idol, Quintilian claims these jests were "not the invention of the orator, but . . . current as public property" (6.3.4). Later in his discussion of wit, however, Quintilian does accuse Cicero of engaging, at least on one occasion, in scurrility (6.3.48). In his *Saturnalia,* Macrobius compares the wit of Cicero with that of Plautus, the comic playwright, and he rehearses a number of jests attributed to Cicero that seem to have come from the collection Quintilian mentions. Although these jests may be, as Quintilian maintains, the product of popular legend, they do nevertheless present Cicero as someone who is particularly addicted to jesting, as someone who, like a buffoon, takes every opportunity to crack wise. In one jest, Cicero sees his son-in-law (who was very short in stature) wearing a long sword, and says, "Who has buckled my son-in-law to that sword?"[35] Several other jests come at the expense of Caninius Revilus who held the consulship for only one day. Reflecting on what Caninius accomplished while in office, Cicero says, "He has at any rate done this: he has obliged us to ask in whose consulship he was consul." To this he added, "We have a wide-awake consul in Caninius, for while in office he never slept a wink" (167). Several more jests take as their butt Vatinius whose consulship was also exceptionally short (only a couple of days). When Vatinius asks Cicero why he did not visit him while he was sick, Cicero replies, "It was my intention to come while you were consul, but night overtook me" (166). Macrobius says that Cicero "welcomed every chance to make a humorous ιеιιιαrk" (167). Perhaps this is one of the reasons why his enemies (including Vatinius) referred to him as "that consular buffoon" (161), a remarkable appellation because it joins what Quintilian and (to a lesser extent) Cicero are determined to keep separate with their many invocations of decorum: the orator and the buffoon, the top of the social scale and its bottom.

Jesting from
the Pulpit

Cicero's answer to the question of whether or not it is appropriate for an orator to jest offers a general model of a jesting exchange: speakers jest in order to create, or reaffirm, an alliance with their audiences at the expense and exclusion of the butts of their jests. Variations of this model appear in many early modern rhetoric and courtesy manuals.[36] It is even implicit in a remark made by Maria in *Twelfth Night* when, vowing to dupe Malvolio, she says, "If I do not gull him [Malvolio] into a nayword and make him a common recreation, do not think I have wit enough to lie straight in my bed" (2.2.133–35). By making Malvolio a "common recreation," Maria not only degrades him but also turns him into a communal object of fun. Those who witness her practical joke and derive pleasure from it will be united by their laughter, a union that comes at the expense and exclusion of Malvolio. But even though Cicero's model persists into the early modern period, it undergoes permutations by which one function or relationship in a jesting exchange is emphasized over other functions and relationships. These permutations are in part the product of changes in the situations available for oratory in the period, the general dynamics of those situations, and the needs of speakers to operate in them successfully.

Early modern rhetoricians preserved in theory the three genres of oratory familiar from classical rhetoric (forensic, deliberative, and epideictic speeches), genres that corresponded to actual sites for public speaking in antiquity: the law courts, senate and public assemblies, and ceremonial gatherings. Jesting fits into these arenas for speech making (particularly the law courts) as a "model of the larger oratorical situation."[37] In early modern England, while lawyers still argued legal issues in the courts and politicians debated matters of state in Parliament, there was a shift in attention (a shift that had already begun in medieval rhetorical theory) to other sites and media for communication, including the pulpit, the royal court, letter writing, poetry, drama—even informal conversation was a subject of theoretical consideration.[38] As these other sites and media increased in importance, writers of rhetoric and courtesy manuals adapted and modified classical discussions of jesting (particularly Cicero's) accordingly. In these adaptations, early modern writers also presented jesting as a "model" of communication, but for these writers, jesting did not model situations in which rival orators verbally sparred in the law courts. Instead, it modeled situations in which people of divergent social and geographic origins meet. While such encounters constitute the early modern jesting situation in its most general formulation, there are other, more specific instances of this situation. One of these is jesting from the pulpit. Here the relationship of interest is not the one between orators and their opponents, but between preachers and their lay congregations where jesting allows preachers to transcend differences between themselves and their parishioners in preparation, one would guess, for that ultimate transcendence.

Jesting from the pulpit is problematic, however. Thomas Wilson embraces the notion wholeheartedly, and Thomas More and Erasmus, while they harbor serious reservations, eventually endorse the practice. Preachers Hugh Latimer and John Hooper even gained reputations for their "mocking and railing" sermons.[39] Ultra-Protestants and Puritans, however, forbid preachers from moving laughter during sermons, arguing that the pulpit is no place for, as John Northbrooke puts it, "frivolous vaine things, full of scurrilitie and baudrie."[40] These competing views over jesting from the pulpit revolve around issues of decorum, both as a guide to practice and as an ideology that limits and constrains the behaviors of preachers and their listeners. Wilson, More, and Erasmus acknowledge (with varying degrees of enthusiasm) the need for churchgoers to be occasionally refreshed with a merry tale: preachers who fail to provide such refreshment are not being responsive to the immediate rhetorical situation and, as a consequence, risk losing the attention of and perhaps even alienating their audiences. Ultra-Protestants and Puritans are also concerned with the needs of churchgoers, but from their perspective, those needs do not include hearing funny stories and witty remarks. More generally, while these competing views on preachers jesting are, in some measure, a continuation of debates among medieval theologians and preachers over the relationship between jest and earnest, they are also related to several central issues that arose during the English Reformation.[41] For one, jesting from the pulpit has it roots in medieval, and hence Catholic, preaching practices, and it seems that some writers want such practices to go the way of other forms of "holy play" associated with the unreformed church. For another, the controversy over preachers jesting participates in a more general rivalry between pulpit and playhouse, a rivalry that later intensified and resulted in the closing of the London theaters during the Puritan Interregnum. As we have seen, evidence for a similar rivalry—that is, one between the rostrum and stage—appears in the Roman rhetorics. But where Quintilian and (to a lesser extent) Cicero aim to preserve distinctions between these two arenas, some Protestants and most Puritans call for the latter's complete destruction. Finally, with the Reformation, preaching came to take precedence over other elements of the liturgy. It was considered the primary vehicle for making scriptural truth available to parishioners, and anything (including jesting) that distracted listeners from that truth was expressly forbidden.

Perhaps the most enthusiastic advocate of preachers jesting from the pulpit is Thomas Wilson who quotes, paraphrases, and reworks Cicero's defense of jesting to suit the needs of a situation quite different from the "fighting line" of the Roman forum. Wilson begins his adaptation by raising the same question Cicero uses to introduce his defense of jesting: "whether it standeth with an orator's profession to delight the hearers with pleasant reports and witty sayings, or no" (165–66). Wilson, following Cicero, answers in the affirmative, arguing for the pragmatic value of jesting: it enhances a speaker's ethos because those who can jest well are "compted to be fine men and pleasant fellows"; it also secures the "goodwill" of an audience, "for what is he that loveth not mirth?"; finally, a speaker can target an opponent and undermine his credibility because "we see that men are full oft abashed and put out of countenance by such taunting means" (166). What is remarkable about Wilson's rendition of his classical source is that immediately after he introduces the question of whether or not it is appropriate for an orator to jest and just before his paraphrase of Cicero's defense, he inserts a rather long digression in which he admonishes speakers "evermore to have regard to . . . [their] audience." In particular, Wilson singles out preachers whom he accuses of ignoring this rule: "Yea, the preachers of God mind so much edifying of souls that they often forget we have any bodies. And therefore some do not so much good with telling the truth as they do harm with dulling the hearers, being so far gone in their matters that oftentimes they cannot tell when to make an end. . . . And now because our senses be such that in hearing a right wholesome matter we either fall asleep when we should most harken, or else are wearied with still hearing one thing without any change, and think that the best part of his tale resteth in making an end, the witty and learned have used delightful sayings and quick sentences ever among their weighty causes" (166). Here Wilson seizes on Cicero's relatively brief reference to jesting's capacity to relieve dullness and tone down austerity, and he amplifies it into a tirade against preachers who ignore the needs of their listeners.

In the process, Wilson focuses on what he sees as the practical difficulties and pitfalls of delivering sermons. He suggests that "truth" and a "right wholesome matter" are not enough by themselves to keep churchgoers attentive,[42] for the dullness of their minds and bodies are obstacles that work against a preacher's professional and spiritual duty to edify the souls of his congregation. If a preacher is "far gone" in lofty matters and fails to adapt his discourse to the needs of his congregation, he risks not only losing their attention or putting them to sleep, but also irritating them to the point where they just want him to shut up and "make an end." Indeed, he might lose his congregation altogether: "Such quickness of wit must be showed, and such pleasant saws so well applied, that the ears may find much delight, whereof I will speak largely when I shall entreat of moving laughter. . . . For except men find delight, they will not long abide: delight them, and win them, weary them, and you lose them forever. And that is the reason that men commonly tarry the end of a merry play and cannot abide the half-hearing of a sour-checking sermon. Therefore even these ancient preachers must now and then play the fools in the pulpit to serve the tickle ears of their fleeting audience, or else they are like sometimes to preach to the bare walls" (47). The need to delight an audience is one of the three offices that Cicero assigns to the orator: that is, to teach, to delight, and to persuade.[43] But here Wilson conflates jesting with delight, elevates this office above the other two, and suggests that delighting listeners is *the* crucial ingredient of the persuasion process: "delight them, and win them, weary them, and you lose them forever."

More interesting is the example Wilson uses to illustrate the pragmatic value of delighting audiences—that is, his comparison between a "merry play" and a "sour-checking sermon." As we have seen, Cicero and Quintilian both acknowledge the power of comic performances to fascinate and delight audiences, but they also caution orators against incorporating theatrical fooling into their public speeches (even if Cicero did not always follow his own advice in his actual practice as an orator). Wilson is less troubled by confusing distinctions between the pulpit and the stage, and even recommends that preachers take a lesson from the latter's success. His doing so is not without precedents. Wilson's emphasis on the power of jesting in combating sleep and boredom and keeping listeners from wandering off are adaptations of elements of the medieval *ars praedicandi* and the practices of medieval preachers. In his *Forma Praedicandi* (1322), Robert of Basevorn includes jesting as an "ornament" of a sermon and says that it should be used "when . . . [listeners] begin to sleep."[44] Also a medieval preacher's collection of *exempla,* such as Petrus Alphonsus's *Disciplina clericalis* or the *Gesta Romanorum,* often included humorous anecdotes that might be used in sermons to illustrate theological topics or to keep the wayward mind awake and attentive.[45] Moreover, although the medieval preacher competed with "both actor and acrobat in the open" over the attention of listeners, the relationship between drama and the church was not necessarily an antithetical one: mystery plays, pageants, and other ritual festivities involving performances were an important part of the liturgical calendar.[46] Even in Wilson's day such performances were still relatively common, especially in remote locales. In addition, the first generation of English Protestants (contemporaries of Wilson) often appropriated cultural forms (including religious drama) associated with Catholicism and turned them against Catholicism itself.[47] For these reasons, Wilson's comparison between the pulpit and the stage may not have been all that shocking to some. As we shall see, however, writers before and especially after Wilson would have certainly bristled at his recommendation that preachers take a lesson from comedy's success and "now and then play the fools in the pulpit."

Wilson is not alone in recommending that preachers jest from the pulpit and incorporate theatrical elements into the delivery of their sermons. As late as 1596 when Protestantism had gained a secure foothold in England and (as we shall see) more sober methods of delivery were demanded of its clergy, Leonard Wright says in his *Patterne for Pastors* that preachers must be able to "stirre up" their listeners and "delight [them] pleasantly." Toward these ends, Wright advises preachers to be "well furnished with canonicall authorities, pretie sayings, apt similes, fit comparisons, familiar examples, and pithie histories meete both for comfortation, persuasion, and delectation."[48] Such pleasant devices will assist preachers in overcoming the distance between themselves and their listeners by appealing directly to their needs and dispositions. These listeners, says Wright, include a "diversity of natures, and commonly the most part ignorant and foolish, who, though the doctrine bee never so wholesome, yet without varietie are soone dulled and wearied, so greatly is the nature of man delighted with novelties, that without change and varitie, nothing seemeth pleasant to his lothsome appetite" (45–46). To enhance the entertainment value of these "novelties," Wright goes on to recommend that they be accompanied by an engaging performance on the part of the preacher, for listeners are "as much mooved and delighted" with alterations in "voice, gesture and countenance" as they are "with doctrine itself" (46). Although he lacks the compassion that Wilson expresses toward churchgoers, Wright's reasoning is the same. Sound or "wholesome" doctrine is not enough in itself to capture the attention of parishioners. Preachers, if they are to be responsive to the situations they face, must also incorporate "novelties" and performative elements into their sermons. Those who fail to do so, Wright suggests, might not gain a hearing at all.

Although Wilson is not alone in offering such advice, some lack his enthusiasm. Thomas More and Erasmus, both of whom clearly influenced the substance, though not so much the tenor, of Wilson's remarks on preachers and jesting, are more reluctant about preachers' moving laughter during sermons, and although they eventually sanction the practice, their acceptance is grudging at best. The reluctance of More on this issue is somewhat surprising since he was both celebrated and criticized for his wit.[49] Even so, in *A Dialogue of Comfort against Tribulation* (1553), a work that More composed while imprisoned in London Tower before his execution, the author's mouthpiece, Antony, assumes a somewhat cautious and conflicted stance toward mirth. Antony says, "[For] a man to take now and then some worldly mirth, I dare not be so sore as utterly to forbid it, sith good men and well-learned have in some cases allowed it, specially for the diversity of men's mind."[50] His mention of "diversity of men's minds" seems to refer to a postlapsarian or post-Babel world, when divisions arose not only among humans but also between humans and God. Before such a time, "no doubt but that unto any man the most comfortable talking that could be, were to hear of heaven." Now, however, "our wretchedness is such, that in talking awhile thereof, men wax almost weary, and as though to hear of heaven were a heavy burden, they must refresh themselves after with a foolish tale" (86). Although preachers who made use of such "foolish" tales would be accommodating their sermons to the "diversity" of their listeners, keeping them from waxing "almost weary," and thus serving decorum on its most practical level, they would also be, Antony's lamenting tone suggests, making a concession (perhaps even contributing) to their listeners' "wretchedness," a concession that seems at odds with preachers' spiritual duty to comfort the listeners with hearing of heaven. Antony's conflicted attitude over worldly mirth appears again in a story he rehearses about a preacher who first promises to tell his listeners a funny story, but then reneges. Realizing that his listeners had fallen asleep and desiring to get their attention, this preacher suddenly called out, "I shall tell you a merry tale." This tactic worked, and upon hearing mention of a "merry tale," the previously inattentive audience raised "up their heads and hearkened unto that." The preacher, however, refused to tell them the tale and rebuked them for their "untoward minds" (87). This story, with its offer then denial of a "merry tale," mirrors Antony's own reservations about "worldly mirth," especially when it is mixed with religious instruction. Unlike the preacher of the story, however, Antony finally acquiesces and sanctions the use of jesting from the pulpit, but not without a final complaint: "I can no more say but he that cannot long endure to hold up his head and hear talking of heaven, except he be now and then between . . . refreshed with a foolish merry tale, there is none other remedy, but you must let him have it. Better would I wish it but I cannot help it" (87–88).

A somewhat more complex meditation over preachers' jesting appears in the second book of Erasmus's *Ecclesiastae* where the author addresses this issue during his more general discussion of the three offices of oratory (*docere, delectare, flectere*).[51] Although Erasmus acknowledges the importance of delighting listeners in general, he is reluctant to let preachers use jesting to accomplish this end. He begins his remarks by directing his readers to Cicero's and Quintilian's discussions of wit for more detailed instructions on jesting, but then says, "I leave it to others to determine whether this [practice of jesting] is appropriate for our preacher [*conveniat Ecclesiastae nostro*]" (124). Not only does this statement frame Erasmus's treatment of this issue in terms of decorum, but it also points in two opposing directions, which reflect the author's own conflicted position. On the one hand, it is an allusion to the question that, as we have seen, Cicero (and then later Wilson) poses at the beginning of his defense of jesting, a question to which Cicero answers in the affirmative. On the other hand, and perhaps more indirectly, this statement alludes to a passage from Paul's letter to the Ephesians (5:4) where

Paul, discussing behavior that "becommeth Saintes," prohibits "foolish talk-ing . . . [and] jesting, which are things not comelie."[52] Caught between Cicero and Paul, Erasmus sifts through and shifts between pagan and Christian authorities as he explores both sides of this issue. Ironically, he often uses pagan authorities in arguments against preachers jesting from the pulpit, while he refers to the Church fathers in passages that seem to condone the practice. First of all, Erasmus says there are no Biblical precedents for jest-ing: a reader might find irony in Scriptures, but "nowhere jokes [*iocos nusquam*]" (124). After establishing this point with several examples, Eras-mus goes on to survey the practices of several Church fathers, including Jerome and Augustine, who often used ridicule against "the vanity of the heathen . . . for some things are better refuted by mockery than by argument [*refutantur irridendo, quam argumentando*]" (124). But these "preachers of old" did more than just rail against enemies of the church; they also used jests in their sermons in order "to delight the people [*ut delectarent populum*]" (124). Having offered precedents for jesting in the practices of these "preach-ers of old," however, Erasmus calls upon Quintilian and Tacitus in an effort to excuse and discount them: "Secular rhetoricians, especially Quintilian and Tacitus, complain that men's characters were once so depraved that judges, not content with learning what pertained to the case, sought to be delighted by an orator; if this did not happen, they felt that they had been insulted, not without risk to the case. In addition, the common people at the time were accustomed to theatrical tales and mimes [*theatricis fabulis, ac mimis*] which were all performed for pleasure's sake; there the people as spectator played judge [*iudicem*] with whistles, stamping of feet, thumbs, applause and accla-mations. Significant traces of this custom long remained among Christians, so that bishops were forced [*cogere[n]tur*] to make great allowances for the ears of the common folk" (124–25). From Erasmus's perspective, there was considerable confusion—in terms of performance conventions and audience expectations—among the law courts, stage, and pulpit in late antiquity. The crowds these early bishops faced were used to witnessing the jests and antics of orators and mimes, and as Erasmus suggests, audience expectations associated with these established and familiar media—secular oratory and mime—were transferred to the relatively new medium of preaching. Eras-mus does not blame the "preachers of old" for this confusion, nor does he hold them responsible for playing to the multitude. Rather, they were "forced" to do so as if acting against their better judgments. But Erasmus does acknowledge that preachers who did incorporate "fictitious stories or foolish jokes" into their sermons not only managed their audiences success-fully but also "were celebrated" (125).

Erasmus goes on to consider how the issue of jesting from the pulpit bears on the contemporary preaching scene, and in doing so, he shifts the blame from listeners who "forced" preachers in the past to conform to their expectations to the preachers themselves, accusing them of lacking a sense of decorum. Moreover, he insists upon there being different standards of behavior appropriate to the pulpit, the stage, and even the forum. "Now," says Erasmus, "theatrical customs have been expelled from churches [*the-atricis mores e[x] templis eiecti sint*]," and with them should go those stories and jests that preachers once used to entertain their audiences. Even so, "there is still no lack of those who too frequently, not to say shamelessly" jest from the pulpit. Using criteria familiar from classical discussions of wit, Erasmus characterizes these jesting preachers as if they were buffoons. In addition to jesting too often and without shame, these preachers "intrude" into their sermons "foolish" jests "fit for old women and hardly modest, with no consideration of those before whom they speak or of the place of their theme." Although these jesting preachers may think they are following the example of Demosthenes who "roused his sleepy judges in a capital case by unexpectedly bringing in a joke about the shadow of an ass," this ancient orator "did once in the marketplace [*in foro*] what those men do almost everyday in church [*in templo*]" (125). Echoing Cicero and Quintilian who insisted on different standards of behavior in the forum and theater, Eras-mus takes the next step and insists on differences between the church *and* the forum *and* the theater. Even the example of Demosthenes himself cannot serve to sanction the behavior of these jesting preachers.

It would seem that, for Erasmus, there should be no jesting from the pulpit. But the man who authored *Praise of Folly,* who translated and sup-plied commentary for the many jests and witticisms appearing in his *Apoph-thegmata,* and who admired the wit of his friend Thomas More cannot bring himself to forbid the practice completely. After censuring those buffoonish preachers mentioned above, Erasmus rehearses in full, even as he condemns, two indecorous jests which he says he witnessed himself. The first was told by a Franciscan, and it involves a wife who, against her husband's instruc-tions and in order to satisfy the curiosity piqued by those instructions, washed her face in a "small pool of foul and ill-smelling water by the dungheap."

Distraught by the experience and its outcome, she asks her husband why he had given his mysterious instructions in the first place, and he replies, "So that what happened wouldn't happen to you" (125). The second jest Erasmus recalls hearing as a boy. It was told by a friar "to rouse sleepers," and it plays on the theme (so popular during the period) of the supposedly insatiable appetite of women for sex. A nun was ravished in her room, and when the Abbess asks her why she did not cry out for help, the nun replies, "I would have done that, but it happened in the dormitory, where breaking silence is forbidden" (125). Erasmus includes these jests to substantiate his claims about what he sees as the indecorous behavior of certain contemporary preachers, but in recounting them in full, he comes dangerously close to engaging in the very practice he is condemning. This possibility does not escape Erasmus who exclaims, "But enough, to keep from becoming foolish myself in rebuking foolishness" (126). Collecting himself, Erasmus says that when preachers confront a dozing congregation, it is "more tolerable" for them to "use noise or a word to waken the sleepers" (126). If a preacher insists on jesting from the pulpit, it is possible, Erasmus concedes, to employ funny stories "appropriately." First, he should draw his comic materials, not from the oftentimes bawdy tales told by medieval preachers, but from "ancient" sources, for there he will find some jests having a "serious and wholesome message" (126). Second, he should use such jests "sparingly and without an appearance of affectation, and not without apologizing for combining the humorous with the divine" (126). By employing them only rarely and without elaborate histrionics (that is, "affectation"), and by prefacing them with an apology that presumably seeks to excuse a breach in decorum just before it occurs, this preacher will distinguish his jesting from that of those buffoonish preachers Erasmus criticizes earlier. Finally, the preacher who jests should not be motivated solely by a desire to make his listeners laugh and "draw the lips apart in a grin," but should "apply everything to his hearers' utility, striving in every way to render most pleasant to his audience that which is most wholesome" (126). What these recommendations amount to is a compromise: although Erasmus is not happy about preachers' jesting during sermons and comes very close to condemning the practice altogether, the best he can hope for is a union between the "pleasant" and the "wholesome."

In his discussion of pulpit jesting, Erasmus is standing at a cultural crossroads. Unlike Wilson, who seems closer to the medieval world with his preacher playing the fool in the pulpit, Erasmus wants to distance himself from what he sees as an outdated and indecorous practice. Yet it is a practice that he cannot discard completely because, by his own admission, it is still popular and apparently effective in his own day. For these reasons, Erasmus serves as a transitional figure in the early modern discourse on pulpit jesting. His compromise between the "pleasant" and "wholesome" is, in a sense, a compromise between the past and the present, but it also points forward, anticipating later developments, at least in England, in pulpit oratory. His claim that "theatrical customs have been expelled from the churches" seems, when applied to the English preaching scene, more of a wish than a statement of fact, for such customs persisted throughout the sixteenth century. But it is a wish that is shared, and propagated, by later writers on pulpit oratory, particularly ultra-Protestants and Puritans who mounted a vigorous and sustained attack against the playhouse. Before turning to these writers, however, we need to examine, if only briefly, the actual or perceived needs of preachers and churchgoers in early modern England. For the recommendations of Wilson and the concessions of More and Erasmus do seem to meet the practical requirements of preaching in the period, requirements that later writers are determined to change.

Like his medieval counterpart, the preacher in early modern England often competed with actor and acrobat. Unlike Wilson, however, some preachers were not interested in taking a lesson from the actor's success and, instead, viewed the stage as one of the pulpit's chief rivals. In a sermon delivered at St. Paul's Cross on St. Bartholomew's Day, John Stockwood asks, "Wyll not a fylthye playe wyth a blast of a Trumpette, sooner call thyther a thousands, than an houres tolling of a Bell, bring to the Sermon a hundred?"[53] John Northbrooke offers a similar observation: "God be mercifull to this Realme of England, for we begynne to have ytching eares, and lothe that heavenly Manna, as appeareth by their [the people's] slowe and negligent comming unto Sermons, and running so fast, and so many, continually unto Playes" (66). But the stage was not the only form of recreation that rivaled the pulpit. Preachers also competed with other forms of amusement such as bear-baiting, gaming, archery, and football.[54] The alehouse was a particularly potent form of distraction, especially since it took on, after Henry VIII's break with Rome, several of the more popular ritualistic elements of the Catholic church.[55] Bishop Pilkington laments, "For come into a church on the sabbath day, and ye shall see but few, though there be a sermon; but the alehouse is full."[56] In order to compete, preachers had to be just as entertaining as these other forms of amusement, or even more so. As a consequence, "wholesome" instruction often took a back seat to funny and sensational stories. According to Horton Davies, "The Elizabethans, like St. Paul's Athenians, were eager to hear 'some new thing.' It was not always soundness of doctrine or sincerity of manner that drew them, but humour, wit, even sensationalism."[57]

Preachers did not have to rely solely on their ability to entertain listeners to get those listeners in the door. The Act of Uniformity of 1559 required all of Elizabeth's subjects to attend services on Sundays and holy days, or suffer a fine. It also required them to behave themselves once they were there— that is, "to abide orderly and soberly during the time of common prayer, preaching, or other service of God there to be used and ministered."[58] For the properly faithful, these injunctions were perhaps superfluous. For nonconformists or recusants, however, or for parishioners who would rather spend their Sundays and holy days in the alehouse or engaged in other, more amusing activities, these prescriptions could be a source of irritation, as is evident in the frequent violations of the attendance law during the period. To add to the problem, many of the clergy, especially during the early years of Elizabeth's reign, lacked the education and skill to deliver an engaging sermon.[59] Accordingly, many of those who did attend services often resorted to forms of resistance, some passive and relatively innocuous, others more active and aggressive. It was not uncommon for parishioners to sleep, knit, or gossip while a preacher was delivering a sermon. Nor was it uncommon for parishioners to cough loudly, sing out of turn, heckle, or throw objects at or even storm the pulpit.[60] On such occasions, preachers are not merely contending with the problem of an inattentive audience, but with a hostile and dangerous crowd disgruntled, more often than not, over some point of doctrine. Such seems to be the case when, on one occasion, a parishioner angered by the topic of a preacher's sermon threw a dagger at the pulpit. Happily, the preacher was not hurt; the dagger was caught in the sleeve of one of the preacher's companions who happened to be in the pulpit with him (for protection, perhaps). On another occasion, the parishioners of Sherborne, Dorset, rushed the pulpit and pummeled their pastor with their fists. In this instance, parishioners not only wished that he would "make an end" to his sermon, but made sure he would do so for a good while to come, for the pastor was beaten so severely that he could not "speak loud enough to preach for six weeks."[61]

Despite the reservations of some over preachers' moving laughter during sermons, jesting and creating comic spectacles were available strategies for managing both an inattentive and a potentially hostile audience. Preacher Hugh Latimer was apparently a master of pulpit jesting, and he may have even fueled Wilson's enthusiasm over the practice.[62] According to Lipking, Latimer adopted elements from the medieval *exempla* tradition and made them "a brilliantly effective vehicle" not only for his "Protestant convictions" but also for capturing the attention of his listeners.[63] On occasion, he even calls attention to the function he intends his jests to serve. He concludes one instance of humor by saying he has spoken a "merry word . . . to refresh my auditory."[64] In another sermon, he prefaces his telling of an anecdote by saying, "I will tell you a pretty story of a friar to refresh you withal" (1:524). But his jests and merry tales were hardly incidental to his overall persuasive aims, mere digression in a discourse on "weighty causes." Rather, they often propel his argument forward by demonstrating in a concrete and entertaining fashion some point he is trying to make. In the following passage (taken from a sermon delivered in 1552), Latimer uses a jest to illustrate his larger theme of human imperfection. He begins by observing that "we shall have victory . . . [in] all our doings," and then continues with the jest: "We have a common saying amongst us, 'Everything is as it is taken.' We read of king Henry the seventh, at a time as he was served with a cup of drink, a gentleman that brought the cup, in making obeisance, the cover fell to the ground: the king seeing his folly, saith, 'Sir, is this well done?' 'Yea, Sir,' said he, 'if your majesty take it well.' With this pretty answer the king was pacified. So it is with us touching our salvation. Our works are unperfect, but God taketh the same well for Christ's sake" (2:150–51). The text of Latimer's sermon moves smoothly from religious principle to proverbial saying to jest and back to a restatement and elaboration of the original principle. In doing so, it brings that principle, stepwise, down to the level of his listeners so that Latimer is better able to lift them up to contemplate the relationship between their own imperfections and salvation.

So successful was Latimer at securing the attention and good will of his listeners that he could afford to jest about the practical difficulties of preaching itself. In a sermon he preached before Edward VI, Latimer borrows a jest from *A Hundred Merry Tales,* but he makes it his own and weaves it almost seamlessly into his discourse. Discussing the importance of parishioners' attending church and hearing "God's word" regardless of their intentions for coming, Latimer says, "I had rather ye should come of a naughty mind to hear the word of God for novelty, or for curiosity to hear some pastime, than to be away. I had rather ye should come as the tale is by the gentlewoman of London: one of her neighbours met her in the street, and said, "Mistress, whither go ye?" "Mary," she said, "I am going to St. Thomas of Acres to the sermon: I could not sleep all this last night, and I am going now tither; I never failed of a good nap there." And so I had rather ye should go napping to the sermons, than not to go at all. For with what mind soever ye come, though ye come for an ill purpose, yet peradventure ye may chance to be caught or ye go; the preacher may chance to catch you on his hook" (1:200–201). With this jest, the general dynamics of a jesting exchange help Latimer reaffirm his bond with his listeners, a bond that would be made evident in their collective laughter. The particular subject matter of this jest allows Latimer to accomplish two other purposes as well. Although he indirectly compares his listeners to the "gentlewoman of London," neither the text of the jest itself nor the way Latimer sets it up makes clear who the object of laughter is. Is it the woman who falls asleep during sermons, or the preacher who puts her to sleep. It ultimately does not matter; either way Latimer wins. If his listeners take the woman as the object of laughter, then this jest serves as a gentle corrective against falling asleep during sermons. If they take the preacher as the butt of the jest, then Latimer still wins points. Not only does he display enough self-assurance to crack a jest at the expense of his own profession, but he also shows his ability to understand and see the world from the perspective of his listeners. It is this understanding of "the practical world and . . . [of] the practical needs of conveying his lessons to his audience" that invites Lipking to say: "It seems unlikely that his [Latimer's] listeners often slept."[65]

In addition to jests, comic spectacles were sometimes used to attract audiences and hold their attention. According to Herr, "sermons at Paul's Cross, and perhaps at a few other pulpits, were frequently made more amusing for the audience by the exhibition of people doing penance." Herr goes on to explain how these exhibitions were orchestrated: "At the Cross there was a regular platform, level with the pulpit, built for the penitents to stand upon and receive the jeers of the audience and the gibes of the village wits."[66] Preachers who made use of this second platform not only took a lesson from drama's success but also included as part of the more general occasion something akin to a theatrical stage with the penitents standing in for players. As we have seen in the writings of Cicero, Quintilian, and Erasmus, there is considerable anxiety over confusing arenas for oratory (the forum or *templum*) with those designed for comic performances. This anxiety springs not so much from a concern that spectators will, in fact, mistake a rostrum or a pulpit for a stage, but from a fear that they will mistake the activities, purposes, and identities of orators and preachers for those of stage clowns and players. To avoid this possibility and to check any inclination of speakers toward the extravagant or excessive, these writers invoke decorum as a measure for both control and clarity. With the comic spectacles at Paul's Cross, however, the arena of the preacher's professional activity—that is, the pulpit—comes very close to being spatially coincident with a stage. To add to the confusion, the platforms used at the Cross were built "level with the pulpit" and thus placed both penitent and preacher on the same plane. Would spectators have missed the irony implicit in this arrangement? The preacher here may not be playing the fool, but he is standing next to one.

An incident in which a pulpit does become a stage of sorts is recorded by John Foxe in his *Actes and Monuments*. Hubberdin, a Catholic preacher who had gained a reputation for his antics in the pulpit during the reign of Mary, came riding by a church "where the Youth of the parish were dancing in the churchyard." Upon seeing this sight, Hubberdin—or "this Silenus," as Foxe calls him—leapt from his horse and "by the occasion of their dancing came into the Church, and there causing the bell to toll in the people, thought in stead of a fitte of mirth, to give them a sermon of dancing." The rest of the story is better left to Foxe:

> In the which sermon, after he had patched up certain common texts out of the Scriptures, and then coming to the doctors, first to Augustine, then to Ambrose, so to Jerome, and Gregory, Chrysostome, and other doctors, had made them every one (after his dialogue manner) by name to answer to his call, and to sing after his tune for the probation of the sacrament of the altar against John Frith, Zuinglius, Ecolampadius, Luther, Tindall, Latimer, and other heretics (as he called them); at last, to show a perfect harmony of all these doctors together—as he had made them before to sing after his tune, so now to make them dance also after his pipe—first he calleth out Christ and his apostles; then the doctors and ancient seniors of the church, as in a round ring all to dance together, with "pipe up Hubberdin." Now dance Christ; now dance Peter, Paul;

now dance Augustine, Ambrose, Jerome. And thus old Hubberdin, as
he was dancing with his Doctors lustily in the pulpit against the heretics,
how he stampt and took on I cannot tell, but "crash," quoth the pulpit,
down cometh the dancer, and there lay Hubberdin, not dancing, but
sprawling in the midst of his audience; where altogether he brake not his
neck, yet he so brake his leg the same time and bruised his old bones, that
he never came in pulpit more, and died not long after the same.
(7:477–78)

But the collapsing of the pulpit, and of Hubberdin along with it, is not the
final punch-line. Afterwards, the church-wardens were summoned and
"charged for the pulpit being no stronger." They simply replied that "they
had made their pulpit for preaching, and not for dancing." This reply is significant, for it insists, *contra* Wilson and *contra* practices commonly used at
St. Paul's Cross, on a functional difference between pulpit and stage. Not
only does it suggest that this particular pulpit was unable to physically with-
stand the jumping and leaping of Hubberdin, but it also implies that pulpits
were generally unfit places for such antics.

Like these churchwardens, there were others in the period who
believed the pulpit was no place for foolery, and their prohibitions concerning such behaviors generally follow three, often overlapping, lines of reasoning: first, jesting in the pulpit, like other festive rituals, smack too much of
Catholicism; second, preachers who move laughter during sermons are
making inappropriate use of theatrics and improperly confusing their roles
with actors; finally, jests are themselves a source of distraction and cause the
minds of churchgoers to wander from scriptural truth. The first two of these
reasons are implicit in Foxe's account of Hubberdin's dancing sermon, an
account clearly intended to disparage this Catholic preacher. Although Foxe,
himself a Puritan sympathizer, does not say so explicitly, he does suggest that
Hubberdin's rather outlandish behavior is somehow connected with his religious affiliation. Using conventional anti-Catholic epithets, Foxe prefaces his
account of the dancing sermon by calling Hubberdin "a right painted phar-
isee" and "a right image or counterfeit, setting out unto us in lively colors the
pattern of perfect hypocrisy." He also accuses him of straying "abroad in all
quarters of the realm" performing one-man "pageants," and of accompanying his sermons with "forged tales and fables, dialogues, dreams, dancings,
hoppings and leapings, with other like histrionical toys and gestures used in

the pulpit" (7:477). It seems the performances of Hubberdin and his use of "histrionical toys and gestures" identify him with what Foxe suggests are all the carnivalesque excesses of Catholicism and its preachers. But they also identify him with actors who engage in similar antics on stage, and by giving the churchwardens the final word in his account of Hubberdin's remarkable dancing sermon, Foxe further suggests that these two arenas are incommensurable.

Several Protestant and Puritan writers in the period share Foxe's views, but express them more directly. In Andreas Hyperius's *Practis of Preaching* ("done into English by John Ludham" in 1577), the author insists that preachers "avoide fond and fabulous histories, and the vaine rablement of miracles."[67] Earlier Hyperius censors those who "delight to tell fabulous tales and historyes" and those who tell stories of "Sainctes" for "lucres sake." Any preacher who does employ these devices should be "reprooved" for his "levitie and avarice" (16). Niels Hemminsen takes a similar position in his *Ecclesiasten,* which John Horsfall translated into English in 1574, and forbids the use of any *exempla* that are not taken directly from Scriptures. One of his chief objections to these extrascriptural *exempla* is their association with the preaching practices of "papistes & mo[n]kes."[68] Puritan divine William Perkins also prohibits the use of fabulous and comic tales during sermons, not so much because of their associations with Catholic preaching practices, as because they distract listeners from scriptural truth: "Humane wisedome must be concealed . . . because the preaching of the word is the *Testimonie of God, and the profession of the knowledge of Christ,* and not of humane skill: and again, because the hearers ought not to ascribe their faith to the gifts of men, but to the power of Gods word."[69] For Perkins, as for other Puritan ministers, preaching "Gods word" was their primary duty, and it was not to be overshadowed by the education and rhetorical skill of the preacher.[70] Accordingly, Perkins says that "Greeke and Latine phrases and quirks," among other things, must be avoided not only because their use constitutes displays of "Humane wisedome," but also because they "disturbe the mindes of the audience" and "hindreth the understanding of those things that are spoken" (135). To these Greek and Latin "phrases and quirks," Perkins adds humorous stories and funny sayings: "Here also the telling of tales, and all profane and ridiculous speeches must be omitted" (136). Unlike Wilson who views jesting as a way to secure the interest of listeners and provide the occasional respite throughout a discourse on "weighty causes," Perkins views the practice as a source of distraction itself, either frustrating the understanding or drawing the attention of listeners away from "Gods word."

There is another, closely related reason why preachers should not jest in the pulpit: preachers who jest or engage in other theatrical behaviors risk blurring lines distinguishing pulpit from playhouse. As we have seen, the reservations of Erasmus over pulpit jesting derive in part from what he sees as a similar risk, but Erasmus eventually sanctions the practice. For other writers, however, there is to be no compromise. The Puritan opposition to the stage has been amply documented, but in an interesting study of the cultural changes brought about by the Reformation in England, Patrick Collinson suggests that the Puritan opposition was only the most extreme expression of a larger movement characteristic of Protestantism in general. According to him, religious practices and observances before the Reformation were thoroughly "mimetic" and consisted of "images, concrete symbols, mime, the ritualised acting out of religious stories and lessons." After the Reformation, however, there occurred a gradual shift from this "mimetic presentation of religion" to a concentration on "the invisible, abstract, and didactic word: primarily the word of the printed page, on which depended the spoken words of sermon and catechism."[71] Collinson's argument agrees with, and helps contextualize, the Protestant emphasis on preaching "Gods word" over other liturgical elements, and it also helps explain why some objected to the notion of jesting in the pulpit, especially a form of jesting involving performative elements. Echoing one of Cicero's prescriptions but applying it here to the preacher, Wilson says that speakers who tell funny stories and anecdotes should actually perform the parts of the various characters involved: "The matter is told pleasantly, when some man's nature (whereof the tale is told) is so set forth, his countenance so counterfeited, and all his gestures so resemble, that the hearers might judge the thing to be then lively done, even as though he were there whereof the tale was told" (167).[72] According to Hyperius, nothing was to be "lively done" in the pulpit: the preacher was not to use "tragicall clamours" when admonishing his listeners (163), nor was he to yell loudly or "depart out of the Pulpit" in a fit of rage (164). Rather, while delivering sermons, the preacher must be a "very careful and diligent observer of decorum" (177) lest through any indecorous use of voice and gesture, he become "the common talking stocke and pastime of the people" (178)—that is, a source of laughter for his parishioners. Perkins also insists that the preacher "speaketh soberly and moderately" in the pulpit (141), and although the preacher is allowed to raise his eyes and arm to "signifieth confidence" or to lower the same to suggest "sorrow and heavines," he must, for the most part, remain still in the pulpit, "the trunke or stalke of the bodie being erect and quiet" (143–44).

Even more objectionable than preachers' performing in the pulpit is the fact that jests are themselves representational forms, often depicting indecorous and what may be construed as vicious and sinful actions. Many apologists of the theater argued that, in making sin and vice appear ridiculous on stage, spectators would be less inclined to imitate such behaviors. For Northbrooke, Hyperius, and Perkins, however, any representation of vice and sin was equivalent to endorsing the same. Nothbrooke calls the stage a "schoole for all wickednesse and vice to be learned in" (59). Then after lumping together "Juglers, Scoffers, Jeasters, and Players," he asks rhetorically, "What other thing doe they teache, than wanton pleasure, and stirring up of fleshly lustes unlawfull appetites and desires? with their bawdie and filthie sayings and counterfeyt doings" (65). Applying a similar logic of representation and effect, Hyperius and Perkins forbid preachers in particular from depicting sinful and vicious behaviors in their sermons, especially if those depictions are seasoned with jesting and mirth. When rebuking his hearers, Hyperius warns, the preacher must be careful not to present "sin in his coolours," for in doing so he might "privily tickle [the] mindes of . . . [his] hearers, and . . . egge them to conceyve eyther a certaine new desyre of sinninge, or els to take a certaine pleasure of their sinne lately commited" (163). Here Hyperius is clearly convinced that delightful depictions of vice and sin will titillate listeners, causing them either to relive forbidden pleasures of the past or to conceive of unheard of pleasures for the future. Is there no difference, then, between the pleasures of representation and representations of pleasure? According to Hyperius, there is none, for "Thou shalt finde those that are wonderfully delighted, when they heare these vices pleasauntly described" (163). In *Cases of Conscience* (1609), another work by Perkins, the author launches a more sustained attack against jesting and other forms of recreation involving representations. Although he allows Christians to find release in such activities as archery, foot races, and chess for these are "in the use of things indifferent," he forbids any recreations that make "use of holy things." As a precedent for this prohibition, he cites mystery plays and pageants that were "put downe" during the early years of the Reformation because "they were nothing else, but either the whole, or part of the historie of the Bible turned into a Play." Secular plays which are now "in use in the world," Perkins contends, should suffer a similar fate, for "they are nothing else, but representations of vice & misdemeanours of men"—even worse, they present these delinquent behaviors for the sake of "causing mirth and pastime." As for more compact forms of representation such as "jests," not all are necessarily prohibited among the laity, but those which "are framed out of the phrases and sentences of the Scriptures" must "carefully . . . be avoided." For preachers, though, Perkins is abundantly clear: there is to be no jesting of any kind from the pulpit, for "it is not meet, convenient, or laudable for men to moove occasion of laughter in Sermons" (162).

JESTING AT COURT

Cicero's discussion of jesting in *De oratore* not only offers a tripartite model of a jesting exchange but is itself a model that was paraphrased, adapted, and rewritten by several writers of early modern handbooks on oratory and courtly conduct. We have seen at least part of his influence on Wilson, how this sixteenth-century rhetorician imitates Cicero's defense of jesting and, in the process, adapts Cicero's tripartite model to fit what he sees as the pragmatic needs of an early modern preaching situation. Castiglione is also deeply indebted to this classical source. The organization of his treatment of jesting in *The Book of the Courtier* generally follows that of Cicero in *De oratore*. He also paraphrases—or, in some instances, merely translates—many of Cicero's prescriptions and sample jests. But when he comes to that portion of his treatment where one would expect to find Cicero's defense of jesting, Castiglione departs from his source in an interesting and important way. Instead of phrasing the issue as a question and then offering an answer that argues for the pragmatic values of jesting (as both Cicero and Wilson do), Castiglione presents no immediate defense. Rather, he declares his reservations about courtiers engaging in laughing matters, although elsewhere he clearly endorses the practice: "To make men laughe alwayes is not comelie for the Courtier, nor yet in suche wise as . . . commune jesters do: and though to a mans thinking Courtes cannot be without suche kind of persons [i.e., jesters], yet deserve they not the name of Courtier, but eche man to be called by his name and esteamed suche as they are" (158). It is not always appropriate for a courtier to jest because jesting could lead to confusion about a speaker's social identity. In particular, Castiglione fears that jesting will blur distinctions between courtiers, on the one hand, and "commune jesters," on the other. This fear is shared by other handbook writers in the period. The important point to note here is the emphasis Castiglione places on the connection between jesting and the speaker's social identity rather than on, say, jesting's capacity to defeat an opponent through ridicule. This emphasis is found in other sixteenth-century courtesy manuals, and as we shall see, it derives from what these manuals perceive as the rhetorical needs of courtiers in their interaction with others at the court of a prince. In that setting, the courtier primarily uses jesting to preserve or enhance his own ethos, to present a self that is socially elevated and clearly distinguishable from that of "commune jesters."

As this passage from Castiglione also suggests, this process of self-presentation is not entirely under the control of the courtier. It also depends on the approval of his audience. This dependence is implicit in the passage above where Castiglione seems to be positing a notion of self that is stable, absolute, and unchanging: "eche man [is] to be called by his name and esteemed suche as they are." In the very act of making claims for a stable self, however, Castiglione acknowledges that the identity of the courtier is also constituted by his audience who, in this case, is the implicit grammatical subject of the infinitives "to be called . . . and esteamed." Who one is depends in part on the judgments and estimation of others. Similar notions appear throughout Castiglione and other courtesy manuals of the period. When engaging in sports and games, for instance, a courtier must "accompanye all his mocion wyth a certayne good judgemente and grace, yf he wyll deserve that generall favor which is so much set by" (Castiglione, 54). While accompanying his every action with good judgment and grace, the courtier exerts some control over the ethos he projects, but his actions are for naught if they fail to win the "general favor" of those who watch him perform. In a similar vein, Guazzo's Annibale says that it is through "publicke conversation" that a person gains knowledge of the self: "For if you consider it wel, the judgement which wee have to knowe our selves, is not ours, but wee borrow it of others" (1:115). As Annibale goes on to explain, the courtier fashions a self not by willing it into existence; instead, self-fashioning is the product of many conversational exchanges where the courtier learns to correct his faults and gradually adjusts and accommodates his behavior to his audience. In short, courtiers "frame themselves . . . according to the judgement of others" (1:116).

The interdependence between self-presentation and audience approval is central to Frank Whigham's analysis of the rhetorical dynamics of the

Elizabethan court. According to him, "public life at court was governed by the rhetorical imperative of performance."[73] It came to be so partly because of increases in social mobility, a phenomenon that challenged the official ideology based on a natural, unchanging social hierarchy since it opened up the possibility for social relocation in what was traditionally a rigid system. The established elite sought to protect their ranks from "incursions from below" by reasserting what they saw as their natural and ontological difference from their ambitious inferiors. In order to constitute this difference, they had to block every avenue of mobility available to the would-be aristocrat. Most important, they had to deny the worth of any substantive effort because such efforts, if valued, could be used by the ambitious to legitimate their social elevation. That is, if status were based on merit rather than birth, then anybody possessing "substantive powers," such as "martial force or organizational ability," could "claim the right to relocate."[74] The established elite responded to this disruptive possibility by defining aristocratic identity as something that "cannot be achieved [or earned] by human effort."[75] The criteria that define this identity all de-emphasize substance and effort; instead, they place a premium on style and manner. As a result, "there arose a basic governing principle of the display of *effortlessness,* Castiglione's *sprezzatura,* designed to imply the natural or given status of one's social identity and to deny any earned character, any labor or arrival from a social elsewhere."[76] On the other side of the scramble for position and privilege, the socially ambitious did not challenge the system as such; instead, they tried to work it to their own advantage by appropriating the codes of aristocratic behavior. Their aim, of course, was "to make themselves indistinguishable from their future peers, if possible by persuading those peers themselves."[77]

As performance comes to dominate courtly life, the importance of audience approval increases proportionately. The courtier can only gauge his success by turning to his audience, for they are the ones who grant or withhold that "generall favour" Castiglione says was so sought after. However, as Whigham observes, each member of this audience was himself a performer, "subject to the same unsettling pressures of dependency on audience."[78] As a result, interpretations of others' behaviors become tainted by indeterminacy: "Is he doing that because I am watching him?"[79] Dislodged from any notion of a stable or true self, behaviors are evaluated only in terms of performative criteria, and the "master trope" governing these evaluations is, according to Whigham, *paradiastole.*[80] As Puttenham defines the term, *paradiastole* occurs "when we make the best of a bad thing, or turne a signification to the more plausible sense: as, to call an unthrift, a liberall Gentleman: the foolish-hardy, valiant or couragious: the niggard, thriftie: a great riot, or outrage, an youthfull pranke, and such like terms" (195). Although Puttenham's definition "emphasizes recuperation" by which a term is turned to a "more plausible sense," Whigham points out the trope's more destabilizing effects: "This master trope governs evaluation, positing a matrix in which praise and blame, flattery and slander, interpenetrate absolutely," causing an "ongoing adjustment of public information by redescribing an utterance or action in such a way as to reverse the polarity of its meaning."[81] Theoretically, this trope could lead to an infinite regress in which one interpretation of an action is followed by another interpretation that reverses the previous one's valence, followed by another, and so on.

How does jesting fit into a rhetorical environment where everybody is trying to show himself to best advantage, yet where communication has no solid grounding? First and foremost, it allows the courtier to present a socially elevated self, albeit one that is continually subject to the approval of others. Indeed, a capacity to jest well is an essential component of the courtier's rhetorical equipment. As Castiglione's Federico says, the courtier should be "such a one that shall never wante good communycatyon and fytte for them he talketh wythall, and have a good understandynge with a certein sweetenesse to refresh the hearers mindes, and with meerie conceites and Jestes to provoke them to solace and laughter so that . . . he may evermore delite them" (152). After hearing Federico's reference to jesting, another interlocutor urges him to discuss the subject at greater length: "teach us how we should use these Jestes you have made mention of, and showe us the art that beelongeth to all this kinde of pleasaunt speach to provoke laughter and solace after an honest sort, for (in myne opinion) it is verye necessary and much to pourpose for a Courtier" (153). Guazzo's Annibale also views jesting as both an essential component of good courtiership and a vehicle for self-presentation. According to him, however, the courtier must know not only how to deliver jests, but also how to take them. After discussing the importance of being affable, Annibale says, "Nowe I will joyne for a sister and companion to affabilitie, an other vertue, verie necessarie in Conversation, and it is that, whiche not only with gentle woordes, but with a certaine wittie and readie pleasantnesse delighteth wonderfully the hearers. And as that [affability] is a signe of curtesie, so this is a token of wit, and is used no lesse in jesting merily with others, then in taking jest patiently of others" (1:158–59). While delighting "wonderfully the hearers," the courtier presents a self, this "token of wit," and should a jest be delivered by another at the courtier's own expense, he is still given an opportunity to enhance his own ethos. By "taking jest patiently of others," he shows those others that he has a sense of humor and perhaps is a good sport. In other words, how one responds to a jest also constitutes symbolic behavior subject to interpretation, and a patient, good-natured response may, in some cases, do symbolic work similar to a witty retort that parries the initial comic thrust.[82]

If jesting allows the courtier to present a self, it is one that agrees with the ideal courtly identity. In an interesting analysis of the role of jesting in Castiglione's *Book of the Courtier,* Daniel Javitch suggests a congruence between the operation of jesting and the more general self the courtier hopes to present.[83] While discussing this general self, Javitch says, "One of the foremost characteristics of the courtier is a flexible capacity to embody opposites": to temper pride with modesty, for instance, or to balance fervor with detachment.[84] The performative ideal of *sprezzatura* also requires the courtier, with a single action, to make artful effort appear natural and effortless.[85] Jesting, which Javitch claims is "an integral part of courtliness," allows the courtier to achieve "this desirable equivocation" in a single utterance.[86] With this claim, Javitch hints at something like an incongruity theory of humor by which jesting secures its effects by combining disparate realms of experience into a compatibly incompatible verbal form. In this way, jesting offers the courtier "verbal opportunities" to display traits "so admired in his general behavior."[87] Such is the case with a jest Bacon claims he delivered while conversing with the Queen. Angered by the import of John Hayward's recently published biography of Henry IV, Elizabeth asks Bacon, "Whether there was no treason contained in it?" Bacon, "intending to do him [Hayward] a pleasure, and to take off the Queen's bitterness with a jest," replies, "No, madam, for treason I cannot deliver opinion that there is any, but very much felony. . . . Because he had stolen many of his sentences and conceits out of Cornelius Tacitus."[88] This jest, with its equivocations on the meanings of treason and felony, offers Bacon an opportunity to showcase his wit, his mental and verbal agility in transforming a potential charge of treason into a playful accusation of plagiarism. We should also note that Bacon (if his account can be trusted) uses jesting here to manage a courtly exchange—that is, to do Hayward a "pleasure" by assuaging the anger, and influencing the opinion, of the Queen.

While I agree with Javitch that jesting offers verbal "opportunities" to display attributes of the courtly ideal, I would go farther and say that courtly jesting may operate more like *paradiastole* with all of its destabilizing effects. That is, although Javitch acknowledges that jesting often works obliquely and through dissimulation, he claims that a courtier's jest will nevertheless have one stable meaning to which his listeners (at least, those with the capacity to get the jest) will have ready access: "the courtier's observers, highly responsive to . . . [the] indirection [of jesting], eventually see through his graceful guises but enjoy the artifices that temporarily leave them deceived."[89] What Javitch overlooks is that because jesting secures its effects through ambiguity and incongruity, a single jest will typically involve multiple, often conflicting interpretations that cannot be resolved completely. For a jest to be a jest, these multiple, conflicting interpretations must be kept in play. Take, for instance, a jest appearing in Puttenham where a king responds to a soldier who "praid his reward, shewing how he had bene cut in the face in a certain battell fought in his [the king's] service." The king replies, "Ye may see . . . what it is to runne away and looke backwards" (199). With his initial appeal to the king, the soldier tries to define the situation in such a way that his cut will be interpreted as a sign of courage meriting reward. But the appeal may also be read as an indirect complaint against the king's failure to pay, and thus a form of criticism directed at the king. In response to this latter implication, the king turns the soldier's definition of the situation on its head and redefines the cut as a sign of cowardice, a failure to fight, and thus fitting reward in and of itself. As this anecdote implies, then, jesting can function in ways similar to *paradiastole:* the king's response reverses the valence of the initial remark made by the soldier. However, where Puttenham's conception of *paradiastole* would have one interpretation prevail over another, where the unthrifty man would be seen as a "liberall Gentleman" and this renaming would be a movement toward a more "plausible [or more self-serving] sense," a jest invites its hearers to entertain multiple interpretations or labels simultaneously. According to Arthur Koestler's definition of comic "bisociation," a joke requires "the perceiving of a situation or idea in two self-consistent but habitually incompatible frames of reference."[90] In the case of the soldier-king anecdote, the humor relies on simultaneously seeing the soldier's cut as both a sign of courage and a sign of cowardice. Without this double vision, so to speak, there would be no jest.

Jesting offers other means for the courtier to distinguish himself. If one of the principal strategies by which the courtier shows his gentlemanly status and denies any "arrival from a social elsewhere" is through the performative ideal of *sprezzatura,* or the effortless concealment of art, then such effortlessness can be displayed in spontaneous quips or witticisms. According to James Biester, the unexpected quip or witticism can serve as "an inalienable mark of a natural distinction, like nobility by birth."[91] While discussing these spontaneous forms of jesting, Castiglione says there is no room for "art" because the "quippie ought to be shott out and hit the pricke beefore a man can discerne that he that speaketh it can thinke upon it, elles it is colde and litle worth" (154).[92] As one reading of this passage might have it, the spontaneous "quippie" must issue from the speaker involuntarily and without effort, and if this is so, then there is indeed no room for "art." On closer inspection, however, what the passage actually suggests is that the "quippie" must only *appear* as if it were the product of some involuntary, effortless process—that is, it must hit its mark "beefore . . . [the listener] *can discerne* that he that speaketh it can thinke upon it." The challenge, therefore, of the spontaneous jest—as with *sprezzatura* in general—is not to avoid premeditation, but to erase all signs of premeditation so that listeners will think that the spontaneous jest is a natural extension of the courtier's grace, a trait that sets him apart from his inferiors.[93] The danger with a spontaneous jest is that if it comes across as appearing too contrived or overly calculated—or if it is interpreted as such through a paradiastolic reversal—then not only is it of "litle worth," but it also reflects poorly on the speaker. According to Della Casa, the courtier who "brings . . . [a jest] forthe . . . colde" will either weary listeners, or "if they doe laughe, they laugh not at the jest, but at the jester him selfe" (70). In withholding laughter or in laughing *at* rather than *with* the speaker, the listeners exert their authority over the speaker, an authority not only to evaluate the success of the jest but also to define the character of the one who delivers it.

Jesting may also display an elevated status by the stylistic techniques it employs. Castiglione, Wilson, Peacham, Puttenham, and Day all recommend the use of figures of speech in the production of jests,[94] and several of these writers define the figures in general as deviations from the norms of everyday usage. Wilson, for instance, says a figure is a "certain kind either of sentence, oration, or word, used after some new or strange wise, much unlike which men commonly used to speak" (195). Puttenham offers a similar definition, saying, "Figurative speech is a noveltie of language evidently (and yet not absurdly) estranged from the ordinarie habite and manner of our dayly talke and writing" (171). As these definitions suggest, figures of speech provide a way for a speaker to distinguish his discourse and, by implication, himself from what is ordinary and common, including common people.[95] The same effects, a courtier might hope, would be secured by jests relying on such figures. According to Freud, the more stylistically complex a joke is—the more it relies on such verbal techniques as allusion, metaphor, and irony—the more socially elevated and refined it will appear.[96] In presenting their renditions of the jesting figures, Peacham and Puttenham both associate certain forms of jesting with social refinement. Peacham defines *asteismus* as "wittie jesting in a civill maner" (33), and according to Puttenham, this figure "is mirth full of civilitie, and such as the most civill men doo use" (200). These descriptions of *asteismus* may encourage readers to adopt this figure as part of their own repertoire of rhetorical strategies, hoping to win or preserve (in using it) membership among those "most civill men." Wilson, although he does not name the jesting figures individually in his catalog of figures of speech, does include a figure he calls "Witty Jesting," a figure that, like *asteismus,* he claims is characteristic of and displays a gentlemanly status: "Many a pleasant gentleman are well practiced in merry-conceited jests and have both such grace and delight in therein that they are wonderful to behold" (206). The ambiguous reference of the pronoun "they" is telling, for it suggests an equation between "gentlemen" and the "merry-conceited jests" they tell. Both are "wonderful to behold."

The courtier can also distinguish himself by simply laughing at his social inferiors or causing others to laugh at them, although in laughing at his inferiors the courtier does suggest, however remotely, that those inferiors pose a threat to him. In the soldier-king jest, for instance, the king's redefinition of the "cut" as a sign of cowardice puts the soldier back in his place and reminds him of the king's superiority. That the king felt a need to put the soldier down, however, suggests that he is to some extent a threat to the king and the system of deference he represents. In other words, the double vision required in getting a jest may also appear at a deeper level of motivation. Such is the case in a discussion from Guazzo's *Civile Conversation* where Annibale and the other interlocutor, the author's brother, consider appropriate and inappropriate forms of interaction between gentlemen, on the one hand, and yeomen and others of inferior status, on the other. During this discussion, Annibale raises the subject of upstarts and those who "will not acknowledge and confesse themselves inferior to Gentlemen." Annibale elaborates, saying there are many "common people" who "fall into such blinde arrogancie, and so foolish a vaine, that they will not sticke to vaunt themselves to be that which they are not, and both in their talk and their apparel brave it out like Gentlemen" (1:195). Guazzo shares his friend's concerns and cites instances of this phenomenon in his native Italy where one does not have to look far to see "riche Peasaunts, who are not ashamed to attire themselves like Gentlemen, to wear weapons by their side, and such like ornaments, which are proper only to gentlemen." The problem with such behavior, as Guazzo sees it, is that it leads to interpretive confusion and the blurring of social boundaries: "And this abuse is so in use at this day . . . [that] a man can discern no difference in estates." A tailor, for instance, accustomed "to weare weapons, and to be appareled like a Gentleman, is not knowne what he is, until he be seene sowing in his shop" (1:196). These interpretive problems are partly the product of social mobility—the "riche Peasaunts" who can afford to dress like gentlemen. But they are also, ironically enough, related to one of the strategies by which the established elite sought to reassert their natural superiority: the emphasis on style—verbal and, in this case, physical "ornaments"—over substance created opportunities for the baseborn to appropriate the outward signs of nobility.

To guard against this "disorder and confusion," Guazzo recommends that Italy follow the practice of France and introduce sumptuary laws whereby "severall [different] apparell is worne, according to everie ones calling" (1:197). Annibale agrees and calls upon princes to "put their handes hereto, and cut the combs of these clownish cockscombes, and make them come down from their degree of gentrie, by forcing them to weare such apparel as may be at least different from Gentlemen" (1:197). The necessity for a legal remedy receives further impetus when he says that under the "maske" of misleading apparel "there may be much falsehood wrought." However, if legislation to "refourme that abuse" is not immediately forthcoming, Annibale says gentlemen still have a strategy for dealing with the situation themselves. And that strategy is laughter: "Those who are gentlemen indeed, ought not to be moved with the matter, but rather *laugh at it*" (1:197, emphasis added). Annibale and Guazzo actually adopt this strategy during this discussion and use derision when they speak of those who "brave it out like Gentlemen." As we have already seen, Annibale calls them "clownish cockscombes" and says that when they ape gentlemanly conduct, they act in "so foolish a vaine." He also refers to them as "malepert clownes" who by their presumption disgrace the "honour and degree of gentrie" (1:197). Guazzo even cracks jests at their expense. He compares them to the "poore drudge brought in in the Comedie" who said that "his father was a goldsmith," but when asked what work his father did "belonging to that occupation," he responded that "hee set stones in morter" (1:195). In another comparison, Guazzo says that an upstart is "like the mule who beeing demaunded of his birth, and beeing ashamed to say that he was an Asses sonne, answered, that he was a horses cousin" (1:195–96). In all of these jibes and jests, the objects of laughter are social inferiors who claim positions in status above those ascribed at birth, and one of the functions of these derisive terms and jests is to define those claims as both false and ludicrous. However, in recommending that gentlemen laugh at peasants who "brave it out like Gentlemen," Annibale betrays a fear of those peasants and admits that they pose a real threat to the system. And it is not simply a threat of interpretive confusion, or even of there being "much falsehood wrought." The image that recurs in Annibale and Guazzo's conversation is that of peasants and tailors wearing weapons, and it is this image—one of potential violence—that must have been deeply troubling to those "who are gentle-man indeed."

As the remarks of Annibale and Guazzo amply reveal, the dictates of decorum often coincide with the demands of a social system based on defer-ence and subjection. In other words, violations of decorum, in this and in many other cases, are not simply infractions against taste and delicacy; they are also transgressions against the social hierarchy. By this logic, the decorous jest is one that preserves existing social relations, while the indecorous jest is one that flouts those relations. As we have already seen, the king's reply to the soldier who "praid his reward" works in agreement with the system, and Annibale's interesting recommendation—that in lieu of a royal injunction, gentlemen should laugh at the socially ambitious—is intended as a stopgap measure to "cut the combs of these clownish cockscombes." Courtly jesting, however, does not only work in the service of the social hierarchy, nudging the delinquent back in line; it must also subject itself to the needs of that hier-archy. Put simply, a courtier's jesting, like all of his utterances and actions, must embody the hierarchical relations of all the participants involved.

If decorum is shorthand for the social order, then it inevitably entails that inferiors never jest at the expense of their superiors. In his *Garden of Eloquence,* for instance, Peacham assigns socially conservative functions to all the jesting figures: they are to be used in the maintenance of the status quo. For instance, irony "pertaineth chiefly to reprove by derision" (36); the chief function of *antiphrasis,* a form of irony, is to "reprehend vice, and mock folly" (24); *sarcasmus,* another figure, is to be used to "represse proud folly and wicked insolencie" (38); and the primary use of *mycterismus,* which Peacham defines as a "privie kind of mocke," is to "represse pride, rebuke folly, and taunt vice" (39). Here Peacham uses moral categories to describe the functions of these figures, categories or attributes that are not necessarily specific to one's social status. When he comes to prescribe the limits of their use, however, he often translates these moral categories into social ones and insists that these figures be used only in ways that preserve existing social relations. *Antiphrasis* is not "seemely to be used of all persons, in respect of breach of duty: it were unmeete for the sonne to say, wisely spoken father, for it were as much, as to call his father foole: and likewise for a servant in his anger to use this figure against his master" (25). Similarly, irony is not a "meete form of speech for every sort of person to use, especially of the inferior toward the superior, to whom by some reason he oweth dutie, for it is against the rule of modestie and good manners . . . to deride his betters" (36). These figures are not a "meete form of speech for every sort of person to use" because the trajectory of their force is downwards: to "represse" is to "push down"; to "deride" is to "laugh down" (*deridere*); to rebuke is to "cut down" (from the Old French *buchier*). Inferiors who jest at the expense of their superiors talk down to them and thus flout social relations that are already in place.

While Peacham insists that inferiors should never jest at the expense of their superiors, other writers advise against the reciprocal practice. That is, they recommend that superiors should guard against jesting *with* their inferiors, the risk being that if they are outmaneuvered by an inferior in a contest of wit they will suffer social degradation. In his *Courte of Ciuill Courtesie,* Robson says, "I would not advise any man to jest mutch with his inferiors, unlesse they be such as he knoweth, both can and will use restraint of over malepartnes. For if a Gentleman should be saucily used by jest, by his inferiour, he cannot escape disgrace, whether he beare with it, or quarell for it" (12). According to Bacon, the mere act of engaging an inferior in a battle of wits is enough to cause a speaker disgrace. He says that under no circumstances should a "wise man contend with a fool," for "it is no victory to conquer, and a great disgrace to be conquered." Once the wise man enters such a contest, once that threshold is crossed, degradation will inevitably be the result: "it makes no difference in this kind of contest, whether we take it in jest or in scorn and contempt; for, whichever way we turn, we must lose in dignity and can in no way quit ourselves well of it" (5:38). Implicit in all of these passages is a particular logic of banter, a logic that seems analogous to the one that governs what Pierre Bourdieu calls the "game of honor." According to him, "To make someone a challenge is to credit him with the dignity of a man of honor, since the challenge, as such, requires a riposte and therefore is addressed to a man deemed capable of playing the game of honor, and of playing it well."[97] A speaker who jests *with* his inferior—that is, engages him in banter—is implicitly offering him a challenge (can he match quip for quip?) and thus crediting him with a capacity to play the game of merriment. In doing so, however, he slights the social distance that should always obtain between superiors and inferiors by treating the inferior as a rival, an equal. More than that, he is making himself vulnerable to attack by his inferior. And should the inferior get the better of his superior, it seems that observers are more likely to register the superior's loss of face than the inferior's insolence.

As many of the remarks and examples in this section suggest, the handbook writers view courtly jesting as a force that can either preserve or invert hierarchical relations. What they largely ignore, however, is the possibility that a single jest could perform both functions simultaneously. Even more so than *paradiastole,* which, as Whigham claims, destabilizes evaluations of others' actions, jesting blurs and confuses disparate and incongruous realms of experience, including the decorous and indecorous, the socially conservative and socially disruptive. Such is the case in an anecdote Puttenham uses to explain how "some skurrility and unshamefastness have now and then a certaine decencie . . . by reason of some other circumstance." Sir Andrew Flamock, "king Henry the eights standardbearer," was attending the king as he "entered the parke at Greenwich." The king blew his horn to announce his coming, and Flamock, "having his belly full, and his tayle at commaundement, gave out a rappe nothing faintly." The king, taken aback by the sound of Falmock's fart, said to him, "How now sirra?" And Flamock, "to excuse his unmanerly act," responded, "If it please you Sir . . . your Majesty blew one blast for the keeper and I another for his man." At this remark the king "laughed hartily and took it nothing offensively" (274–75).

This anecdote contains two humorous acts: Flamock's fart and the witty excuse through which he apparently repairs the situation. The first act is socially disruptive, for it collapses several hierarchical oppositions. The king's mouth is equated with Flamock's behind, an equation that topples a cluster of other oppositions that are associated with the head and bottom: the mind and spirit versus the body and excrement, the sociopolitical head versus the sociopolitical bottom, the crown versus the commons. Also, the blowing of the king's horn is placed on the same level as breaking wind. Royal fanfares announce the coming of the king and, perhaps, are a symbol of his potency. Flamock's "rappe," by contrast, implies that what is coming is noxious and offensive and, perhaps, suggests that the king is nothing but a windbag. However, Flamock's witty response to the king's "How now sirra?" seems to repair the situation and reestablish some of the hierarchical distinctions leveled by the "rappe." He addresses the king as "Sir" and "your Majesty," both of which show that Flamock is acknowledging his inferior position relative to the king. Also, by saying that the "king blew one blast for the keeper and [Flamock] another for his man," Flamock uses the hierarchical relationship between these two men to mirror and reaffirm the one between the king and himself. Finally, Flamock's quick recovery redirects the trajectory of the "rappe" from targeting the king to targeting the keeper's man: it is aimed not up at the king, but down at a servant. Thus, it seems that Flamock successfully neutralizes his disruptive act, as the laughter of the king evidences.

The interpretation might close right here with the observation that Flamock's witty response contains and neutralizes the disruptive nature of his "unmanerly act." That, however, would fail to account for the mechanism of the jest itself. For if we think about it, the humor of this anecdote hinges on seeing Flamock's actions as simultaneously socially disruptive and socially conservative. Although Flamock's remark reinstates each participant in his proper social place, this anecdote also invites us to view the recuperative gesture as duplicitous. For, after he farts and then interprets his actions with his witty (and socially decorous) response, we are not likely to say, "Oh! That's what he meant by the fart. He meant it to be directed at the keeper's servant all along." It might be argued that the reader who comes up with such an interpretation does not get the jest. Rather, getting the jest requires the audience to "see that the meaning implicit in the punch line both follows from, and at the same time contrasts with or contradicts, the initial frame of reference."[98] The "initial frame of reference" in the Flamock jest would encourage reading Flamock's "rappe" as constituting a form of transgression. Such a reading is encouraged both by Puttenham's promise to offer "some skurrility and unshamefastness" and by the king's "How now sirra?" a remark implying the king has also sensed that a transgression has occurred. Flamock's witty response, the punch line in this case, "follows from" this initial frame of reference in the sense that he is trying to make the best of a bad thing and "excuse his unmanerly act." However, it offers an interpretation of the "rappe" that contradicts our initial inferences about its transgressiveness. We do not abandon this initial inference and substitute Flamock's recuperative interpretation for it. Instead, we keep both contradictory interpretations in play in order to enjoy the pleasure of the jest.

The story of Flamock's "unmanerly act" appears in Puttenham's more general discussion of decorum. As such, it is itself a textual disruption, a moment in which the indecorous is identified with the decorous, in which "skurrility" may "have now and then a certaine decencie." Although Puttenham offers this story as a special instance or exception, it nevertheless encapsulates and complicates the main issues explored in this chapter. Flamock uses jesting to manage a particular social situation, and his "rappe" and witty excuse affect every participant involved, turning the potential wrath of the king into laughter and transforming Flamock from the king's attendant to his critic back to his attendant again. As we have seen, jesting is also presented in the handbooks as a strategy for managing other situations as well. In the forum, the Roman orator primarily uses jesting to defeat his opponent and enlist listeners as his allies over and against that opponent. In the early modern pulpit, jesting (when it is sanctioned) allows preachers to overcome communicative obstacles between themselves and their lay parishioners, preparing them for (or, in some cases, being a vehicle of) religious instruction. But as Flamock's "unmanerly act" also suggests, the success of speakers rides on their ability to recognize and then submit (or, at least, create the appearance of submitting) to the dictates of decorum. Puttenham describes Flamock's witty excuse as "well becoming the occasion" because it seems to preserve hierarchical relations already in place prior to the jesting exchange. As we have seen, however, much of the humor of Flamock's excuse depends on registering its duplicity; it is simultaneously conservative and disruptive, decorous and indecorous. Indeed, jesting will always confuse and blur boundaries, combining incongruous and disparate elements into a single utterance. This chapter has repeatedly hinted in that direction, recording instances in which jesting threatens to erase distinctions between the classical orator and the low comedian, the Elizabethan pulpit and playhouse, the gentlemanly courtier and the common jester. The following chapters make this property of jesting still more apparent.

The *Topoi,* or "Places," of Jesting

A jest appears in *Tales and Quick Answers* in which an "uplandish man nourished [reared] in the woods" comes to the city and witnesses a royal procession. When he first enters the city, he sees the streets filled with people shouting, "The King cometh!" The excitement of the crowd piques the bumpkin's interest, and he waits for the king's arrival. When the king does come into view with "many nobles and 'states before him," the crowd shouts, "God save the king! God save the king!" The bumpkin, however, cannot identify the king and asks someone to point him out. A person standing nearby responds, "Yonder is he [the king] that rideth upon the goodly white horse." The bumpkin cannot believe that the man on the horse is the king, suspects that this other fellow is playing a joke on him, and delivers what turns out to be the jest's punch line: "Is that the king? . . . What thou mockest me. . . . Methink that is a man in a painted garment." This jest ends, as so many do in this jest book, with a short didactic tag that makes explicit the lesson the jest supposedly illustrates: "By this tale ye may perceive . . . that nourishing, good bringing up and exercise been more apt to lead folk to humanity and the doing of honest things than Nature herself. Those . . . are noble, free and virtuous which in their youth hath been well nourished up and virtuously endoctrined" (Zall, *Hundred Merry Tales,* 274). According to this tag, the object of laughter is the bumpkin whose country-bred ignorance prevents him from being able to identify the king and from knowing how to behave in his presence. The function of this jest, again according to the tag, is conservative. Not only does it represent correct behavior and attitudes toward the sovereign, but it also clarifies and reinforces boundaries between city dwellers and rustics, that is, between the social and geographical center and the social and geographical margins.

However, one wonders: does the tag make explicit the jest's didactic content, or does it impose a particular interpretation on the events related in the anecdote—an interpretation that tries to neutralize the subversive energy of the bumpkin's remark about the king? For it seems this jest is open to another interpretation, one in which the bumpkin's remark is read, not as ignorance, but as unadulterated wisdom that demystifies the king's power and the symbols used to constitute it. The bumpkin's inability to recognize the king, despite the train of "many nobles and 'states" riding before him, the "goodly white horse," the "painted garment," and the shouts of the crowd, suggests that the king's authority is not natural; it is not self-evident so that anybody would be able to recognize it on sight. Instead, it is a rhetorical construct constituted by the symbols the king attaches to himself and his subjects' ability to interpret those symbols. Indeed, the king could be taken as embodying rhetoric itself since his "painted garment" may trigger associations with rhetoric as a "painted" art. Following this alternative interpretation, we laugh, not at the ignorance of the bumpkin, but at the foolishness of the people who make such a fuss over a "man in a painted garment" and perhaps at the king himself who, as the word "painted" also suggests, appears like a fool in motley.

This anecdote, its didactic tag, and my alternative reading illustrate the difficulty in determining the subject matter and function of a jest. It is not that the interpretation implicit in the tag is wrong and that my alternative reading is right, nor is it the other way around. Rather, jokes secure their effects through incongruity, duplicity, and interpretive disjunctions. They are inherently ambiguous and thus resist efforts to stabilize their meaning and effect. In practice, people do attribute meanings to jokes. If they did not, then jokes would lose much, if not all, of their rhetorical efficacy. Still, there is no guarantee what meaning, or meanings, they will attribute. Consider the bumpkin jest again. It is an instance of what humor theorists call "standardized," as opposed to "spontaneous," humor: it is relatively self-contained and can be reproduced in a variety of settings without an elaborate reconstruction of the situation in which it supposedly first occurred.[1] With each new setting in which it is retold, however, a new (and always complex) set of relationships come into play among the joke teller, the listeners, and even the characters within the joke. A speaker's attitude toward his listeners, their attitudes toward him, and both the speaker's and listeners' attitudes toward bumpkins, city dwellers, kings, and painted garments, although they may overlap, may also diverge or even clash. Lines of solidarity, contention, and indifference among the participants in a jesting exchange will always impinge on who laughs at what, or if they laugh at all.[2]

This instability of jesting is further complicated by the fact that jests do not emerge *in vacuo*. They do not issue from some transhistorical comic essence.[3] Rather, they reproduce and produce ambiguities and contradictions in the culture in which they occur.[4] Although I described the bumpkin jest as "relatively self-contained," it is not entirely so. It is deeply embedded in, and gains resonance from, its context of production. It plays upon an ambiguity between the king's identity being natural and self-evident and its being artificial and constructed, and this ambiguity points to and participates in a broader cultural ambiguity over social identity in general. The official ideology of Tudor England may have rested upon the notion of a God-given, natural, and unchanging social hierarchy—one's identity was fixed at birth, and one's civil, even moral, obligation was to stay put and submit to one's betters—but that ideology was seriously challenged in the sixteenth century when England experienced dramatic increases in both social and geographical mobility. Relocation, in terms of both social status and region, occurred with increasing frequency during the period, and as a consequence, the determinants of social identity at all levels of society became increasingly ambiguous. Is identity ascribed at birth and hence natural and absolute? Or is it manufactured, something that can be achieved through education, geographical relocation, or self-fashioning?

The bumpkin anecdote dramatizes both types of mobility and some of the ambiguities that may ensue. The bumpkin, having come from an "uplandish" region, is geographically mobile. When he enters the city, stands among its citizens, and witnesses the royal procession, his mere presence is a source of ambiguity. He is part of the crowd of citizen onlookers, yet he is still an outsider. When he delivers his demystifying (or naïve) comment, he becomes an even more active source of ambiguity, confusing what is supposed to be a royal procession with what he thinks is a rather silly exhibition of a "man in a painted garment." According to the tag, it is his "uplandish" breeding that leads to this confusion. The bumpkin anecdote also dramatizes social mobility, although in a less direct manner. While no character in the jest is actually socially mobile, the bumpkin's remark allows for the possibility of fashioning an elite identity by assuming the signs and trappings of nobility. Even the didactic tag allows for this possibility. As I have already said, the tag suggests the bumpkin is an object of laughter because he fails to recognize the natural identity of the king. But while suggesting this, the tag undermines the notion of natural identity, for it allows anyone, through "nourishing, good bringing up," and virtuous indoctrination, to acquire "noble, free and virtuous" qualities and thus improve on "Nature herself." In a roundabout way, then, the tag makes the same potentially disruptive point as the bumpkin's demystifying remark: namely, identity is an artificial construct that can be achieved through self-fashioning.

The rather lengthy explication of this jest brings out many of the issues and challenges the rhetoric and courtesy manuals confronted while trying to define and determine the subject matter, not of a single jest, but of jesting in general. The manuals define that subject matter to be either physical deformity or deformity in conduct. Like the didactic tag but on a much grander scale, the manuals are trying to stabilize the subject matter of the laughable. In the process of doing so, several of the manuals posit deformity as a general *topos* or "place" of laughing matters and go on to offer a set of particular *topoi* that are meant to specify the various ways the general *topos* of deformity may be drawn upon in the production of jests. From a practical standpoint, the manuals are trying to supply orators and courtiers with a method for inventing jests, a method that is, in theory, analogous, if not identical with, topical invention. While this method of joke production may seem to contradict modern intuitions and beliefs about the creation of jokes, it is nevertheless in keeping with what the rhetoricians see as the ultimate goal of topical invention: the acquisition of *copia,* or an abundance in thought and expression, that allows orators to speak extemporaneously on any subject on any given occasion. In addition to its practical aim, this method of jest production, like the didactic tag, serves social and political ends as well. To define the subject matter of laughter as deformity is to assign jesting a socially conservative function: jesting reinforces the status quo by ridiculing deviations from culturally defined norms. Moreover, the language of topical invention, with its pervasive use of spatial imagery, suggests the manuals seek not only to determine the subject matter of jesting but also to fix its deformed and delinquent objects in clearly bounded spaces, set apart from or safely contained within the official arenas or "places" of rhetoric: the law court, Parliament, the pulpit, and the royal court.

What is interesting about this project is how it plays itself out in the manuals' catalog of the specific *topoi* of jesting and in the sample jests the manuals use to illustrate them. For the most part, the *topoi* of jesting are not *topoi* as they were traditionally conceived, but include figures of speech and what may be called conversational strategies meant to flout or undermine the conventions and proprieties normally governing serious (that is, nonhumorous) discourse. While the identification of figures of speech as *topoi* is not entirely at odds with how Renaissance rhetoricians viewed the figures and their potential use as heuristic devices, their inclusion among the *topoi* of jesting undermines the manuals' attempts to locate and fix the sources of laughter, because the figures are, by definition, deviant and transgressive, producing multiple and oftentimes conflicting meanings. Equally deviant and transgressive are the conversational strategies meant to produce laughter, for they challenge some of the most basic assumptions and practices of conversational exchanges: for instance, they encourage speakers to misread the remarks of others intentionally, to pretend not to understand what others are saying, and to say one thing and mean the opposite. Even more problematic are the sample jests the manuals use to illustrate their method of jest production. As was the case with the bumpkin jest, these jests reveal the difficulty (even impossibility) of determining, once and for all, the subject matter and function of a given jest. In effect, the manuals in their discussions of the subject matter of jesting occupy the same position as the didactic tag does in relation to the jest it comments on. They too are trying to comprehend the subject matter of laughter in ways that accord with existing power relations. While doing so, however, they unleash energies that neither they nor their method of jest production can completely contain.

Let us first piece together the manuals' theory of the invention of jests since bits of it are scattered throughout their discussions of humor. Nearly every early modern handbook that includes a discussion of jesting defines the subject matter of laughter as deformity, either in physical appearance or behavior. Although Plato and Aristotle offer similar definitions, the handbooks' most immediate source is Cicero, who says: "the field or province [*locus . . . et regio*], so to speak, of the laughable . . . is restricted to that which may be described as the unseemly or ugly [*turpitudine et deformitate*]" (*De oratore,* 2.58.326). This definition was very influential in the Renaissance, and repetitions and variations of it appear in many treatises. Wilson, for instance, says, "The occasion of laughter and the mean that maketh us merry . . . is the fondness, the filthiness, the deformity, and all such evil behavior as we see to be in other" (165). This definition includes both physical deformity, for "oftentimes the deformity of a man's body giveth matter enough to be right merry" (173), and deficiencies and deviations in behavior, such as an intellectual lack, moral turpitude, and social misconduct, which the words "fondness," "filthiness," and "evil behavior" respectively imply. Castiglione also offers a definition of the laughable that features deformity: "The place therfore and (as it were) the hedspring that laughing matters arrise of, consisteth in a cetein deformitie or ill favourednesse" (157). As a final example, the anonymous author of *The Schoolemaster* claims that jests typically point out or "touche certayne faultes and deformyties of the bodye."[5] Implicit in all of these definitions of the laughable is a crude sociology of laughter and jesting, one in which deformity and conformity divide the social world into those who laugh and those who are laughed at. The primary function of laughter in a world thus divided would be to keep the deformed and delinquent at bay, while bolstering the solidarity of those who do laugh.

Also implicit in these definitions of the laughable is a method for jest production that several of the handbook writers go on to develop more fully. To say that deformity is a *locus,* that it "giveth matter," and that it is a "place" and "hedspring" of "laughing matters" is to invoke the rhetorical canon of invention where the *topoi, loci,* or "places" for inventing subject matter are outlined. In other words, deformity is a *topos, locus,* or "place" which generates the subject matter of humorous discourse. Indeed, several of the handbook writers, both ancient and early modern, are very explicit about what they perceive as a connection between jest production and topical invention. Cicero says, "Remember this, that whatever subjects I may touch upon, as being sources [*locos*] of laughing matters, may equally well, as a rule, be sources [*locis*] of serious thoughts" (*De oratore,* 2.61.248). According to Quintilian, "From all forms of argument [*ex omnibus argumentorum locis*], there is equal opportunity for jests" (6.3.65).[6] Similarly, Castiglione claims, "You shall understande moreover that out of the *places* jestinge matters are derived, a man may in like manner pike grave sentences" (158, emphasis added). And Wilson: "out of diverse pleasant speeches ancient [i.e., grave] sayings also may be gathered" (168). Positing deformity as a general *topos* or "place" of the laughable and then claiming that the *topoi* of serious discourse

can be used in the production of jests have their advantages. For the practicing orator or courtier, the manuals' definitions of the laughable would seem
to supply a general rule of thumb: if a speaker wants to say something funny,
then his remarks should refer or allude to some kind of deformity. Also, if
the *topoi* of jesting are the same as those of "serious" or "grave" thoughts,
then the orator or courtier could—at least, in theory—commit these to
memory and deploy them as opportunities presented themselves.

However, we might find it puzzling, even paradoxical, that the manuals would propose such a method. Apart from canned jokes of the "did-you-
hear-the-one-about" variety, jesting is typically thought of as a spontaneous
form of discourse that issues from the speaker without much, if any, fore-
thought. Even Cicero and Castiglione, both of whom invest considerable
energy into setting forth an elaborate method of jest production modeled on
topical invention, view spontaneity (or, at least, its appearance) as defining
characteristic of the successful quip or witticism. Cicero says that a "shaft of
wit has to be sped and hit its mark, with no palpable pause for thought"
(2.54.219). In a passage we have already seen, Castiglione echoes his classical
source: "quippie ought to be shott out and hit the pricke beefore a man can
discerne that he that speaketh it can think upon it" (154). A modern formulation of this view is offered by Freud when he says there are significant differences between "making" a joke and performing other kinds of discursive
acts: "We speak, it is true, of 'making' a joke; but we are aware that when we
do so our behavior is different from what it is when we make a judgement
or make an objection. A joke has quite outstandingly the characteristic of
being a notion that has occurred to us 'involuntarily.' What happens is not
that we know a moment beforehand what we are going to make, and that
all it then needs is to be clothed in words. We have an identifiable feeling,
rather . . . a sudden release of intellectual tension, and then all at once the
joke is there—as a rule ready-clothed in words."[7] Although Freud far from
settles the issue of what happens when we "make" a joke, he does advance,
however impressionistically, a theory of joke production that seems radically
at odds with the one found in the rhetoric and courtesy manuals. According
to him, jokes are the results of something like an "involuntary" process; they
cannot be willed into existence by first thinking "beforehand what we are
going to make" and then clothing it in words. However, if we situate the
manuals' remarks about jest production in the context of what they say
about the uses of topical invention in general, then positing a set of jesting

topoi may not seem so strange after all, although (as I will argue below) this method is still plagued by a crippling flaw.

The words *topos, locus* or "place" figure prominently in ancient, medieval, and early modern discussions of rhetorical invention.[8] Although these terms have a "bewildering diversity of meanings," they generally refer to regions or locales in one's mind or notes where arguments reside.[9] Cicero and Quintilian both define the *loci* as "seats of arguments [*sedes argumentorum*]," suggesting they are containers from which arguments may be drawn.[10] In his *Rule of Reason,* Wilson defines a "place" as "the restyng corner of an argumente," and then goes on to offer a playful analogy between searching out the "places" and hunting for foxes by looking for their boroughs, "wherein if any one searche diligently, he maie find game at pleasure."[11] Theoretically, all an orator would need to do in order to generate the substance of his speech would be to run the subject or issue under consideration through the *topoi, loci,* or "places," gathering whatever arguments seemed most relevant and discarding the rest. In *De inventione,* a treatise that greatly influenced later developments in topical invention, Cicero divides the *loci* under two general headings: attributes of the person and attributes of the act (1.24.34). The first includes such *loci* as name, nature, manner of life, fortune, and interests; the second includes *loci* concerned with the nature of the act, the occasion upon which it was performed, and its consequences. If an orator were defending a client, he would go to these *loci* to find arguments for his client's defense. Under the *locus* "manner of life," for example, the orator would consider "with whom he [the client] was reared, in what tradition and under whose direction, what teachers he had . . . with whom he associates on terms of friendship, in what occupation, trade, or profession he is engaged" and so on (*De inventione,* 1.25.35). Under the *locus* concerned with the nature of the act, he would inquire, among other things, "by what means, and why, and for what purpose the act was done" (*De inventione,* 1.26.37). After going through all of the *loci* of person and act, the orator would then have a wealth of arguments from which he could chose those most advantageous to his case. Moreover, because the *loci* or "places" of argument are relatively portable, the orator could use them repeatedly on different occasions to produce, theoretically, an endless number of speeches.

Set out in this manner, topical invention may seem a rather mechanical and prolonged exercise, one that would seem to hinder and stifle the spontaneity, flexibility, and "sudden release" often required in jesting. The ultimate aim of training students in the topics, however, was not to enslave them to a complex and halting method of invention. Rather, it was to give them an abundance of thought and expression—*copia* or "ready copy"— which they could then deploy extemporaneously as the case or occasion demanded. At the beginning of *De Duplici Copia Verborum ac Rerum,* an elementary textbook setting forth a vast array of techniques (including the topics) for developing *copia,* Erasmus says that learning these techniques "will make no insignificant contribution to the ability to speak or write extempore, and will prevent us from standing there stammering and dumbfounded, or from disgracing ourselves by drying up in the middle."[12] Erasmus, like other rhetoricians before and after him, did not think *copia* would come easily to the beginner, but would have to be cultivated through practice and exercise. Discussing the topics in particular, Erasmus says, "Anyone training with a view to acquiring eloquence will have to look at all the possible topics in turn, go knocking from door to door so to speak, to see if anything can be induced to emerge; but with practice the right ones will come to suggest themselves naturally, without this process being necessary" (606). In other words, the acquisition of *copia* by means of the topics involves a learning curve: students would have to begin slowly (and perhaps clumsily) searching through all the topics, but as they became more proficient in their use, they would come "naturally," as if involuntarily. Quintilian makes a similar point with a suggestive analogy between using topical invention and playing the lyre: "But it is only by constant practice that we can secure that, just as the hands of the musician, even though his eyes be turned elsewhere, produce bass, treble or intermediate notes by force of habit, so the thought of the orator should suffer no delay owing to the variety and number [*verietas et . . . copia*] of possible arguments, but that the latter should present themselves uncalled and, just as letters and syllables require no thought on the part of a writer, so arguments should spontaneously follow the thought of the orator" (5.10.125). With this analogy, Quintilian is trying to capture the mental processes (or their seeming absence) of one who has mastered the topics after years of training. Like the virtuoso musician who, after long and continual practice, transforms the playing of a song into something like a muscle memory, the master orator plays the topics, so to speak, to ensure that arguments are always ready at hand and seem to spring "spontaneously" from his lips.

Viewed in the context of what the manuals say about the deployment of the *topoi, loci,* or "places" in general, the use of topical invention as a model for jest production may seem less strange. Practice in the *topoi* of jesting, like practice in the argumentative *topoi,* will help the orator cultivate the "planned spontaneity," as Richard Lanham calls it, that gives evidence of mastery in speaking on both serious and laughing matters.[13] Indeed, the attention the handbook writers devote to the "places" (either of argument or of jesting) evidences a profound difference between early modern and modern cultures. According to Walter Ong, the "places" serve important functions in either oral or residually oral cultures where there is frequently an "information storage problem." In such cultures, "the oral performer, poet or orator, needed a stock of material to keep him going," and the doctrine of the "places" served as "the codification of ways of assuring and managing this stock."[14] In the early modern period, with the invention of print, the "drive to collect and classify" the "places" increased dramatically and was given a "potential previously undreamed of." Now as never before, examples illustrating the "places" could be "culled from any and every writer," and the "results . . . once achieved, could be multiplied" in a potentially endless number of copies. Moreover, print facilitated information retrieval because "printed collections of . . . [the] commonplaces could be handily indexed."[15] The advent of print, however, also marked "the beginning of the end of the commonplace tradition." As Ong explains, "Commonplaces had their deepest roots in the noetic needs of an oral world. The Renaissance preoccupation with texts, inherited from the Middle Ages, but intensified by print, tended to shift the focus of verbalization from the world of sound to the surface of the page, from the aural to the visual. This is not to say there were not competing tendencies in the Renaissance, such as the accentuation of the oral fostered by the cult of the classical orator, but the effect of print was ultimately to prove overwhelming."[16] Signs of this "shift" in focus can be found in the handbooks' discussions of jesting. Many of the sample jests that appear there are taken from printed sources, including Cicero's *De oratore,* Macrobius's *Saturnalia,* and early modern collections of *facetiae, apophthegms,* and jests. While discussing the importance of using "gestures" and a "livelie voice" when telling funny stories, Castiglione even refers his readers to stories from Boccaccio's *Decameron* where the "force" of the spoken word is captured "in writing" (161). Even so, the handbook writers still viewed jesting as primarily an oral practice, and the *topoi, loci,* or "places" of jesting were to assist orators and courtiers in oral performance.[17]

Although the manuals' method for jest production makes sense in terms of the ultimate aim of topical invention and its place within the "noetic" economy of early modern culture, it nevertheless breaks down, particularly in its failure to account for what makes a jest a jest and to recognize that serious and humorous forms of address are fundamentally different. As I have already said, jesting secures its effects through incongruity, ambiguity, and interpretive disjunctions. However, it is precisely these same features that "are often treated as problems during serious discourse, and attempts are made to remove them or lessen their impact."[18] In his *Arte of English Poesie,* Puttenham includes a catalog of what he calls "vices" of speech, which are "always intollerable" and are "generally to be banished out of every language." Many of these involve linguistic forms that frustrate comprehension "such as it is not possible for a man to understand the matter without an interpretour" (256). For instance, *amphibologia* or "the Ambiguous" occurs "when we speake or write doubtfully and that the sence may be taken in two wayes." This vice creates a confusing diversity of interpretations and thus should be avoided unless, Puttenham goes on to say, it is used "for the nonce or for some purpose" (267). He does not elaborate on this qualification, but we may assume that doing it "for the nonce or for some purpose" might include jesting, for many forms of jests (think of the pun!) involve speaking "doubtfully" or in "two wayes." In his discussion of another "vice" of speech, Puttenham explicitly equates doing it "for the nonce" with the "intent to moove laughter" (260). Although he never comes out and says it (and despite his initial categorical exclusion of the vices as "always intollerable"), Puttenham's prohibition of certain forms of speech seems only to apply to serious forms of address (the examples he uses to illustrate *amphibologia* merely involve ambiguously placed modifiers). In other words, while Puttenham's qualifications seem to recognize jesting as a special form of discourse different from statements made in serious manner, the rhetoricians, in their use of topical invention as a model for jest production, blur or elide that difference by allowing serious and humorous statements to be generated by the same method.

In addition to ambiguous and contradictory significations, jesting differs from serious discourse by flouting conventions, assumptions, and proprieties that typically govern conversations. In other words, a jest may also issue from undermining expectations concerning interactional, rather than semantic, aspects of communication: for instance, making unexpected or apparently irrelevant remarks, talking out of turn, and intentionally or unintentionally misreading the utterances of others.[19] Although Della Casa treats the subject of jesting in his *Galateo,* his acceptance of this form of discourse is at times grudging. One of his objections to it is that it involves conversing in an (apparently) uncooperative fashion.[20] While talking with others over dinner, Della Casa says, participants must always "answer after a gentle sort" and never be "clownishe nor lumpishe" like those who "never give a man a good countenaunce . . . [and] say, No, to all things" or who "refuse it all, what soever is presented or offered unto them." For instance, "if a man say: 'Sir, suche a one your friend, asked me how you did,'" then it is inappropriate to reply, "Let him come feel my pulse," for such an answer is "carterlike and clownish" and ill befits "all good and honest company" (34–35). Implicit in these admonitions is a hierarchical distinction: to respond in a "carterlike and clownish" fashion is to behave like a peasant or lower-class buffoon, while answering "after a gentle sort" displays a more socially elevated identity. Della Casa also seems to recognize a distinction based solely on interactional criteria: jesting, whether in a courteous or discourteous fashion, often involves violations of proprieties that normally guide the conduct of conversation, while serious forms of address seek (or should seek) to adhere to them scrupulously. Topical invention, however, with its emphasis on generating the subject matter of discourse, has little, if anything, to say about the proprieties that should or should not govern that discourse.

A final way in which jesting differs from serious discourse derives from the fact that jests frequently interrupt the flow of conversations and signal that interruption with various linguistic and paralinguistic markers. A jest itself can be considered a "place" or, rather, a rupture in the flow of serious discourse; it is an "episode," as William Fry calls it, framed by verbal and nonverbal cues. Verbal cues might include conventional openings such as "Did you hear the one about" or "I heard a good one last week," while nonverbal cues might include certain gestures, facial expressions, and changes in voice inflection.[21] These cues and markers signal a departure from serious discourse and create a space where the "bisociative" principles, to use Koestler's term, of jesting are operative, where incongruous or opposing elements merge in fittingly unfitting combinations, where interpretive reversals and inversions are not unusual, but the norm. Latimer illustrates this phenomenon when he prefaces one of his jests with a verbal cue ("I will tell you a pretty story to refresh you withal"), and he ends another with a similar framing device (he spoke a "merry word . . . to refresh my auditory"). Although the rhetoricians have little to say about such linguistic and paralinguistic cues, several of them do suggests that jests are identifiable episodes in, or distinguishable departures from, the discourses in which they occur. In the preface to his *Apophthegms New and Old,* Bacon says that *apophthegms* have several uses, including "to be interlaced in continued speech" (7:123). The metaphor here implies that *apophthegms* are threads woven into the texture of "continued speech," but it can also suggest alternating between two types of discourse, the jesting and the serious. Wilson seems to have the latter sense in mind when he says that in order to secure the goodwill and admiration of their listeners, "the witty and the learned have used delightful sayings and quick sentences ever among their weighty causes" (166). Not only does this alternation between "delightful sayings" and "weighty causes" help keep listeners attentive and well disposed to the speaker, but it also presupposes recognizable differences between humorous and serious forms of address. If there were no discernible differences, then neither speaker nor audience would be able to tell what was spoken in earnest and what was spoken in jest.

While the handbook writers frequently view jesting as a special form of discourse, distinct from serious modes of address, their conflation of jest production with topical invention tends to blur this important distinction, but not entirely. As they catalog the various *topoi* or "places" of jesting, these writers seem engaged in a struggle to make jesting accord with topical invention, and evidence of this struggle can be found in a gradual slippage in terminology whereby the *topoi* or "places" of jesting look less and less like *topoi* or "places" proper, and more and more like figures of speech and disruptive conversational gambits. When we come to examine the sample jests used to illustrate the various *topoi* or "places," we shall find that the notion of "place," while somewhat useful in identifying recurrent objects of laughter, fails to account for the subject matter of jests. Because any given jest is susceptible to a wide diversity of interpretations, its subject matter will always exceed any boundaries meant to comprehend it.

On some occasions, the manuals suggest that the "places" of jesting will generate subjects of laughter or, more specifically, that they will assist orators and courtiers in selecting the butts of their jests. In this way, there does seem to be a relatively close affinity between the "places" of jesting and Cicero's formulation of the topics which are generally to be used in the "discovery of materials for argument."[22] As we have already seen, the author of the *Table Phylosophie* says that laughing matters "touch certayue [*sic*] faultes and deformyties of the bodye." After offering this definition, he gives several examples such as "the crookednesse, rysing up, or flatnesse of the nose" (M2ᵛ). In this instance, the "place" of jesting corresponds quite literally with a place or region on the body and can be used as the subject matter of a jest. Other writers identify, in addition to regions on the body, types of behavior as sources or "places" of laughter. Wilson says, "Folly and lack of natural wit . . . give good *matter* of mirth sometimes" (179, emphasis added). Castiglione also says that "foolishe matters" will supply speakers with subjects of jesting, and he offers the following story as an example. One day, Duke Federico is discussing what he should do with a large pile of dirt that has just been "caste up to laye the foundacyon of . . . [his] Palayce." An Abbot, who happens to be present, devises a solution: "My Lorde, I have well beethoughte me where you shall beestowe it [the dirt], let there be a great pitt digged and into that may you have it cast without any more ado." Laughing at this suggestion, Federico asks the Abbot, "And where shall we beestowe then the quantitie of earth that shall be cast out of the pitt?" The Abbot answers, "Let it [the pit] be made so large that it may well receive both the one and the other." The jest ends, as did the one about the bumpkin, with a brief tag: "Now see what a good forecast this Abbot had" (163–64). The verb "see" subtly disguises one of the functions of this tag, which is to control the listeners' interpretation of the story. In effect, the joke teller is inviting his listeners to look for themselves, but then precludes the necessity of any such looking by suggesting in advance what they will see: the stupidity of the Abbot.

With this jest (and with many other jests that supposedly target stupidity), foolishness does not necessarily "give good matter of mirth"; rather, mirth is generated by the ways in which speakers and audiences interpret types of behavior. If we accept the tag's interpretation of the Abbot jest, then this is not a situation in which an orator "invents" a witty observation or response: presumably the Abbot does not intend for his remarks to be funny; instead, they are interpreted as such by Federico and others who are involved in subsequent rehearsals of this story. In other words, the Abbot's "foolishe" suggestion constitutes an instance of found, or what Mulkay calls "natural," humor: "Humour is possible wherever participants can accomplish an interpretation of events, actions or texts in accordance with the bisociative principle of humorous discourse."[23] With found humor, the creative work of invention is performed by the onlookers or listeners and the "interpretive procedures . . . [they] bring to bear" on the situation.[24] However, there is no guarantee what "interpretive procedures" they will bring to bear, or even if they will bring to bear the same "interpretive procedures." In this case, they may perceive an incongruity (or "bisociation") between the irrational logic of the Abbot, on the one hand, and a commonsense logic about the digging of holes and the displacement of dirt, on the other. However, the jest is about much more than the foolishness of the Abbot or Abbots in general. It dramatizes an encounter between a duke and a member of the clergy, and by doing so, it triggers a host of incongruities associated with these two social types: secular authority versus scared authority (and, more remotely, a noble "Lorde" versus the Lord); conspicuous expenditures versus vows of poverty; palace versus monastery; and, in early modern England after the dissolution of the monasteries, the newly enfranchised versus the recently disenfranchised. All, some, or none of these additional incongruities may impinge on any given interpretation of this jest. For this reason, the "place" of this jest is extremely vast and encompasses much more than the heading "foolish matters" would allow.

In addition to viewing the *topoi* or "places" as storehouses of generic subjects of laughter, the manuals identify them as figures of speech and thought. Cicero and Castiglione, for instance, include such figures as antithesis, metaphor, understatement, overstatement, and irony as *loci* or "places" of jesting. [25] Immediately after listing a number of *loci,* including genus, species, antecedents, and consequents, and saying they give "material [*materia*] for jests," Quintilian adds that jests may also be derived from "all forms of trope" and thus suggests that both the *loci* and the tropes serve as means for inventing jests (6.3.66).[26] Not to be forgotten are the writers of stylistic rhetorics, such as Sherry, Day, Puttenham, and Peacham, some of whom thought "the figures . . . [were] derived from the topics of invention," and all of whom included a set of figures specifically designed for humorous purposes.[27] Peacham characterizes all of the figures (including the jesting figures) as "mightie streames of eloquence" and thus as sources of persuasion and not mere ornament (AB3^v). By suggesting that these figures will help in the production of jests, these writers obscure traditional distinctions between the *topoi* proper and the figures that are traditionally the province of style.

More important, this slippage in terminology deflects attention away from issues of substance or subject matter and focuses, instead, on formal devices that can actually create problems in serious discourse. According to Puttenham, the figures are "abuses or rather trespasses in speach, because they passe the ordinary limits of common utterance, and be occupied of purpose to deceive the eare and also the mind, drawing it from plainesse and simplicitie to a certaine doubleness" (166). They are so transgressive, according to Puttenham, that judges of the Areopagus in ancient Greece "forbid all manner of figurative speaches to be used before them in their consistorie of Justice" because the figures "inveigle and appassionate the mind" and thus undermine "upright judgement" (166). While the figures may serve invention, they are metaphorically conceived elsewhere, not as bounded *loci* or "places," but as violators of boundaries so volatile that they were driven (or thought to be driven) from one of the literal "places" of forensic rhetoric—the court of the Areopagus.

It seems the handbook writers had to resort to the figures because the technical vocabulary provided by topical invention was inadequate for describing all humorous phenomena. An example from Castiglione will illustrate this inadequacy. After cataloging the "manie places, out of which a man may picke pleasaunt and wittie sayinges" (179), Castiglione adds a few more to his list. One of these "places" is hyperbole, which is usually classified not as a *topos,* but as a figure either or thought or speech. As an instance of this figure, Bernardo, one of Castiglione's interlocutors, tells how the Magnifico Giuliano, another interlocutor present, described his skinny servant: this servant "was so lean and drie, that in the morning as he was blowing the fire to kendle it, the smoke bore him up the chimney unto the tonnell, and had gone awaye with him had he not stook on crosse [crosswise] at one of the holes above" (179). Using the terms the manuals supply, we might say the "place" or subject matter of this jest is the bodily deformity of the servant—his skinniness. However, that alone is not enough to make it a jest; Giuliano could have expressed roughly the same thought by saying, "My servant is very skinny." What, in part, makes it a jest is how that subject matter is stylistically transformed, how hyperbole is used to create a disjunction between commonsense notions of how the world works (a commonsense physics of sorts) and the improbable scene of a man, leaf-like, being blown up a chimney. One consequence of describing the servant jestingly rather than matter-of-factly is that it challenges a fundamental rule of serious discourse:

statements should have a stable, unequivocal meaning. This jest, by contrast, produces an excess of meaning and invites its hearers to view the hyperbolic description of the servant as simultaneously real and unreal, probable and improbable, fitting and unfitting.

A third and final way in which the rhetoric and courtesy manuals use the word "place" is to designate what can be called discursive strategies that undermine the conventions and proprieties normally governing conversations. Lacking a precise vocabulary to name these strategies, the handbook writers typically describe the technique involved. Wilson, for instance, says, "When we see a notable lie uttered, we check the offender openly with a pleasant mock" (182). The "notable lie" is itself a breach of conversational propriety, and thus checking it "openly" with a mock, although it too may be considered tactless in some situations, would nevertheless seem appropriate or fitting at a higher level—that the obvious lie warrants exposure.[28] Other strategies, however, are clearly more disruptive: for example, "when they [other participants] look for one answer and we make them a cleane contrary, as though we would not seem to understand what they would have" (168); or "when we gather another thing by a man's tale than he would gladly we should gather" (176). To illustrate the former strategy, Wilson rehearses an anecdote in which a man who has just been cuckolded asks another, "Ah Lord, what think you, sir, of him that was taken in bed of late with another man's wife?" The other responds, "Marry . . . I think him to be a very sluggard" (168). Apparently, the cuckold was seeking, albeit very obliquely, some confirmation of his disdain for the adulterer. The other man's response does and does not conform to the cuckold's expectations: while he condemns the adulterer, he does so not on moral grounds as the cuckold would seem to hope, but for getting caught or, perhaps, for a sluggish performance. Castiglione describes similar strategies: for example, "whan we give eare to heare one thinge, and he that maketh answere, speaketh an other and is alleaged contrarye to expectacion" (169); and "whan a man of the verie communication of his fellow taketh that he would not" (182). All of these strategies disrupt the flow of conversation and send it along unexpected paths. While such unexpected disruptions may be sources of pleasure for some, for others they could be sources of frustration or even offense. Della Casa censors those who "speake and make answer, otherwise then a man would lightly look for" because such jests come across as too "grose" and "rude"—that is, too discourteous.

In many ways these strategies are like the jesting figures, for they often involve playing with language and turning words and phrases to different and unexpected senses. As such, they also produce a diversity of meanings that would exceed any "place" meant to comprehend them. Unlike the jesting figures, however, these strategies frequently occur across conversational exchanges rather than being embodied in a single utterance. While illustrating the strategy of delivering an answer that is "clean contrary" to the one anticipated, Wilson recounts a story in which a man, while traveling to the fair to buy a horse, meets an acquaintance. He asks this acquaintance "how horses went at the fair," meaning what was their going price. The acquaintance "merrily" answers: "Some trot, sir, and some amble, as far as I can see. If their paces be altered, I pray you tell me at our next meeting" (168). If we tried to locate the "deformity" that this jest targets, we might be hard pressed to find it, since the pleasure of the acquaintance's remark seems to derive more from playing with language than from laughing at some bodily deformity or delinquent behavior. Even so, perhaps a hint of affectation can be detected in the first man's use of the word "went": that is, it might seem a bit pretentious for the man to use this word rather than express himself more simply and directly. The acquaintance calls attention to this affectation and brings it to bear on the situation by punning on "went" (without mentioning the word himself) and intentionally misinterpreting it according to a more common, less affected meaning, as in "to go." This jest seems to be about much more than affectation, however, for it toys with, even challenges, several assumptions and conventions meant to ensure the smooth operation of serious exchanges and shows just how fragile those assumptions and conventions are. The pun on "went" upsets the conventional assumption that each word has one, and only one, signification, an assumption that sustains the fiction that one's meaning can unproblematically be conveyed to another if one selects the proper word. More interesting is how the acquaintance manipulates the conventions of politeness and how he creates a disjunction between the manner of his response and the action it performs. His response exhibits several markers of polite discourse: the words and phrases, "sir," "as far as I can see," and "I pray you," all create the appearance of showing deference to the first man and thus seem to position him as a superior. The outcome or action performed, however, is that the acquaintance puts the first man down, and he does so by flouting the even more fundamental convention of responding faithfully to the utterances of others.

This slippage in terminology from the "places" of jesting meaning sources of generic objects of laughter to their meaning figures of speech and disruptive conversational strategies suggests a failure on the manuals' part to assimilate jesting to topical invention, in particular, and serious discourse, in general. Jests are far too idiosyncratic and far too open to a diversity of interpretations for anyone to determine, once and for all, their subject matter and function. However, I do not think the notion of *topoi* of jesting should be abandoned completely. Despite the problems involved in determining the subject matter of any given jest, we can still identify recurring (or stock) characters and situations in early modern jests. For this reason, the notion of the *topoi* of jesting may be of use, provided we keep in mind its limitations. For one, this notion offers a theoretical apparatus for mapping out what a particular culture or community generally finds funny. That is, a set of jesting *topoi* might constitute common ground (*communis locus*) that allows the content and point of jests to be shared. For another, attention to the *topoi* at which people laugh might also reveal boundaries between groups and show how these boundaries are policed—who is included and who is excluded. As Kenneth Burke says of Castiglione's treatment of jesting, "In displaying his sense of the 'right' things to laugh at, the courtier thereby displayed the marks of his class."[29] Finally, one would expect the *topoi* of jesting to shift not only across groups or cultures, but also across time. Patterns in the ways these *topoi* are reproduced, revised, forgotten, or replaced could serve as indices of social change.[30]

It should by no means be thought, however, that these *topoi* of jesting are stable entities unto themselves. As has already been suggested, the ambiguities and contradictions through which jesting secures its effects preclude the possibility of locating *the* comic object. What is needed then is a way to talk about the subject matter of laughter that recognizes and accounts for the peculiar nature of jests and their social embeddedness. Mary Douglas offers a partial solution. In her study of the "social control of cognition," Douglas uses jokes as examples of symbolic expressions to argue that "the pattern of social forms limits and conditions the apprehension of symbolic forms."[31] In other words, people's experiences in specific social and historical situations determine what they say, think, and perceive. Despite the problems with the unidirectional determinism of her model, Douglas does make several important contributions to humor theory. One of these is relevant to the present discussion, for what she is talking about, although in different terms, is the invention of jokes and how this process is conditioned by situational factors. Moreover, she tries to accommodate her theory of joke production to the mechanisms and operations of humor, unlike the handbooks on oratory and courtly conduct, which try to adapt jesting to a method for inventing serious discourse.

She begins her analysis of joking with a description of the formal properties and operations of jokes, claiming that humor almost invariably issues from the perception of an incongruity: a joke "brings into relation disparate elements in such a way that one accepted pattern is challenged by the appearance of another which is in some way hidden in the first."[32] In the Abbot jest, for instance, Douglas might identify the central incongruity to be an opposition between the rational and the irrational. The Abbot's irrational suggestion challenges supposedly rational modes of thought and action. After offering this description of the formal characteristics of a joke, Douglas goes on to argue (as I did in the case of the bumpkin jest) that a relationship exists between the incongruities of a joke and the incongruities in a given social structure and that the former is a symbolic expression of the latter: "a joke is seen and allowed when it offers a symbolic pattern of a social pattern occurring at the same time. . . . All jokes are expressive of the social situations in which they occur." Douglas even claims a joke will not be identified as such, unless it expresses an incongruity in the social structure: "The one social condition necessary for a joke to be enjoyed is that the social group in which it is received should develop the formal characteristics of a 'told' joke: that is, a dominant pattern of relations is challenged by another. If there is no joke in the social structure, no other joking can take place."[33] If we translate Douglas's argument into rhetorical terms and shift her emphasis from reception to production, then we have a model for the invention of jokes that not only accounts for the formal operations of jokes but also recognizes their subject matters as historically and socially specific. The incongruities, ambiguities, and contradictions present in the social structure of a particular culture or group are available *topoi* for jokes.

There are problems, however, with this model. As I have already said, it is deterministic. According to Douglas, jokes *reflect* social ambiguities and contradictions; the witty speaker is nothing more than a conduit through which these ambiguities and contradictions are channeled and given expression. There is no room in her theory for the possibility of a joke's actually producing, and not merely reflecting, an ambiguity or contradiction, nor room for the creative powers of the speaker who brings together disparate elements of the social realm in new, incongruous, and surprising combinations. Douglas's model is deterministic in another sense: jokes are inherently subversive. A joke requires "two elements, a juxtaposition of a control against that which is controlled, this juxtaposition being such that the latter triumphs." On this point, Mulkay takes issue with Douglas. Like Douglas, he subscribes to an incongruity theory of humor and concedes that some humor is socially disruptive. However, he argues that most humor operates in a way that sustains existing social relations: "The humour that occurs in formal [social] structures is closely linked to . . . [those structures'] inherent contradictions. Overwhelmingly, however, this humour is employed in accordance with the requirements of the existing systems, and in a way that supports that system."[34] For Mulkay, humor predominately serves socially conservative ends.

Douglas's and Mulkay's models for the relationship between jokes and social structure are powerful analytical tools, and they offer promising ways to approach the issue of the subject matter of jesting. But perhaps there is an alternative to what may seem to be their reductive binarisms. Perhaps the incongruous elements out of which jests are made could be set in a dialectical relationship, rather than a combative one in which one element must triumph over another. This alternative model would view the incongruous elements of a jest as circulating, more or less, freely. How they are put together and how they come to serve a particular purpose are the result of a process of negotiation among the participants involved in a particular jesting exchange. One advantage of this alternative model, in addition to a gain in complexity and depth of analysis, is that it allows us to move beyond the reductive conservative-disruptive binary: if the function of a jest is no longer seen as part of its inherent makeup, then a jest can serve a host of functions simultaneously depending on the situation in which it is deployed and on the interpretive work participants in that situation perform. Another advantage of this model is that it preserves the multiple interpretations to which a particular jest is susceptible. In this way, it recognizes jests, not as repositories of stable meanings, but as sites where meaning is negotiated and contested.

Looking at several early modern jests that feature stock characters and situations reveals that jesting strays even further beyond the grasp of topical invention, and even beyond the official arenas of rhetoric—that is, the "places" of forensic, deliberative, courtly, and religious discourse.[35] The

Roman rhetorics typically offer sample jests modeling confrontations between competing orators. That is, the characters in these jests are of roughly the same status; hierarchical distinctions between them are established by the jests themselves when, for example, one orator scores a verbal victory over another. In the early modern handbooks on orator and courtly conduct, by contrast, the characters in the sample jests are often already socially differentiated in some respect, and thus the jests in which they appear model encounters between persons of different orders of being. In this way, these jests are primed for enacting inversions and reversals, exploring areas of ambiguity or tension in the social structure, and capturing liminal moments when two social types communicate across the boundary that normally separates them. In addition to capturing liminal moments of exchange, these encounters are typically set in liminal spaces. Unlike the jests in the Roman rhetorics, which are usually set in the official arenas or "places" of the forum or senate house, the jests found in the early modern handbooks often take place in unofficial settings. As we have already seen, the "how-horse-went" jest is set on a roadway, the characters are between destinations, and one of the characters is on the way to the fair. The skinny-servant jest invites listeners to imagine the servant wafting up a chimney, which is itself a place of interchange between inside and outside, high and low. The Abbot jest takes place as the Duke is breaking ground for his new palace. And even in the jest about Flamock, he commits his "unmanerly act" as he and the king cross the threshold of the "parke at Greenewich." In short, early modern jests often act out their liminal status in the flow of serious discourse.

These liminal, unofficial settings are not incidental to these jests, but create a context in which the pressures of hierarchy, or of inside and outside, are less powerfully felt. In the bumpkin jest, the procession in which the king participates is a portable context that preserves and displays hierarchical distinctions, even as the king travels to outlying regions of his kingdom. However, this portable context has less force (less protective power) than would a more official setting—that is, for example, the royal court where the place itself exerts pressures ensuring that participants model their speech and behavior in accordance with existing power and social relations. In the jests we have already examined and in those to come, the unofficial contexts in which they are typically set might be said to free participants from at least some of the constraints of hierarchy and thus facilitate the circulation of the incongruous elements of which these jests are made.

Encounters between clergy and lay folk are a staple of early modern jest books, and they frequently appear in the manuals. The rhetorical (and social) functions they serve are perhaps as numerous as the situations in which they were told. They could be used to criticize delinquent members of the clergy for their avarice, lechery, and gluttony. They could be used to attack not only delinquent members of a particular faith, but also the faith itself: any one of the many religious factions in early modern England could target other factions as a way to assert their difference from (and superiority to) those factions while bolstering solidarity among their own members. They could also be used as vehicles for religious instruction. In *A Hundred Merry Tales,* there appear several jests which rehearse the Ten Commandments, the Twelve Articles of Faith, and the supposed meaning of the Ave Maria. Jests about the clergy could even, as Thomas argues, be seen as expressions of religious skepticism, especially on the part of the lower orders of Elizabethan society.[36] As an example, Thomas quotes the following jests from *Tales and Quick Answers:* a curate preaching to his parishioners said that "our Lord with five loaves fed five hundred people"; a clerk, catching the curate's mistake, whispered in his ear, "Sir, ye err. The gospel is 'five thousand'"; the curate replied, "Hold thy peace, fool. . . . They will scantly believe five hundred."[37]

However, it would be too reductive to say that a jest is about "such-and-such" or that it serves "such-and-such" a function. If social incongruity and contradiction are the materials of jesting, then judgments about a particular jest's subject matter and function will always be provisional and subject to renegotiations.[38] Wilson rehearses an anecdote that dramatizes an encounter between a friar and a lay parishioner. The friar, "disposed to tell mysteries, opened to the people that the soul of man was so little that eleven thousand might dance upon the nail of his thumb." A parishioner, "marveling much at that," asked the friar, "I pray you master friar . . . where shall the piper stand then, when such a number shall keep so small a room?" (174). What the parishioner accomplishes with his question is to bring together, in a single utterance, a host of incongruous realms of social experience, including the secular and the sacred, the material and the spiritual, the playful and the serious, and the literal and the figurative. Perhaps most prominent here is the incongruity that results from the parishioner subjecting one of the "mysteries," which are supposedly religious truths beyond the reach of human reason, to a literal-minded logic. By doing so, he sets in motion a chain reaction of possible associations and cultural allusions.

For instance, this jest appears in Wilson's overtly Protestant *Rhetoric,* which itself was published in a Protestant (at least, officially) England. The parishioner's response to the Catholic friar's mystery could invoke a variety of issues associated with the conflict between Catholics and Protestants. The jest could be interpreted as participating in Protestant attacks on what they viewed as superstitious and idolatrous beliefs and practices. Or, it could be about the tenacity of such beliefs and practices since, despite legislative efforts, Catholicism persisted in England, especially in rural areas.[39] Even more specifically, the parishioner's literal take on the mystery of the souls could invoke the conflicts over Biblical exegesis, conflicts in which many Protestants argued for literal and historical readings of Scriptures rather than the four-tiered interpretations associated with medieval, and hence Catholic, exegesis.[40] This jest could also be about preachers and their often conflictual relationship with congregations. That is, the parishioner's remark could be read as an instance of the recalcitrance of churchgoers in general.[41] Or the jest could be about the conflicted roles of preachers. On the one hand, preachers supposedly offer religious instruction and moral guidance to their parishioners. On the other, they are performers of sorts. The identification of the preacher in this joke as a "Friar" is particularly telling. Before Henry's break with Rome, friars would typically preach during open-air assemblies where they would compete with clowns, actors, and acrobats for the attention of onlookers. Not only might such a setting encourage confusing these social identities, but it might also encourage preachers to become overly absorbed in their roles as performers. Such seems to be the case with the friar, for in his discourse on souls, he actually inserts himself into the description and thus becomes part of the wonder to behold: it is "his thumb" upon which the souls dance. In short, this jest is a vortex that swallows its situation of utterance.

In addition to encounters between the clergy and the laity, early modern jests often involve encounters between foreigners and natives. Such jests could serve as powerful strategies for mediating tensions that arose because of increases in geographic mobility, New World exploration, trade and commerce, on the one hand, and the centralization of power and an emergent nationalism, on the other. According to Christie Davies, writing about the related topic of ethnic humor, the tellers of such jokes usually target neighboring peoples "who are often part of the same linguistic and cultural family or are in the process of becoming so."[42] From the teller's perspective, these targets are "anomalous, and ambiguous, a contradiction of the joke-tellers' sense of ethnic and linguistic order and unity, a blurring of the clarity of boundaries."[43] Following this line of reasoning, we could say that one function of ethnic jokes is to disambiguate their targets by pigeonholing them as stupid, incompetent, canny, stingy, etc. However, in many instances (as was the case with the bumpkin anecdote), a jest of this sort may unleash the (oftentimes threatening) perspective of the outsider, a perspective that the joke teller cannot completely control or discredit.

In *A Hundred Merry Tales,* a jest appears that ostensibly targets the stupidity of the Welsh; however, it could also be read as a satire of English authorities. A knight had a servant who was found guilty of committing a "felony" for which he was shortly to be hanged: "Wherefore in all haste he [the knight] sent a letter by a welchman, a[nother] servant of his, unto the King's Justice of the King's Bench." The purpose of this letter was to beg pardon from the Chief Justice for the first servant's crime. When the Welshman arrived at the Chief Justice's palace, he saw at the gate "an ape sitting there in a coat made for him." The Welshman took off his cap, "made courtesy to the ape and said: 'My master recommendeth him to the lord your father and sendeth him here a letter.'" The ape took the letter, opened it, and appeared to read it, while "making many mocks and moves as the property of apes is to do." The Welshman, thinking that his task was completed, returned to his master, the knight, and said that he had "delivered the letter unto my Lord Chief Justice's son which sat at the gate in a furred coat." When the knight asked the Welshman what "answer he had," the Welshman said that the ape "gave him an answer but it was either in French or Latin, for he understood him not." The Welshman went on to assure his master, "But sir . . . ye need not to fear for I saw by his countenance so much that I warrant you he will do your errand surely to my lord his father." The knight, thinking that he had done all that he could on behalf of his other servant, "made none other labor," and thus, within two days, the first servant was hanged. The didactic tag appended to this jest reads, "By this tale, ye may see that every wise man ought to take heed that he send no foolish servant upon a hasty message that is a matter of weight" (Zall, *Hundred Merry Tales,* 108–9).

According to Christie Davies, the butts of ethnic jokes "represent a comic unthreatening form of ambiguity."[44] Not so with the Welsh, for Wales had long been perceived as a turbulent country and threat to the English crown.[45] Jests about the Welsh, thus, could be seen as a way to manage that perceived threat, yet they would always presuppose the power of the people they target. Laughing "'puts people down' in signalling that they are put down, but that could not happen unless they were originally perceived as 'up'—as in some way holding power over and thus . . . potentially threatening the laugher."[46] In the case of the Welshman-ape jest, I would go a step further and claim that this threat is located not only in the perceptions of the laughers, but also in the text of the jest itself. The exchange between the Welshman and the ape occurs at the gate of the Chief Justice's palace. This gate physically represents the many thresholds and boundaries that impinge upon this encounter: high and low; inside and out; English and Welsh; man and ape; master and servant, law and lawlessness (the Tudor settlement, in part, was motivated by the fact that the Welsh were effectively *outside,* or beyond the reach of, English law); language user and non–language user; learned and unlearned; etc. The Welshman's mistaking the ape for the Chief Justice's son blurs these distinctions and allows these terms to circulate across the boundaries that normally keep them separate. To say that a person "ought to take heed that he send no foolish servant upon a hasty message" is to insist that these terms be arranged in a particular (and, in this case, a socially conservative) way. However, the mechanism of the jest—what had set these terms in circulation in the first place—allows for another arrangement, one in which the Chief Justice's son, and hence the father, is indeed a chattering ape.

Just as popular as jests about the clergy and foreigners are jests representing interaction between masters and servants. Like the other kinds of jests we have examined, the functions of master-servant jests are diverse and complex. Jests that ostensibly target the foolishness of servants, for instance, might be taken as warranting those servants' inferior positions and thus as affirming the traditional system of paternalism and deference that demanded servants' unconditional obedience. Or those same jests could be about servants who role-play—that is, who work the system to their own advantage by manipulating the outward signs of deference.[47] Wilson rehearses and then comments on a jest in which a master asks his servant, after they have just returned from church, "what he has brought home from the sermon," meaning what has he learned. The servant replies, "Forsooth, good master . . . your cloak and your hat." Wilson takes this answer as evidence of a "honest, true dealing servant" who, although "plain as a packsaddle," is faithful nevertheless. Wilson then contrasts him to "privy picking" servants who "under the color of hearing [sermons] . . . bring other men's purses home in their bosoms in the stead of other men's sermons" (169). However, perhaps the first servant is himself operating under a "color." By saying, "Forsooth, good master . . . your cloak and your hat," perhaps he is giving his master what he wants or expects to hear, and perhaps this answer is itself a "cloak" concealing other motives and actions. In other words, perhaps the "honest, true dealing" servant is not unlike "privy picking" ones and uses signs of deference and simplemindedness to block or deflect his master's questions. Or perhaps this jest is about master-servant relations in general. During the sixteenth century and beyond, the traditional conception of masters' and servants' being bound by a set of mutual, albeit unequal, obligations was being displaced by a new conception resembling (and anticipating) modern employer-employee relations. While this new conception entailed a loss of security for masters and servants alike, it did free them, to some extent, to pursue their own (usually financial) interests more aggressively.[48] The contrast Wilson draws between "honest, true dealing" servants and those who pick pockets at least hints at these changes in master-servant relations.

Jests involving foolish servants (apparent or otherwise) were not the only brand of master-servant jests in the period. On the contrary, many of these jests involve clever or canny servants who get the better of their masters. From the perspective of masters, these jests could be read as cautionary tales: "Beware of crafty servants!" or "Tighten your grip, or your servants will try to get the better of you!" From other perspectives, however, these jests could be taken as celebrating the insolence of servants or, even worse, offering readers models of insolence to be imitated. Jesting is a particularly powerful means of criticizing a superior, for the verbal form of a jest often attracts attention away from what may be construed as an irreverent implication. Moreover, since jesting often works by way of allusion and indirection, it may allow a servant to disown that implication ("It was only a jest") or even to disown the jest itself ("There was no jest. Therefore, I'm not in trouble"). Guazzo rehearses a master-servant jest in which a servant, having first been mocked by his master, delivers a quip involving a verbal reversal that, in turn, suggests a reversal, if only temporarily, in the relational positions of the participants. One day when this master called his servant "King of fooles," the servant answered, "I would to God I were King of fooles, I would not doubt then, but I should beare rule over hym which is better than

myself" (2:103–4). By calling his servant "King of fooles," the master sought
to ridicule him, to put him down. However, to be "King" implies ruling over
—that is, being above—something or somebody. This ambiguity between
putting down and elevating gives the servant an opening and allows him to
define his master as his subject. Moreover, the rejoinder includes a bit of
clever and strategic wordplay. The phrase "better than myself" suggests not
only that the servant, as "King of fooles," will rule over his social "better"
but also that he will rule over one who is "better" at being a fool. Also, the
antecedent of "hym" is ambiguous. If the servant had said, "beare rule of
you," then the pronoun reference would have been definite: it would clearly
refer to the master. By using "hym" instead, the servant creates a small
degree of uncertainty in the pronoun's reference and thus gives himself a little room in which to maneuver should the master take him to task for his
apparent insolence.

In addition to offering examples of master-servant jests, Guazzo actually includes a discussion of the practice of masters and servants jesting with
one another. Late in the third book of *The Civile Conversation,* Guazzo's two
interlocutors discuss how masters and their servants are to behave when
together and even when they are apart. At one point, the discussion turns to
the question of whether or not servants who possess "imperfections," such as
being rude, foolish, or insolent, ought to be tolerated or dismissed from their
masters' services (2:103). One of the interlocutors, Annibale, at first comes
down on the side of dismissal, saying, "I thinke suche servantes better lost
then found, and the house the worse that they are in" (2:103). But then he
qualifies this statement and says that he knows "some honest gentlemen,
who so long as their servantes are faythfull and trusty, care not though they
be fooles, vaine talkers, or jesters to make them merry" (2:103). Having said
this, Annibale alters the initial question in two respects. First, the servants he
mentions here are not just rude and insolent; they are also "faythfull and
trusty," attributes that might be said to mitigate their other, less desirable
qualities. Second, the phrase "to make them merry" suggests their masters
take some degree of pleasure in their servants' jesting and fooling even
when, Annibale goes on to say, their "mockes and scoffes" are directed at the
masters themselves (2:103). By reframing the question in this way, Annibale
far from settles the issue; in fact, he complicates it. That is, he opens up the
possibility that the servants' unruly behavior simultaneously works against
and reinforces the hierarchical relationship that should obtain between

masters and servants. For by being unruly, these servants *are* serving their masters: they are making "them merry." And the masters, by giving off signs of delight even when they are the ostensible objects of laughter, not only sanction such behavior but also give it further encouragement.

Immediately after Annibale raises the issue of unruly servants and fails to resolve it, the second interlocutor, the author's brother, chimes in with a jest that also fails to settle the matter. Instead, it reinforces, through its indeterminate subject matter, the ambiguous and conflicting dynamics of masters and servants who jest with one another. It also suggests the difficulties that may be encountered when trying to figure out what exactly is being laughed at: "There was a gentleman at Parris, who going forth of hys Lodgyng, wylled hys servaunt to go to a Butcher named David, to buy some tripes, but the Butcher having soulde all his tripes, hee retourned to his Mayster, who was at Church hearing a sermon, and by chaunce as hee entered in at the Churche, the Preacher (meaning to alleadge some text of Scripture out of the Psalmes of David) sayde, what sayth David? Mary sayth he, that hee hath sold all his trypes" (2:103). After rehearsing this jest, Guazzo's brother says, "I know not whether that ought to be termed foolishnesse, or pleasantnesse." His indecisiveness issues from an indeterminancy of the jest's subject matter and function. Who is the object of laughter? Is it the servant who not only mistakes (either wittingly or unwittingly) the preacher's rhetorical question for a direct one, but also supplies an answer that is way off the mark (although, for the sake of the jest, it comes at an opportune moment)? Is it King David, author of the Book of Psalms, whom the servant confuses with David, the local butcher who sells tripe? Is it the preacher whose sermon has been interrupted and who, we might suppose, was knocked off balance by the sudden disturbance? Moreover, since the preacher is, in a sense, the mouthpiece of David in this instance, maybe he too is equated, through the logic of the jest, to the local butcher, his sermons being the verbal equivalent of tripe. Perhaps some of the laughter is also directed at the master: since he is accountable for the actions of his servant, he might be considered laughable by association. Or is the master secretly laughing to himself, taking pleasure in the disruption his servant has caused and in the discomfiture of the preacher? No single answer will completely satisfy the question, "Who or what is the object of laughter?" for the subject matter and function of this jest are ultimately beyond determination.

A practical joke recounted by Castiglione was ostensibly played at the expense of a "coople of great Ladyes," but as we shall see, strays into the dangerous territory of laying bare some of the contradictions at the heart of the Renaissance orator's and courtier's entire project. At some unnamed court, "there arrived a manne of the Countrie about Bergamo, to be in service wyth a Gentilman of the Court." This rustic "was so well sett oute with garmentes and so finelye clad" that although he knew no other occupation but looking after cattle, "a manne that had not heared him speake would have judged him to be a worthie Gentilman." As a prank, the two "greate Ladyes" were told that this cowherd was the "best Courtier in all of Spaine," and they, having heard of his great reputation, "longed verie much to speake with him." A meeting was arranged, and "after they had receyved him honorablye, they caused him to sit downe, and beegan to entertaine him with verie greate respect in the presence of all menne." Although there were a few men present who did not know he was a mere "Bergamask Cowherd" and who were thus not in on the prank initially, they soon caught on once they heard his rustic speech. Seeing those "Ladies entertaine him [the cowherd] with such respect, and honour him so muche, [these men] fell all to laughing, the more bicause the seelie felowe spake still his natyve language, the meere Bergamaske tunge." The ladies did not catch on because the courtier who had arranged this prank had "first toulde those Ladyes that emonge other thinges he [the cowherd] was a great dissembler and spake all tunges excellentlye well, especially the Countrie speache of Lumbardye, so they thought he feigned." As it turned out, "thys communication lasted so long that everye mans sydes aked for laughinge, and he could not chouse himself but uttre so manye tokens of his nobleness of birth, that at length those Ladies (but with much ado) beleaved he was the man that he was in deede" (Castiglione, 192–93).

In many ways, this prank is a variation on the bumpkin-king jest with which this chapter began. In this instance, however, it is the bumpkin, and not the king, who is dressed in a painted garment. Moreover, in the first bumpkin jest, the king travels, as the focal point of a royal procession, through outlying towns and cities in a spectacular display of his power. While he is in one city he comes within proximate contact of the bumpkin who confuses him with a man in a fancy getup. Although the bumpkin's response to this procession can be read as demystifying the power of the king, it occurs at a relatively safe distance from the procession and would presumably be lost amidst the shouts of the crowd. In the cowherd jest, by contrast, it is the bumpkin who invades the space of the court and becomes the centerpiece of an elaborate prank. It would seem that one of the functions of this prank, as was the case in the first bumpkin jest, is to clarify and reinforce boundaries between the center and the periphery, between the high and low. With their laughter, the courtiers separate themselves from the cowherd and the ladies, while simultaneously uniting themselves as a group whose members are not only different from, but also superior to, the ostensible comic objects. In orchestrating this prank, however, the courtiers allow distinctions that preserve their supposedly absolute and fundamental difference from peasants to be blurred, and by doing so, they reveal these distinctions to be ultimately artificial. The joke, in short, is on everybody.

The success of this prank depends upon manipulating various symbolic resources and behaviors for rhetorical effect; however, whenever these resources and behaviors are manipulated they are shown not only to have multiple, contradictory significations, but also to be artificial. The rich "garmentes" are both a sign of nobility and a disguise that conceals the cowherd's supposedly true identity. The good report—that the cowherd is the "best Courtier in all of Spaine"—that precedes his arrival is both compelling evidence (at least for the ladies) of his worth and a lie manufactured for the sake of the prank. And the "verie great respect" paid to the cowherd by the ladies is both a sign of deference and a ridiculous exhibition. All of these symbolic resources and behaviors, while carefully managed for the sake of the jest, are also the stock and trade of courtiers in general. By showing how they may be manipulated to deceive others, this prank severs the link between them and what they supposedly signify—the elevated social identity of the courtier.

There is one symbolic resource, however, that is presented as if it were an irrefutable marker of one's social status, and that resource is speech. Throughout his recounting of this prank, Castiglione repeatedly refers to speech, suggesting that it will always reveal one's ascribed status or identity. The cowherd would have been taken for a "woorthie Gentilman" by anybody who had "not hearde him speake." Also, it is the cowherd's rustic language that gave him away to those few men who had not been told beforehand that he was a bumpkin. Even the person who orchestrated the prank had to supply the ladies with information that would account for the cowherd's "natyve tunge." In the end, what finally convinced the ladies that this man was not an accomplished courtier but a cowherd was his speech:

"he could not chouse himselfe but uttre so manye tokens of his noblenesse of birth, that they [the ladies] beleaved he was the man that he was in deede." This statement suggests that he was not in control of what he said and how he said it—that is, with his speech, he could "not chouse" but give his true identity away. This statement is also ambiguous. The phrase "noblenesse of birth," when applied to the rustic, is sarcastic, a final poke at the cowherd. However, this statement would presumably apply to supposedly true gen- tlemen as well. That is, because of his absolute, ontologically given status, a noble also "could not chouse" but "uttre so many tokens of hys noblenesse of birth" so that anyone that heard him speak would be convinced that "he was the man that he was in deede."

This confidence in speech as an unmistakable marker of social status would seem to neutralize any threat the cowherd might embody. Seemingly, there is no danger that he will be taken for a gentleman because speech will always separate the courtiers from cowherds. However, this confidence is at odds with an anxiety that runs throughout *The Book of the Courtier,* an anx- iety that the courtier will say or do something that will disgrace him, that his speech and behavior will reveal cracks in an otherwise carefully managed presentation of self. This anxiety is shared by other handbook writers as well. In his *Galateo,* Della Casa says, "In speech a man may fault many wayes." He then catalogs these many faults, not for the sake of mere descrip- tion, but as a warning to is reader so that he will never say anything that "ill becomes an honest gentleman" (37). Similarly, Puttenham fears that his courtier-poet will "shew . . . himself a craftsman, and merit to be degraded, and with scorne sent back to the shop, or other place of his first facultie and calling" (305). This confidence in speech as a reliable index of social status is also at odds with another view of the rhetorical and social functions of speech found in the handbooks. According to this other view, speech is not an irrefutable index of social status, but something an orator or courtier can put on, like a garment, to present a variety of selves, but especially one that is socially elevated. This view is implicit in the ladies' initial response to the speech of the finely clad cowherd. That is, they interpreted his "Bergamaske tunge" not as an indication of his being a rustic, but as evidence of his being a thoroughly accomplished courtier. One of the ladies said, "What a won- derfull matter is this, howe he counterfeyteth this tunge" (193). If there were an absolute and ontological link between speech and social status, then the handbook writers would have virtually nothing to write about. And the would-be orator or courtier would have no hope of ever leaving "the shop, or other place of his first facultie and calling."

In addition to being a variation of the bumpkin anecdote, the cowherd jest can also be read as an allegory of the manuals' attempts to assimilate jesting to topical invention in particular and the official discourses of rhetoric in general. The cowherd is the embodiment of the comic: he is deformed, filthy, and low. His admittance to court parallels the admittance of jesting into the official arenas of forensic, deliberative, courtly, and religious rhetoric. His arrival at court provides the courtiers an opportunity to reinforce distinctions between themselves and all that is ignoble and base. Jesting too is supposed to maintain similar distinctions, those between high and low, inside and out, proper and improper. As we have seen, however, the cowherd also blurs many of the distinctions his presence is meant to preserve. Within the logic of the jest, he is both a "woorthie Gentilman" and a "Bergamask Cowherd," and his speech is both that of a rustic and that of a masterful courtier. In order to enjoy the pleasure of this prank, the onlookers must continually dance back and forth between these two sets of opposing possibilities. Similarly, as all of the sample jests in this chapter suggest, jesting in general blurs distinctions. The manuals, by invoking the language of topical invention, try to stabilize the laughable and deposit its objects into bounded spaces, that is, the "places" of jesting. However, jesting will always exceed any bounds meant to encompass and comprehend it. It opens up a space of its own, a space whose limits are violated and transgressed by the operation of jesting itself, a space—in short—where cowherds are courtiers and courtiers are cowherds.

3

Point out Something Unseemly in No Unseemly Manner

To the question that several of the manuals themselves raise about whether or not it is appropriate for an orator or courtier to jest, the manuals answer in the affirmative, apart from a few reservations and qualifications. They defend the use of jesting on the basis of the practical advantages it can secure: jesting enhances the power of speakers and is an available resource for managing diverse social situations, provided that those speakers observe decorum and adapt their jests to the immediate occasion and the larger social context. The way in which these writers framed their defenses of jesting, however, betrays a certain nervousness over orators' and courtiers' engaging in laughing matters. In other words, even to ask whether or not it is appropriate for an orator or courtier to raise a laugh presumes that the appropriateness of an orator's or courtier's jesting is at issue, that there are some who would object to his using humor or that there are reasons for prohibiting him from indulging in laughing matters. As we have seen, some writers in the period do forbid preachers from moving mirth during sermons. But these are exceptions. Here I am concerned with writers who clearly endorse the use of jesting but nevertheless seem somewhat anxious over the practice.

This anxiety springs from at least two sources. First, jesting involves practical risks that could undermine a speaker's ethos and hence his efforts to persuade his audience: a jest could be ill aimed and target someone whom the audience does not regard as a fitting object of laughter, it could also fall flat and fail to raise a laugh, or it could fail on account of a poor delivery on the part of the speaker. Second, and more important, the manuals fear that an orator or courtier who jests will be taken for a common buffoon or jester. In both ancient and early modern handbooks, the buffoon embodies everything an orator or courtier must distance himself from in his jesting: the low, deformed, disorderly, and ambiguous. It is precisely these things, however, with which an orator or courtier must come into contact while jesting. The subject matter of an orator's or courtier's jesting is deformity: it is the "hedspring" and fount of all his witticisms and funny stories. In this way, Cicero's prescription that jests "point out something unseemly in no unseemly manner" actually expresses the predicament of an orator or courtier who jests. How can he ensure that his manner of jesting is seemly enough to be distinguished both from the unseemly jesting of buffoons and from the unseemliness of the persons and actions he ridicules? The manuals invest considerable effort into making and preserving distinctions between the seemly and the unseemly, between the orator or courtier and buffoon. For the early modern manuals, such distinctions are especially important to maintain because the professional arenas of orators, courtiers, and buffoons are more likely to coincide than in Roman antiquity. Moreover, the position of the orator in early modern England is more unstable and tenuous than that of the Roman orator who, at least during the Republic, wielded considerable power and influence. Despite these additional risks, several of the early modern handbooks occasionally blur the very distinctions that are meant to separate orators and courtiers from their buffoonish counterparts. Similar confusion can be found in representations of several real-life courtiers in the period and characters from the Elizabethan stage—all of whom suggest that possibility of combining wit and buffoonery, the seemly and unseemly, in a single persona.

Practical Risks

In order to talk about the practical risks of jesting, we must first discuss the possibility of a jest's failure, a subject that is oftentimes ignored in theoretical treatments of humor. Jerry Palmer makes the significant observation that "any theory of humour, jokes and comedy which does not have the principle of potential failure built into it . . . is a defective theory."[1] The importance of such a principle, according to Palmer, is that it will gauge thresholds of humor, boundaries that mark the lines between success and failure and are constantly being negotiated by the participants involved in a humorous exchange.[2] However, not only are these thresholds and boundaries subject to negotiation in particular rhetorical situations, but they are also subject to negotiation over long periods of time so that what may count as a successful joke at one historical moment may be deemed a complete failure at another. I will limit myself here to those thresholds, or practical risks, of jesting that come up in the manuals, always keeping in mind their historical specificity.

Although a seemingly unlikely place to begin, Norbert Elias's *Civilizing Process* offers a convenient (and historically conscious) way into a discussion of the practical risks of jesting since the thresholds of humor identified in the manuals often coincide with, though they sometimes violate, what Elias calls the thresholds of shame, embarrassment, repugnance, and delicacy. One of Elias's central arguments is that from the latter Middle Ages into the Renaissance, the frontiers of shame and delicacy gradually expanded, and as a result of this expansion, increasingly greater restraints were imposed on individual conduct and behavior. Especially relevant to our purposes is what Elias says about the restraints imposed on aggressive behavior. In the medieval phase of the civilizing process, the expression of aggressive impulses was relatively uninhibited. "Outbursts of cruelty did not exclude one from social life. They were not outlawed. The pleasure in killing and torturing others was great, and it was a socially permitted pleasure."[3] As governments became increasingly centralized and obtained a monopoly on violence, however, more and more restrictions were placed on aggressive behaviors. Elias says, "Once the monopoly of physical power . . . [had] passed to central authorities, not every strong man . . . [could] afford the pleasure of physical attack."[4] The effects of these restrictions on the life of the nobleman were especially dramatic. No longer the warlord, the nobleman becomes a courtier: "A new constraint, a new, more extensive control and regulation of behavior than the old knightly life made either necessary or possible, is now demanded of the nobleman. . . . He is no longer the relatively free man, the master of his own castle, whose castle is his homeland. He now lives at court. He serves the prince. He waits on him at table. And at court he lives surrounded by people. He must behave toward each of them in exact accordance with their rank and his own. He must learn to adjust his gestures exactly to the different ranks and standing of the people at court, to measure his language exactly, and even to control his eyes exactly. It is a new self-discipline, an incomparably stronger reserve that is imposed on people by this new social space and the ties of interdependence."[5] The nobleman does not abandon the art of war, for he will need it to defend his prince from internal and external enemies. However, much more emphasis is placed on cultivating the art of good conduct. As a result, aggressive energies and impulses once given relatively free rein are absorbed and redirected by the royal court.

Although his work predates that of Elias, Freud sees joking as an important component of the civilizing process, as one of the modes of expression into which aggressive behavior was channeled. According to him, certain kinds of joking are the product of ever increasing restrictions on our expressions of hostility. Since the "childhood of human civilization, hostile impulses against our fellow men have been subject to the same restrictions, the same progressive repression, as our sexual urges."[6] No longer are we likely, if angered by an enemy, to bash him or her over the head with a club. In place of such "brutal hostility," we "have developed a new technique of invective": what Freud calls "hostile jokes."[7] In a roundabout way, a hostile joke will make available the "pleasure in killing" that Elias attributes to medieval culture, although it will do so in a socially acceptable way and without causing physical harm to our opponent: "A joke will allow us to exploit something ridiculous in our enemy which we could not, on account of obstacles in the way, bring forward openly or consciously; . . . [it] will evade restrictions and open sources of pleasure that have become inaccessible."[8] What Freud identifies, although hardly in a historically rigorous way, is a threshold between a period in which expressions of physical hostility were socially sanctioned and a period in which some of this hostility was rechanneled into the form of jokes.[9] The traversing of this threshold marks a stage in the civilizing process.[10]

There are thresholds, however, within the practice of jesting itself, between acceptable and unacceptable jests, between success and failure, which change over time. Traces of such a transformation appear in a passage from Castiglione where he explains why a courtier should always make a good first impression. The people who are most likely to fail in this respect are those who "make profession to be very pleasaunt and with this their meerie facion purchase them a certeine libertie, that lawfully they may saye and do what commeth to minde, without thinking upon it" (146). Thinking that this "meerie facion" frees them from all restrictions concerning proper conduct, these "good fellowes," as they style themselves, observe no limits in their jesting and horseplay: "Many times they shoulder one another downe the stayers, and hurle billets and brickes at one an others head. They hurle handfulles of dust in mens eyes. Thei cast horse and man into ditches, or downe the side of some hill. Then at table, potage, sauce, gelies, and what ever commeth to hande, into the face it goith. And afterwarde laughe, and whoso can doe most of these trickes, he counteth himselfe the best and galantest Courtyer, and supposeth that he hath wonne great glo-rye" (146). This passage bespeaks the transformational character of the Renaissance in the "civilizing process." Castiglione's compulsion to forbid his courtier from engaging in such behavior simultaneously suggests that such behavior did occur at court, yet was beyond the pale of what constituted good manners. In other words, the aggressive jesting and roughhousing of these self-proclaimed "good fellows" are anachronisms in the courtly society of the Renaissance and seem better suited to a previous time when such thinly disguised forms of aggression were less inhibited. This passage also qualifies Freud's analysis of aggressive jokes. Merely packaging aggression in the form of a joke or horseplay does not guarantee its social acceptance, and the criteria of that acceptance are not fixed. They are always shifting, subject to historical pressures, negotiations, and transformations in social relations.

Although thresholds of humor do not remain fixed from one historical period to another, and although they may even change from one situation to another in the same historical period, the manuals identify several boundary lines that mark the difference between success and failure, the seemly and the unseemly, in the practice of jesting. One practical risk is that a speaker's jest could be ill aimed or target a person whom the audience does not regard as a fitting object of laughter.[11] Cicero and Quintilian solve the problem by delimiting the range of appropriate objects of laughter, advising orators not to jest at the expense of the wicked, wretched, and well-beloved (Quintilian adds the politically powerful or *auctoritates* to his list [6.3.33]). Their concern is that if an orator does target an inappropriate object of laughter, then it might reflect poorly on that orator's character and cause him to fall in the estimation of his audience. Several early modern writers repeat the advice of Cicero and Quintilian on this issue almost verbatim. Here is the original passage from Cicero (which I did not quote in full earlier) followed by Wilson's imitation:[12]

For neither outstanding wickedness, such as involves crime, nor, on the other hand, outstanding wretchedness is assailed by ridicule, for the public would have the villainous hurt by a weapon rather more formidable than ridicule; while they dislike mockery of the wretched, except perhaps if these bear themselves arrogantly. And you must be especially tender of popular esteem, so that you do not inconsiderately speak ill of the well-beloved. (*De oratore,* 2.58.237)

No such should be taunted or jested withal that either are notable evil livers and heinous offenders, or else are pitiful caitiffs and wretched beggars. For everyone thinketh it a better and a meeter deed to punish naughty packs than to scoff at their evil demeanor; and as for wretched souls and poor bodies, none can bear to have them mocked, but think rather they should be pitied, except they foolishly vaunt themselves. Again, none such should be made any laughingstocks that either are honest of behavior or else are generally well beloved. (Wilson, 166–67)

The thresholds of jesting charted in these two passages are informed by an Aristotelian logic of the golden mean. Laughing at criminals is too little, while ridiculing the unfortunate is too much. More appropriate objects of laughter lie somewhere in between these two extremes and, according to Cicero, involve "those [things] which call for neither strong disgust nor the deepest sympathy" (*De oratore,* 2.59.238). As regards the well beloved, they too are positioned, at least in Cicero, as one extreme on another spectrum with the unfortunate again occupying the other end: "all laughing matters [suitable to the orator] are found among those blemishes noticeable in the conduct of people who are neither objects of general esteem nor yet full of misery" (*De oratore,* 2.59.238). The application of Aristotle's golden mean should not distract us from what Cicero and Wilson suggest is a more practical issue: the influence of the audience in determining thresholds between appropriate and inappropriate objects of laughter. As I observed earlier, it is listeners who regard these three groups of people as ill suited to laughing matters. For instance, listeners generally consider compassion, and not laughter, as the proper emotional response to the wretched. However, Wilson does not fail to mention (as Cicero does before him) that the thresholds between appropriate and inappropriate objects of laughter are negotiable under special circumstances—that is, if the poor and wretched "foolishly vaunt themselves, then they become fair game. Their presumption in acting in ways above their socially defined condition or station outweighs all other considerations. If such circumstances obtain, a speaker is justified, even obliged, Wilson suggests, to take them down a notch.

Although there is considerable overlap between classical and early modern manuals in regard to who is and who is not a fitting object of laughter, the early modern handbooks frequently reveal their own historical specificity. Robson's *Courte of Civill Courtesie,* for instance, and Della Casa's *Galateo* both contain striking departures from classical discussions of inappropriate objects of ridicule. Like ancient and other early modern treatments of jesting, Robson's states that the wretched, the defenseless, the unfortunate, and "those that be in miserie" are off-limits (11). But Robson drops from his list of unsuitable targets the wicked and the well-beloved and adds social types that do not appear in the classical rhetorics. One of these is women, who should not be the object of a speaker's jest "further then the boundes of modestie and curtesie" permit (10). Robson's near exclusion of women from the realm of the laughable can be explained in part by their *inclusion* in the courtly life of early modern England. In antiquity, women did not have access to the official arenas of rhetoric: the law courts, senate, and public assemblies. Because they generally did not participate in oratorical contests where one orator might try to overcome his opponent by making him appear ridiculous, there was no need for classical rhetoricians to consider the suitability or unsuitability of laughing at women. In early modern England, by contrast, women did have access to the court and frequently participated in courtly conversations and pastimes. Their involvement in courtly life thus created a need for rules and prescriptions governing interaction between male and female courtiers.[13] These rules and prescriptions did not empower women; instead, they generally ensured their subordination to their male counterparts. This tendency is evident in the reason Robson gives for refraining from laughing at women, a reason that is couched in the gentlemanly code of honor: "a man to jest so farre with them [women] as they may not for shame answere, nor for unsufficiencie quarrel for, wilbe accompted a dishonorable battell, wherein the vanquished hath more honor than the vanquisher" (10).[14] In other words, women are not worthy opponents. Limited by "shame" and supposedly inferior physical strength, women are insufficiently equipped for what Robson constructs here as manly contests of wit.[15] In what seems to be a surprising turnaround, however, Robson goes on to say that women can be "jested with, if their wit be sutch as they delight in the like, and can in good sporte enterchaunge in the same manner" (13). As we saw with Wilson's remarks about the poor and wretched who "foolishly vaunt themselves," the thresholds of jesting are negotiable under special circumstances. In the present instance, the circumstances require a woman disposed to merriment with an able wit sufficient to meet the challenges of a jesting "enterchaunge." But even if these conditions obtain, Robson still imposes limits on the jesting behavior of the participants, insisting that the "boundes of curtesie be observed (that is) that there be no cause of blushing given" (13). Presumably, this restriction is meant to safeguard what Robson considers to be the frailty, and hence inferiority, of the female participant.

In addition to women, Robson also includes another group whom he regards as unfitting objects of laughter: those who are "deformed, for want either of bewtie, favour, or other blemishes in their shape, stature, or limmes" (10). A similar prohibition appears in Della Casa who says, "They that scoffe at any man, that is deformed, ill shapen, leane, litle, or a dwarfe, ar[e] much to be blamed for it" (66). With this group, Robson and Della Casa exclude what other handbook writers regard as a ready source of the laughable—physical deformity. As we saw in the previous chapter, bodily deformities and deformities in conduct are *topoi* of humor and are to be drawn upon in the orator's or courtier's production of jests. Wilson, for instance, has no reservations about laughing at people who are physically deformed: "Sometimes we jest at a man's body that is not well proportioned, and laugh at his countenance if . . . it be not comely by nature" (165). Robson disagrees, saying that "none of these things [deformities] be faultes of . . . [the deformed persons'] own making, neither lieth in their power to amend them"; therefore, "we ought rather to bee moved thereby to thanke the maker of us all, for dealing much better with us, then with them" (10). According to Della Casa, this issue primarily concerns modes of behavior befitting a nobleman, for a speaker who does laugh at the deformities of others is "unworthy to beare the name of an honest gentleman" (66). By excluding bodily deformity from the realm of the laughable, Robson and Della Casa not only narrow the range of permissible objects of laughter, but also give evidence of a new sensibility—a new social restraint—developing in the period. According to Keith Thomas, during "the Tudor and Stuart age" there was a "growing conviction that men should not be knocked for unavoidable misfortune and that deformity and suffering were matters for compassion not laughter."[16]

This "conviction," however, was by no means pervasive. There were still jests targeting "every disability, from idiocy and insanity to diabetes and bad breath," and these "reflected the actual practice of a world where most professions were closed to the physically deformed, where visits to Bedlam were a standard form of entertainment, and where idiots were maintained in noble households for amusement's sake."[17] Even so, the insistence of Robson and Della Casa that physical deformity is not to be laughed at suggests an emergent sensibility, a shift not only in the thresholds of jesting, but also in the thresholds of what was considered, at least by some members of early modern society, to be good conduct beffiting an "honest gentleman."

Although advising speakers not to direct their jests at the wretched, the wicked, the well-beloved, the powerful, and (for some) women and the deformed may serve as a general rule of thumb, it may fail to account for situations in which the thresholds between appropriate and inappropriate objects of laughter are less clearly defined. An example from Puttenham will illustrate just how difficult it sometimes can be to know in advance where those thresholds lie and just how damaging it can be to a speaker should he inadvertently cross one of them. In the previous chapter, we saw how Sir Andrew Flamock successfully used a jest to repair the damage caused by his "unmanerly act"—how he stepped over a threshold of jesting and managed to step back across relatively unscathed. In the present example, Flamock does not fare as well, for he delivers an obscene jest in the presence of Henry VIII, one that comes at the expense of a lady whom the "king greatly favor[ed]" (275–76). The king and Flamock were approaching a tower by barge where a "fayre Lady whom the king loved was lodged." The king, "disposed to be mery," said to Flamock, "let us rime" and then began to sing: "Within this towre, / There lieth a flowre, / That hath my hart." At this point, Flamock took over and continued the song with verses Puttenham refuse to quote in full because they were so scurrilous: "Within this hower, she will, etc. with the rest in so uncleanly termes, as might not now become me by the rule of Decorum to utter." Apparently, the import of Flamock's verse was that this "fayre Lady" and the king would soon be engaged in a sexual liaison. The king was so offended with this jest that he called Flamock a "varlet" and told him that "he should no more be so neare unto him." Perhaps, the king's anger was partially fed by having his true intentions, in regard to the lady, exposed. That is, perhaps the king's rhyming was the first phase of his planned seduction of the lady in the tower. Flamock's obscene suggestions, although they did not exactly blow the king's cover, at least did not help keep up appearances. Nevertheless, as Puttenham explains the incident, Flamock misread the "kings expectation" and talked of the lady in "very rude and uncivill" terms, while the king had begun his rhyme as nothing more than a "pleasant and amorous proposition." But we could also say that Flamock misread what his audience, the king, would deem a fitting object of laughter. Although the king was "disposed to be mery" and even invited Flamock to "rime" with him, his mood did not sanction a jest that took as its object a lady whom the king greatly esteemed. Flamock's mistake cost him, at least temporarily, the favor of the king.

Another practical risk the manuals see speakers taking while jesting is that a jest may fail to raise a laugh, not because it is aimed at an inappropriate target, but because it either defies comprehension or simply bombs. According to Palmer, one of the most basic requirements a joke must meet in order to succeed is comprehensibility: if a joke is not understood, then it fails.[18] In jesting, comprehensibility is almost always at risk since jests usually secure their effects through semantic ambiguities, conceptual contradictions, indirection, and allusion—in short, verbal techniques that strive to frustrate comprehension, if only for an instant, so that when the implicit connection is made or the missing piece of information is supplied by the hearer, the pleasure of getting the joke is all the more intense. If some implicit connection escapes the hearer, or if the hearer does not possess some piece of crucial information necessary for understanding a joke, then that hearer will not get that joke.[19] In some instances, it may not simply be a matter of listeners failing to understand a joke; instead, there could be confusion over the motives behind a given joke or over the spirit in which it was delivered. For this reason, Della Casa recommends that we not "use such parts [in our jesting], as bring men in doubt and suspicion what our intention and meaning is in them." What he fears in particular is that if one participant is "in doubt" over the intentions or disposition of the other, then a jesting exchange may degenerate into an exchange of physical blows: "It many times chaunceth, in boording and Jesting, one tackes in sporte, the other strikes again in earnest: & thus from playing, they come to fraying" (67). With this outcome, thresholds of both jesting and good conduct are breached: not only has the jest for all practical purposes failed, but both participants are exercising a form of power that, according to Elias, was increasingly becoming the sole province of the state.

Peacham is also concerned over the issue of comprehensibility and jesting, and while he acknowledges how damaging it is to a speaker if his audience does not get one of his jests, he also suggests that obscurity and incomprehensibility may have, in some situations, strategic value. These alternate attitudes are implicit in Peacham's description of one of the jesting figures, *mycterismus*. He defines this figure as a "privie kind of mocke, or maner of jesting, yet not so privie but that it may well be perceived" (38). Even in his definition of this figure, Peacham is conscious of the possibility of failure—that a jest of this sort may not succeed because it evades perception. He elaborates on this risk when he comes to list the cautions that a speaker must observe when using this figure: "This figure must not be too obscure or darke, for by that it may loose the vertue and use, if it be not perceived" (39). Again, comprehensibility is at issue and marks a threshold between failure and success. What Peacham fears in particular about the potential failure of this figure is that the person at whom it is aimed—that is, the person being mocked—might not realize that he or she is, in fact, being mocked. In this way, it fails to achieve its assigned function: "to represse pride, rebuke folly, and taunt vice" (39). For this reason, a speaker should not direct it toward "simple and ignorant persons, which do want the capacitie & subtlety of wit to perceive it" (39). In other words, because these "simple and ignorant persons" will more than likely fail to understand this "privy kinde of mocke," the speaker will fail in rebuking them and be denied the satisfaction of seeing the shame registered on their faces.

However, does not Peacham's characterization of this figure imply that *mycterismus* could serve another function, and could we not imagine a situation in which incomprehensibility is precisely the effect a speaker strives after? A speaker delivers a jest that is purposefully beyond the comprehension of some of his hearers in order to distinguish himself from, and display his superiority to, those hearers. Their incomprehension would then mark them as outsiders, not "privie," as an insider would be, to a "privie kinde of mocke." According to Whigham, incomprehensibility and opacity were strategies that the governing classes could use to give "evidence of a discontinuity in the sociointellectual scale."[20] A similar effect could be secured by a jest that, while comprehensible to the speaker's peers and superiors, is beyond the reach of his inferiors. Such seems to be the case in an anecdote relating how Lord Burghley visited the home of an unnamed gentleman who "was shallow and credulous, and easy to be deluded."[21] The home of this gentleman was packed with pictures, statues, medals, gems, tapestries, etc. After showing Burghley these lesser treasures, the gentleman led him into a room where he showed him "a piece of infinite valew for the antiqui-tie, and that was Solomon's statue." While the gentleman believed that the statue was authentic and even "cut" while Solomon was still alive, it was, in fact, "an old weather-beaten statue of some ancient Philosopher." Under the statue was a motto reading "*omnia VANITAS*"—that is, with the first word printed with small letters and the second written in large. Observing the dis-parity in the size of the print and "purposing to put a grave sly squibbe upon" the gentleman, Burghley said, "Sir . . . this does not well; I would advise you to alter by any means; for methinks *omnia* is very little and *VANITAS* exceeding greate." The gentleman, "not apprehending the acute dilemma of his speech," replies, "My Lord . . . it shall be done, for to speak truly, *VANITAS* hath been here a long time, and I crowded in *omnia,* but I'le have my painter make them all one before your Lordshippe comes againe." The gentleman misses the point of Burghley's jest which comes at the gen-tleman's own expense, but his doing so is not an indication of its failure. Instead, it seems the success of the jest depends upon—and is even enhanced by—the gentleman's inability to comprehend Burghley's "sly squibbe."[22]

In some cases, then, the absence of laughter is not necessarily an indica-tion of failure. In other instances, however, its absence can be utterly disas-trous not because listeners do not understand a jest, but because they dislike it. Laughter supplies important evaluative information about the success of a jest; it usually (but not always) communicates a listener's appreciation.[23] As Della Casa says, listeners who laugh at a jest make "a kind of admiration of it" and, presumably, of the speaker who delivers it (71). Listeners who with-hold laughter, therefore, may be registering their dislike of a speaker's jest and, by implication, their dislike for the speaker. As we have already seen, if a jest is particularly offensive to one of the recipients, then he and the speaker may go "from playing . . . to fraying." The issue of withholding laughter will be explored more fully in the next chapter where I focus on the rhetorical dynamics between speakers and listeners in a jesting exchange. Neverthe-less, because this issue is relevant to the present discussion and does consti-tute a threshold between success and failure, I will comment on it briefly here. At the end of his rather lengthy discussion of inappropriate objects of laughter, Robson adds a final "admonition," one in which he warns his read-ers to make sure in advance that their jests will evoke laughter: "Who so in his entertainments shall endevour to tell any tale to move laughter (specially in straunge companie) had neede to be sure that it carrye that life or quickness with it, as he be not so much deceaved of his expectation, that he be faine himselfe to laugh alone: for that will be so great a disgrace, as in steede of laughing at the table, they will smile in theyr sleeves at him" (12). Jesting is indeed risky business, for it may constitute a defining moment for both speaker and listeners. The reputation and character of a speaker is entangled with, and may even be determined by, the jests he tells. This seems to be especially the case in "straunge companie" where listeners lack other personal information regarding the speaker and thus may use his jests as carriers of such information. For this reason, listeners who withhold laughter (or "smile in theyr sleeves") communicate their lack of appreciation not only for the jest but also for the one who delivers it.[24] Moreover, they define themselves as being in some way apart from (and perhaps superior to) the speaker. For as Robson implies, the desired outcome of a jest is "laughing at table," a phrase suggesting (particularly with its mention of "table") the communal and inclusionary aspects of laughter. The opposite—that is, the absence of laughter—results both in the "disgrace" of the speaker and in his social isolation: he is one who "laugh[s] alone."

While Robson recommends that a speaker determine in advanced whether or not his jest carries "that life or quickness with it," Della Casa suggests that such a determination cannot be made prior to a jest's delivery. If this is so, then jesting is even more risky than Robson implies. Near the end of his treatment of jesting, Della Casa says he will not "discourse of the best and the worst kind of jestes" because "other men have written treatises thereof much more lernedly and better" than himself. Besides, he continues, "jestes and tauntes, have at first sight, a large and sure proofe of their grace or disgrace . . . for where the jest is pretty and pleasaunt, there a man straite is merry, and shews a liking by laughing" (71). The "sure proofe" of a jest's success, according to Della Casa, is not determined beforehand but comes after it is delivered and manifests itself in the laughter of its hearers. Similarly, as Rosaline says to Berowne in *Love's Labor's Lost*, "A jest's prosperity lies in the ear / Of him that hears it, never in the tongue / Of him that makes it" (5.2.857–59). If the success of a jest depends largely upon audience ratification, then an orator or courtier cannot predict with certainty how a jest will fare until it has left his tongue. If it fares poorly and "the company geves foorth no liking of thy sportes and conceites," then della Casa advises, "hould thy selfe still . . . and jest no more" (72). Here the thresholds of jesting and those of good conduct again converge. A speaker, seeing that his "company geves foorth no liking" of his jests, should hold himself still and cease from jesting if he is to show himself sensitive to, in Elias's words, "the impulses of others." Reciprocally, the social pressures that make him feel and think that this is the appropriate course of action may be the ingredients of a new form of shame and embarrassment. For what Della Casa also seems to be capturing in this admonition is that flashing instant (perhaps too familiar to some of us) when a speaker realizes not only that his jest fails to provoke a laugh, but that once spoken, it is irretrievable.

A final practical risk a speaker takes when jesting is that a jest could fail owing to some inadequacy or lack of skill in the speaker's delivery or performance.[25] Here we enter the realm of such issues as timing, voice, gesture, diction (some of which will be discussed below when we come to the topic of buffoonery). In a sense, this reason for failure is the most general of all since it could easily subsume the other practical risks we have examined: the selection of an inappropriate object of laughter or the incomprehensibility of a jest, for instance, could be attributed to poor performative skills on the part of a speaker. Still, we can identify several risks that primarily concern performative failure, and chief among these is delivering a jest in a premeditated and overly rehearsed or strained fashion. According to Quintilian, "there are no jests so insipid as those which parade the fact that they are intended to be witty" (6.3.26). In other words, the speaker who puts too much effort in making a joke only shows his incompetence as a witty man. Instead, the jesting of a speaker should appear spontaneous as if it springs naturally from the immediate situation. Perhaps this demand for spontaneity in jesting explains Quintilian's preference for witty retorts over witty attacks: "wit always appears to greater advantage in reply than in attack" (6.3.13), for remarks "designed for attack are usually brought ready-made into the court, after long thought at home, whereas those made in reply are usually improvised [*reperiuntur*] during a dispute" (6.3.46). A witty retort, because it is a response to a previous utterance, must, of necessity, spring from the immediate situation. In this way, it displays a speaker's mental and verbal agility, his seemly and seemingly effortless adaptability to situations even when they are adverse, and his ability to "find" (*reperire*) materials in the situation that he can then refashion improvisationally into the form of a jest.

Improvisational jesting (or, at least, the appearance of such jesting) is also highly valued in early modern handbooks, especially those on courtly conduct, not only because of the tactical advantages it supplies in witty exchanges, but also because it evidences *sprezzatura,* the defining attribute of ideal courtiership. According to Castiglione, there is "one rule . . . above all other[s]" that applies "in al thynges belongyng to a man in worde or deede," and that is "to use in every thyng a certain Reckelesness, to cover art withall, and seeme whatsoever he doth and sayeth to do it wythout paine, and (as it were) not mynding it" (59). *Sprezzatura,* which Hoby translates here as "Rekelesness," governs all of the courtier's activity, "al thynges . . . in worde and deede." One of its primary purposes is to "cover" or conceal effort, and by doing so, reveal its opposite, *grazia* or "grace": "[From *sprezzatura*] grace is much deryved, for in rare matters and wel brought to passe every man knoweth the hardness of them, so that a redines therin maketh great wonder. And contrarywise to use force, and (as they say) to hale by the hear, giveth a great disgrace, and maketh every thing how great so ever it be, to be litle esteemed. Therefore that may be said to be a very art that appeereth not to be art, neyther ought a man to put more diligence in any thing then in covering it: for in case it be open, it loseth credit cleane, and maketh a man litle set by" (Castiglione, 59).[26] Jests offer courtiers "verbal opportunities" to display *sprezzatura,* and they embody, in highly economical forms, opposing and contradictory qualities not unlike those required by the exercise of *sprezzatura.* For if the best jests point out "something unseemly in no unseemly manner" and if, moreover, they appear to slip effortlessly and spontaneously from the lips of the one who makes them, then they display—and formally embody—the very qualities demanded of a good courtier—the investment of effort only to conceal all effort.

If an ability to improvise (or create the appearance of improvisation) defines excellence in jesting, then any jest showing signs of premeditation or effort risks failure. As Cornwallis says, speakers who "take paines, and . . . earne a Jest with labour" are "in worse case then a Ballad-singer" (47)—that is, a lowly performer who works (perhaps too visibly hard) for the entertainment of others. An example of a speaker straining for a laugh appears in an anecdote recounted by Castiglione.[27] Several men are at the house of a friend who happened to have lost an eye some time back. The friend asks the others to stay for dinner, but they all decline except for one who says, "I am well pleased to tarye [for dinner], for I see a voide roume for one." As he says this, he points at the "hole where his [the friend's] eye had bine" (170). In addition to targeting an inappropriate object of laughter, this jest fails, according to Castiglione, for two reasons: first, it is delivered without provocation, and second, it seems premeditated: "See how bytter and discourtious this [jest] is passynge measure, for he nipped him [the friend] without cause and wythout beeinge first pricked himself; and he saide the thynge that a man might speake against [all] blinde men. Suche generall matters delyte not, bicause it appeereth they are thought on purpose" (170). This jest is "bytter and discourtious" because it breaches thresholds of good conduct. It is an unprovoked attack and thus violates restrictions emerging, albeit slowly and unevenly, during the early modern period meant to limit the expression of aggressive "affects," as Elias would say. Moreover, Castiglione describes this jest as "cold" and says that it appears "thought on purpose," suggesting that it fails to live up to the standards of *sprezzatura*. It was as if this speaker had this jest ready at hand and was merely waiting for an opportunity to use it. As a consequence, it appears out of place under the given circumstances (certainly, a dinner invitation is not adequate grounds for an attack), and the signs of his effort to make it fit were much too visible.

Let us end this section with an example that qualifies our previous discussion of the practical risks of joking. As we have seen, these risks often coincide with thresholds of delicacy and good taste. For instance, speakers should not target the wretched and, according to some writers, the deformed, because in doing so they risk offending the sensibilities of their listeners. Also, some forms of roughhousing, such as throwing bricks at others' heads, are much too aggressive and ill suited to a courtly setting, even though they are performed in a "meerie facion." In some instances, however, jesting may permit a speaker to transgress thresholds of delicacy. That is, a "meerie facion," or the way in which an utterance is packaged may in fact grant speakers some liberties and allow them to say or do things that would be inappropriate if delivered or performed in a serious mode.[28] Framing devices, such as "Did you hear the one about," and other linguistic and paralinguistic features cue listeners that what follows will probably be (or, at least, is intended to be) humorous and will likely violate normal expectations concerning, for example, logical consistency, practical knowledge of how the world works, and, most important, good taste. Freud even argues that the verbal form of a joke acts as a distracting mechanism that permits the expression of aggressive or sexual impulses normally kept in check by internal inhibitions and external restrictions.[29]

Castiglione offers a sample jest that, because of its manner of delivery, allows a speaker to breach a threshold of good taste. Toward the end of his discussion of jesting, Castiglione raises the issue of whether or not it is appropriate for a speaker to crack a jest that calls into question a woman's sexual propriety. One of Castiglione's interlocutors, Bernardo, answers that to do so is clearly inappropriate: "above all . . . [a speaker should] have respect and reverence, as well in this [jesting], as in all other thinges, to women, and especially where the staininge of their honestie shall consist" (199).[30] However, Bernardo concedes that in special circumstances this rule may be violated, and he cites a jest told earlier as an example. A Spanish courtier, named Alonso Carrillo, commits some harmless misdemeanors and is ordered by the king to spend the night in prison. On the next day when he returns to the king's court, a lady named "maistresse Boadilla" approaches him and says jokingly, "M. Alonso, I tooke great thought for this mishap of yours, for al knew you were in feare least the kinge would have hanged you." Alonso quickly replies, "Indeede maistresse, I was in doubte of the matter my selfe to[o], but yet had a good hope that you would have begged me for your husband." This response implies that Boadilla is a whore, for, as Bernardo explains, "in Spaine . . . the manner is, whan a manne is lead to execution, if a commune harlot will aske him for her husbande, it saveth his life" (184). Because Alonso's witty response suggests that the lady is a "commune harlot," it would seem to violate the rule never to impugn a lady's honor, even jokingly. In this instance, however, Bernardo excuses the violation because this potentially indecorous suggestion is packaged in a verbally decorous manner. Although the response "somewhat touche [the lady's] honestie, yet doeth it not discontent me, bicause it is fett farr inoughe of[f], and is so privie, that it may be simplye understood, so, that he [Alonso] might have dissembled the matter, and affirmed that he spake it not to that ende" (201). The seemliness of Alonso's response, the verbal techniques of indirection and innuendo that would allow Alonso, if pushed into a corner, to disown the jest's indecorous suggestion, sanctions his violation of the rule not to impugn a lady's honor because it creates distance between the speaker and his unseemly suggestion.

What Bernardo fails to mention in his interpretation, however, is that the genders of the participants in this jesting exchange also sanction the jest. Alonso's reply could only be made by a man to a woman. The jest would not work—perhaps, would not even be conceivable—if a woman directed it toward a man. For one, there is no reciprocal practice by which a woman about to be executed could hope to be saved by a male prostitute begging her to be his wife. For another, and more important, the implicit and culturally defined balance of power in the exchange is skewed in favor of men. As Susan Purdie argues, speakers who jest declare their "discursive power" over the objects of their jesting—that is, "the right to define the *nature* of their objects."[31] If a culture denies this "discursive power" to women, then any jest made by a woman is a "false claim to power which must be resisted" and shames "any man who lets . . . [her] get away with it."[32] This is precisely what occurs in the exchange between Boadilla and Alonso. Boadilla cracks a jest at the expense of Alonso and, in this way, claims "discursive power" over him. The situation almost demands Alonso to expose this claim as false. Alonso's retort not only accomplishes this task, but also represents Boadilla in the inferior position of a prostitute begging him to be her husband.

Orators, Courtiers, and Buffoons

The practical risks of jesting, then, often coincide with thresholds of good conduct that were expanding in the early modern period. Further support for that argument comes from examining a social type who is a perpetual presence in the manuals' treatment of laughter and jesting: the common buffoon. Like their classical sources, the early modern handbooks repeatedly advise orators and courtiers to avoid all manners of jesting that smack of buffoonery, and to ensure that their advice is followed, these writers invest considerable effort into distinguishing forms of jesting suitable to orators and courtiers from those characteristic of buffoons. Their reasons for doing so, however, are not limited solely to the pragmatic pitfalls of jesting nor to the consequences of breaching standards of good conduct. Instead, these writers are themselves engaged in a rhetorical act, and the buffoon (or rather, their construction of the buffoon) gives them tremendous rhetorical leverage. The vilification of the buffoon in the courtesy manuals is intended to preserve the integrity and purity of the nobility (to which the ideal courtier belonged), and to do so in the face of widespread increases in social mobility. More generally, it participates in a larger social process by which the nobility gradually withdrew from popular culture (with which the buffoon was closely associated) in an effort to establish their fundamental and absolute difference from the lower classes. The motives behind the rhetorics' insistence that orators avoid all forms of buffoonery are not altogether different, although the social position of the men who wrote rhetoric manuals in the period (a position that greatly influenced their representations of the orator) gives them a somewhat different perspective. As "men on the make," they are trying to create a place of power and privilege for orators in Elizabethan society, and the buffoon offers them a convenient and socially resonant character type against which they can construct an elevated social identity for the orator.

Differences between a witty orator or courtier and buffoon, between the seemly and unseemly, are not always as clear-cut as the manuals would have them. In some instances and from the perspective of some sixteenth-century writers, they can be quite fuzzy. Several of the handbook writers themselves occasionally confuse or even conflate orators with buffoons, suggesting that both are either disorderly or ridiculous. In addition, the behaviors, accounts, and popular representations of several well-known courtiers, including John Skelton, Thomas More, and John Harington, often skirt, if not cross the line, between wit and buffoonery. Finally, several characters from the stage—most notably, Shakespeare's Falstaff—complicate the handbooks' categorical distinctions between orators and courtiers, on the one hand, and buffoons, on the other. In doing so, they suggest the complexities in how audiences might respond to buffoons, complexities the handbook writers fail to acknowledge and confront.

The rhetoric and courtesy manuals stipulate a number of criteria that distinguish an orator's or courtier's jesting from that of a buffoon, and the principle that generates these criteria is decorum. Buffoons characteristically violate the rules of decorum while orators and courtiers observe them (or should observe them) scrupulously. According to Castiglione, the courtier who jests "must have great respect to the place, to the time and to the person with whom he talketh, and not like a common Jester pass his boundes" (161). Earlier in his discussion of jesting, he says, "There are manye . . . that in to[o] much babling passe sometimes their bounds and wexe unsavery and fonde, because thei have no respect to the condicion of the persons they commune withal, to the place where they be, to the time, to the gravity and modestye which they ought to have in themselves" (153). Wilson offers a similar warning, although in a more condensed form: "good it were to know what compass he should keep that should thus be merry. For fear he take too much ground and go beyond bounds" (166). Those who do "go beyond bounds," Wilson goes on to say, typically engage in "gross bourding and alehouse jesting . . . [and] foolish talk and ruffian manners, such as no honest ears can once abide, nor yet any witty man can like well or allow" (167). A similar concern with maintaining proper boundaries while jesting is expressed by the author of *The Schoolemaster:* "pleasaunt wordes and apt sayings, not exceeding the boundes of honestie, do much cheare the table, & solace the company" (M3ᵛ). These warnings to observe decorum, or some synonymous concept such as "honestie," remind speakers that jesting is always socially situated—that jesting requires a careful balancing of every element in a given situation. More interesting is that in all of these passages, decorum is imaged as a bounded and compassed space, an arena that limits and defines the proper comic behavior of the orator or courtier. Outside of, or transgressing, these bounds is the buffoon or "common Jester" who has no regard for the place, time, or persons with whom he jests. In effect, decorum erects a boundary around and carves a space for the orator or courtier over and against the buffoon or jester.[33]

The space thus erected is not simply one delimiting appropriate forms of jesting, but lends itself to several metaphorical extensions. Most notably, this space stands for one's position or place in the social hierarchy. We have seen hints of such an extension in several of the passages we have just examined. Castiglione's use of the adjective "common" to modify "Jester" has obvious class associations, suggesting the buffoon's lowly position. The phrases "gross bourding" and "alehouse jesting" also suggest lowly and base behaviors, for the early modern "alehouse" was the haunt of "thieves and coney-catchers, impoverished second sons and declasse knights"—that is, those who were at the bottom of the social scale or were on their way down.[34] Later, while discussing the limits to be observed when counterfeiting the behaviors of others for comic effect, Castiglione makes it very clear that the bounds of decorum coincide with boundaries determining one's social status. Echoing Cicero's remarks concerning mimicry, Castiglione says, "It is not meete for a Gentlemanne to make weepinge and laughing faces, to make sounes and voices, and to wrastle with himselfe alone as Berto doeth, to apparaile himself like a lob of the Country as doeth Strascino, and such other matters, which do well become them, bicause it is their profession [that is, as buffoons]. But we must by the way and privilie steale this counterfeiting, alwayes keaping the astate of a gentilman" (161–62). Making faces and strange voices, wrestling with oneself, and dressing like a rustic (that is, one who resides beyond the city limits) exceed not only the bounds of decorum but also the bounds demarcating the "astate" or "place" of a gentleman. In order to preserve that "astate" or "place," the courtier is not forbidden, Castiglione says, from employing techniques similar to those used by buffoons, but he can only do so indirectly—that is, "privilie"—so that there is no confusion over his social status.

Other excessive forms of jesting are likewise to be avoided not only because they transgress the bounds of decorum, but also because they degrade the speaker socially and make him appear like a buffoon. Jesting too frequently, for instance, violates proprieties of time and moderation and thus constitutes another way in which the socially elevated orator or courtier is distinguished from the lower-class buffoon. According to the manuals, buffoons will crack a jest every chance they get—in fact, they are so addicted to jesting that they cannot help themselves from trying to raise a laugh even when it is in their best interests not to do so. A recurrent theme in Peacham's treatment of the jesting figures is that they should be used only in strict moderation. Puns, for example, should not "fall . . . into excesse, or untimely use, which folly and boldness do oft commit" (57); irony too should not be "often used, lest he that useth it be . . . taken for a common mocker" (36). With the latter rhetorical device, it is not so much the kind or manner of jesting employed as the frequency of its employment that turns one into a "common mocker." Similarly, Castiglione advises his courtier not to jest too often, for "it bringeth a lothsomnesse if a man stand evermore about it, all day in all kind of talke without pourpose" (190). Here the risk is that if a speaker jests too frequently and without regard to the occasion, he will discredit himself and drive his listeners away. In a letter of advice to his son, William Cecil (Lord Burghley) warns against being "scurrilous in conversation," saying that he has "seen many so prone to quip and gird as they would rather lose their friend than their jests, and if by chance their boiling brain yield a quaint scoff they will travail to be delivered of it as a woman with child."[35] The simile with which this admonition ends suggests that what is ultimately at stake is self-control (or even bodily control)—the "scurrilous" jester cannot keep his jests in. Wilson also regards this issue as being one of self-control and restraint: "consideration of time, and moderation of pastime, and seldom using of dry mocks, even when need most requireth it, make a difference and show a several understanding betwixt a common jester and a pleasant wise man" (168). The "pleasant wise man," unlike the buffoon, will often resist the temptation to jest even when the opportunity presents itself. By allowing such opportunities to pass, he is given another opportunity—that is, to show he is in control of his impulses and can keep them within compass, attributes that distinguish him from and elevate him above a "common jester."

Another form of excessive jesting associated with buffoonery (and thus with matters that are base and ignoble) includes jests that make use of foul or obscene language. As we have already seen, Wilson insists that orators avoid "gross bourding," a phrase suggesting both coarseness and excessiveness (that is, being large or bloated). Earlier in his treatise, he warns against using "scurrility," which can mean insolent or obscene language and which, as we have seen, derives from the Latin word for buffoon—*scurra* (47). Puttenham is even more explicit about the connection between obscene language and the buffoon or *scurra*. In his treatment of "vices and deformities in speech and writing" that should be "banished"—that is, driven out—from "every language" (256), Puttenham includes *cacemphaton* or the "figure of foule speech," which occurs when a speaker uses words that "may be drawn to a foule and unshamefast sence" (260). Puttenham's courtly poet must, for the most part, "shunne" this figure "least of a Poet he become a Buffon or rayling companion, the Latines called him *Scurra*" (261). Other writers, while they may not directly link obscenities to buffoonery, are nevertheless clear about its class associations. Della Casa, for instance, says that a speaker must never use "foule and filthie words" in his jesting, because they do not become, and are presumably beneath, a "gentleman" (72). Castiglione goes one better, saying "they that be filthye and bawdye" in their jesting ought "to be excluded out of everye Gentylmans companye" (178). The implication here is that because those who jest in a "filthye and bawdye" manner are acting out of bounds, it is only fitting that they be kept beyond both the physical and social bounds of a "Gentylmans companye."

Although the manuals agree that foul or obscene language should be "banished" from an orator's or a courtier's jesting, several of them do allow speakers to engage in risqué humor, provided that the manner or style of their jesting is sufficiently distanced from any obscene suggestion. As we saw in the previous section, Bernardo was willing to condone Alonso Carrillo's somewhat racy response to "maistresse Boadilla" because its import was, as Bernardo explains, "fett farr inoughe of[f]"—that is, disguised by its seemly verbal packaging. Puttenham too, even as he condemns those who use "foule and unshamefast" language, says that an obscene jest is "in some cases tollerable" when, for instance, speakers "give it some strange grace" or when the jest is "not altogether so directly spoken" (260–61). Freud's analysis of obscene jokes offers a good gloss on these passages especially in regard to their class implications; however, it also betrays Freud's elitism (an elitism that the early modern handbook writers would not, I believe, find strange or unwarranted). According to Freud, speakers can distance the manner of their jesting from lower forms of humor (and members of the lower classes) by packaging their jokes in complex verbal forms. For example, undisguised or blatant obscenities are "universally popular . . . among the common people." However, if a speaker uses verbal techniques, such as allusion or analogy, that mask and attract attention away from a joke's smutty content, then the joke will appear to its listeners to be more urbane: "the greater the discrepancy between what is given directly in the form of smut and what it necessarily calls up in the hearer, the more refined becomes the joke and the higher, too, it may venture to climb into good society."[36] Setting an unseemly and obscene suggestion far enough off or giving it a "strange grace" creates distance between the form and meaning of a jest, and this verbal distance, in turn, translates into social distance between the high and the low, the seemly and the unseemly, and the gentlemanly and the baseborn.

A final class of jests associated with the excessive buffoon involves those that are inordinately cruel, bitter, or severe. In the previous section, while discussing jests that fail owing to a poor delivery or performance, I discussed an anecdote rehearsed by Castiglione in which a one-eyed man is ridiculed after inviting his friends to stay for dinner. One of the reasons why this jest fails is that it comes across as premeditated and stiff, but it also fails because it is, as Castiglione says, "bytter and discourtious . . . *passynge measure*" (170, emphasis added). Earlier Castiglione explicitly warns against jesting "to[o] bitingly," for nipping a person with undue harshness is a "token . . . of a commune jester" (162). The distinction here is not categorical—that is, between jests that are bitter and jests that are not. Rather, it is an issue of degree, of being *too* bitter.[37] How then does one gauge thresholds between the appropriately and the excessively bitter jests, especially when so many of the handbooks claim deformity is the source of the laughable and thus imply that jesting, by definition, expresses aggressive, cruel, or bitter impulses? Peacham offers one answer when he says that the force of a jest (that is, the degree of bitterness it expresses) must be commensurate with the act that provokes it. In his discussion of the jesting figures, he includes the *asteismus,* or "wittie jesting in [a] civill maner" (33), and *mycterismus,* or "a privie kind of mocke" (38): the aim of the former is to produce pleasure and supply refreshment in "private companie"; the latter is to be used as a mild and indirect rebuke of deviations in conduct. He reserves the jesting figure of *sarcasmus,* which he defines as "a bitter kind of derision," for situations requiring a strong corrective, one not unlike the "most bitter corrections in Phisicke . . . which although they be painfull and bitter, yet for the most part bring profit." More specifically, *sarcasmus* should be employed when the speaker faces "some great cause which may well deserve it, [such] as arrogancie, insolent pride, wilfull folly, shameful lecherie, ridiculous avarice, or such like." If he does not face vicious acts of this magnitude and if his intentions are not to "bring profit," then he should refrain from using *sarcasmus.* For it is "both folly and rudenesse to use derision without cause," and the man who does so may gain a reputation for being a "scorner and common mocker"—that is, a buffoon (Peacham, 38).

Other writers of the period offer somewhat different answers to the question of how bitter a jest can be and still remain within the bounds of decorum. And even though these alternative answers approach the problem in ways that are different from Peacham, they nevertheless rely (however remotely) on a fundamental distinction between high and low, inside and outside, urbane gentlemen and lowly buffoons. According to Della Casa, there are two kinds of bitter jests: ones that "bite . . . like a sheepe," and others that bite "like a dogge." The latter are to be scrupulously avoided because they are "*beyond* all honest measure" (69, emphasis added). Therefore, "gentlemen . . . should seldome or very easily nip or taunt any man" (69–70). The author of *The Schoolemaster* makes a similar division at the beginning of his discussion of jesting during meal times, saying there are two kinds of jests: "The one a plaine rayling, or checking. The other a figuratively shadowed speach covered cleanly with myrth & civility, sou[n]ding one thing, & covertly meaning another, but not proceedyng to expresse bytternesse. The fyrst kynd is altogether to bee banished [from] the table" (M2^r).[38] At first glance, this may seem a categorical distinction between jests that are bitter and those that are not. However, the author goes on to add that the second kind, "which is covert, may also be sauced with sharpnesse" (M2^r), thus bringing the question back, at least in the case of some jests, to an issue of degree.

What distinguishes these two kinds of jests seems to be their form: the first kind is characterized by a "plaine" or direct style, while the second is "figuratively shadowed." As was the case with "tollerable" obscenities, formal differences also imply social differences. The first kind of jesting involving "plaine rayling, or checking" suggests behaviors characteristic of the lower-class buffoon (remember Puttenham's "rayling companion"). The second kind, as the words "covered cleanly" and "civility" imply, is more refined and thus more appropriate to gentlemen. The figurative shadowing and clean covering distance a speaker not only from a jest's potentially bitter import, but also from the "rayling" of a buffoon.

If decorum, imaged as a compassed space, can be extended metaphorically to one's social "place" or status, then it can also be used to discuss how the speaker manages his body—particularly its boundaries—while jesting. Using Bakhtin's opposition between the classical and grotesque body as an interpretive heuristic, Rebhorn explores representations of the body in Castiglione's *Book of the Courtier,* focusing particularly on the body of the courtier and that of the buffoon. Rebhorn finds that the courtier's body is consistently presented as one that is totally under control with its boundaries clearly defined: it is supple, strong, agile, and—most important—it is "finished, limited, and closed off from the outside world." The grotesque body of the buffoon, by contrast, appears out of control and continually violates its own boundaries: it is "contradictory and in process, constantly transgressing its limits and open to the universe."[39] These opposing representations of the body, Rebhorn argues, were part of a larger ideological campaign waged by members of the nobility (and others who identified with the noble classes) in an effort to distinguish themselves from the lower orders of early modern society, and the two opposing representations of the body—the classical and grotesque—served as a powerful symbol of that campaign.

Rebhorn's interpretation of images of the body in Castiglione applies equally as well to other manuals of the period. In his *Courte of Civill Courtesie,* for instance, Robson says that a young gentleman, when dining, should not fill "his mouthe so full of meate as he cannot holde his lippes together" while chewing, "for otherwise, men shall looke into his mouthe, and see the meate rowle up and downe" (34). In rather graphic detail, Robson presents a body that is not "closed off from the outside world"; moreover, the "outside world" can look in and see operations that Robson suggests should be kept from sight. The rhetorical, social, and, as Elias would say, "affective" consequences of chewing with one's mouth open seem to be that it will degrade those who do so and offend others who must witness the sight. Similar consequences may result, according to Della Casa, if a gentleman improperly manages his body and its motions as he makes his way down a street: "I would not have a gentleman to runne in the streate, nor go to[o] fast: for that is for lackies, and not for gentlemen to doe. Besides that, it makes a man weary, sweate, and puff: which be very unsightly things for suche men to doe. . . . And when a man walkes, it is no good sight to see a man shake his bodie to[o] muche . . . nor yet cast & fling his aremes up & downe, in such sort as a man would weene, hee were soweing of Corne in the field" (107). This passage moves back and forth across three different, but interrelated, domains: the social, the bodily, and the affective. First, running down the street or flinging one's arms up and down are not behaviors appropriate "for gentlemen to doe," because they are associated with behaviors characteristic of the ignoble and base: in the first instance, servants or footmen who run alongside their masters' carriages; in the second, farmers out in the fields sowing seeds. Second, these behaviors cause the body to exceed its own limits—to sweat and puff—or to appear out of control— shaking or flailing too much. Finally, these behaviors are "unsightly" and of "no good sight to see," a word and phrase suggesting that such behaviors not only reflect poorly on the man who performs them, but also cause discomfort to those who see them. The phrases "unsightly" and "no good sight to see" imply that these behaviors have their most powerful impact on others. It is as if an excessive or disorderly body creates a rippling effect that radiates out well beyond the boundaries of its source (that is, the body) and invades and disturbs the space of others.

Similar restrictions about managing the body should also be observed by orators and courtiers while jesting. The high standards of bodily decorum that Della Casa requires of a man walking down the street also apply to a man who wishes to "make other men merie." He says that a man should avoid "ilfavoured gestures, distorting his countenaunce, & disfiguring his bodie," for that is "an arte for a Juggler & jester to use" and "doth not become a gentleman to do so" (72). We have seen similar restrictions in a passage quoted earlier where Castiglione says that it is indecorous for a "Gentlemanne" who jests to make "weepinge and laughing faces," produce strange noises with his voice, and wrestle with himself. All of these gestures and behaviors should be avoided because they cause the body to appear out of control and as a consequence, make the person who performs them look like a buffoon. More important, they identify a speaker with what the manuals view as the principal source of the laughable—that is, deformity. By distorting his face or disfiguring his body, the orator or courtier becomes an object of laughter rather than a source of wit. In short, people laugh *at* rather than *with* him. And this seems the ultimate disgrace.

Using decorum, in general, and social status and bodily management, in particular, to distinguish orators and courtiers from common buffoons is not a Renaissance innovation in rhetorical theories of jesting. The distinctions we have examined here all have precedents in antiquity, as do some of the motives behind these distinctions. Quintilian and (to a lesser extent) Cicero both insist on preserving differences between the professional arenas and activities of the socially elevated orator and those of the lowly buffoon, comic actor, and mime. Their insistence is in part a response to the fact that there was some confusion between these arenas and activities in ancient Rome. Not only did several prominent politicians socialize with actors and mimes, but it seems (at least by Quintilian's account) that orators were adopting comic techniques from the stage and using them in their public speeches. Cicero, who allowed his orator to borrow a "suspicion of mimicry" (*De oratore,* 2.59.242), was not above playing the stage comedian himself on occasion, and according to Macrobius, his enemies often referred to him as "that consular buffoon." In the early modern period, the professional arenas of orators, courtiers and buffoons actually coincided in the space of the court "where they would meet on a daily basis . . . [and] participate in the same games and pastimes."[40] Courtiers and buffoons also serve similar social functions at court: "both are witty performers who create comical spectacles" to entertain and win favor from their peers and social superiors.[41] Castiglione even says that "Courtes cannot be without such kinds of persons [jesters]," but he immediately adds that court jesters do not "deserve . . . the name of Courtier" (158). The spatial proximity and similarity in function between courtiers and buffoons put tremendous pressure on courtiers (and on those who wrote handbooks on courtly conduct) to display their difference from their ever present counterpart.

Other motivations inform the manuals' vilification of the buffoon, motivations that are specific not only to the early modern period but also to each kind of manual. As I argued in the introduction to this study, the courtesy manuals were written, at least initially, by members of the social elite in an effort to suppress social mobility. Their construction of the buffoon contributes in important ways to this effort. For one, it allows them to define with greater clarity and sharpness their ideal courtier. The buffoon embodies everything that is to be absent in the courtier, and reciprocally, the courtier personifies everything lacking in the buffoon. For another, the characteristics attributed to buffoons offer the established elite strategies for dealing with their ambitious inferiors who wish to enter their ranks. As we saw earlier in Guazzo's discussion of upstarts, the best way (apart from a royal injunction) to deal with those who wish to "brave it out like Gentlemen" is "not to be mooved with the matter, but rather to laugh at it" (1:197). In other words, one way gentlemen can undermine the efforts of the socially mobile is to define those efforts as ridiculous and buffoonish. As we have seen, this is precisely what Guazzo's two interlocutors do while addressing this issue: that is, they call socially mobile merchants and tailors "malapert clownes" and crack jests at their expense. Finally, the courtesy manuals' vilification of the buffoon signals and participates in the nobility's gradual withdrawal from popular culture to which the buffoon is closely associated. Peter Burke examines this withdrawal and characterizes it as a gradual and uneven process that took place all over Europe roughly between the years 1500 and 1800. According to him, the principal cause for this ever widening gap between the ruling and subject classes was the emergence and rapid rate of change of learned culture, a rate of change so fast that popular culture lacked the "institutional and economic basis" to keep pace.[42] While Burke's account may be true, it seems to overlook other, more ideologically informed motivations. While discussing rigid standards of bodily decorum found in the courtesy manuals, Keith Thomas claims this "new etiquette was meant to distinguish the elite from the vulgar," to "establish that dignified style which contemporaries thought necessary for the maintenance of social respect."[43] Within the logic of this "new etiquette" and in order to shore up boundaries between the noble and ignoble classes, the buffoon and his unseemly behaviors had to go.

The motives informing the rhetoric manuals' remarks concerning buffoonery are just as complex, although they differ somewhat from those of early modern handbooks on courtly conduct. The social role of the orator in early modern England is tenuous at best. In antiquity, the place and function of the orator in society was, for the most part, clearly defined. He was at the center of society in Athens and in Rome during the Republic, and he participated in making important political and legal decisions.[44] In early modern England, by contrast, the social position of the orator was not so well established; he was a newcomer, brought over to England in the first wave of humanism near the beginning of the sixteenth century. As a result, writers of rhetoric manuals had to write into their rhetorical theory a place for the orator in English society. One of the most typical ways in which the handbooks sought to accomplish this task was by invoking the Ciceronian myth of the origins of eloquence in which the orator is portrayed as a civilizing force and protector of order.[45] Wilson recasts his version of this myth in Christian terms and locates the origins of eloquence in a postlapsarian world: "After the fall of our first father, sin so crept in that our knowledge was much darkened, and by corruption of this our flesh man's reasons and intendment were both overwhelmed." Corrupt and lacking reason, humans found themselves in a world of chaos: "all things waxed savage: the earth untilled, society neglected, God's will not known, man against man, one against another, and all against order." Seeing his creatures living in such a state, God sought to "repair mankind" and thus gave to "his appointed ministers . . . the gift of utterance, that they might with ease win folk at their will and frame them by reason to all good order" (Wilson, 41). Armed with this "gift of utterance," these "appointed ministers" civilized the savage world and persuaded people, through the force of eloquence, to live in society within the confines of law and order. Richard Rainolde offers another version of this myth, which picks up after the savage world had been tamed by eloquence and which advertises, more explicitly and more forcefully, the abilities of orators and their value in running a commonwealth: "Nothyng can bee more excellently given of nature than Eloquence, by which the florishyng state of commonweales doe consist: kyngdomes universally are governed, the state of every one privatelie is maintained" (A1ʳ).[46] Then, after citing several examples from antiquity in which famous orators defend their commonwealths from internal as well as external enemies, Rainolde proclaims: "a common wealth or kingdome *must* be fortified, with famous, grave, and wise cou[n]sailours [orators]" (A2ʳ, emphasis added). The modal *must* is revealing: not only does it suggest the necessity of orators in maintaining the social order, but it also implies that they have not yet been assigned that role. In other words, the modal transforms this statement into an impassioned plea for the orator's inclusion in English society. The buffoon, with all of his disruptive and unruly characteristics, is a source of disorder and confusion.

If his attributes are amplified, he seems the personification of the chaotic world Wilson says existed before eloquence. For these reasons, he must be contrasted negatively with the orator who both civilizes society and stands as a force guaranteeing its continued maintenance.

There are ways, however, in which the orator does resemble the buffoon. Like his lowly and vulgar counterpart, the orator is also occasionally portrayed as a transgressor of boundaries and a disrupter of order. In his version of Cicero's myth, Rainolde goes on to say that orators "pluck doune and extripate affecio[n]s and perturbacions of the people," and they "speake before Princes and rulers, to perswade them in good causes and enterprises, to animate and incense them, to godlie affairs and business, to alter the cou[n]sail of kinges" (A1ᵛ). Here Rainolde places orators above the "people" whom they make compliant through their oratorical skill, but their relation to princes is ambiguous. In terms of their social status, they are presumably below princes and rulers, but in terms of their powers of persuasion, they are above them and have the ability "to alter" a king's counsel. So although Rainolde presents the orator as a civilizing force and champion of order, he also suggests that the orator is, at least potentially, a disruptive presence: someone who flouts existing social relations and enacts a kind of hierarchic inversion by assuming a position above the sovereign.

Thomas Wilson even writes into his representation of the orator skilled in jesting an appeal for the social advancement of that orator based on the skills that his jesting displays. In contrast to the ideal courtier found in handbooks on courtly conduct who uses jesting to defend an already established identity—that of a gentleman—the identity constructed by Wilson for the witty speaker is one that is in the process of becoming and that seeks official recognition and placement in a fixed social position. Wilson says that a capacity to make others laugh "declares a quickness of wit worthy [of] commendation" (165). Also, the speaker who can gracefully deliver a humorous anecdote "is worthy to be highly esteemed" because "undoubtedly no man can do any such a thing except they have a great mother wit and by experience confirmed such their comeliness" (173). Phrases such as "worthy [of] commendation" and "worthy to be highly esteemed" read like advertisements for the orator's ability. They also suggest that recognition is pending: although the witty speaker is *worthy* to be commended and esteemed, he has yet to be so. And what merits commendation, estimation, and—in short— preferment is not birth, title, or martial prowess, but intellect—that is, the "quickness of wit" the speaker displays in jesting. In these passages, Wilson is positing a hierarchy of intellect, and although it runs dead against arguments advanced by the established who (while trying to preserve the purity of their ranks) clung to the traditional notion of a hierarchy based on birth and landed wealth, it allows Wilson to argue forcefully for the social advancement of his witty speaker.[47] In doing so, however, Wilson presents the orator as a violator of boundaries who transgresses lines demarcating differences in social rank.[48]

If Wilson undermines one distinction between these social types by suggesting that orators and buffoons transgress boundaries, he delivers an even more devastating blow by suggesting that the difference between these two character types is a rhetorical construct. In his discussion of rhetorical amplification, Wilson illustrates techniques for "augmenting" or "diminishing" one's subject matter through verbal manipulation and strategic word choice. For example, the speaker who wants to malign "a covetous man" might call him a "devil" instead, or call "a naughty fellow [a] thief or hangman, when he is not known to be any such." In another example, Wilson says that a speaker can belittle "a pleasant gentleman" by referring to him as "a railing jester" (152). On the one hand, this example suggests a difference between witty gentlemen and railing jesters. If there was not a difference, then this strategy would lose its rhetorical efficacy. On the other hand, however, Wilson suggests that these two character types are in some way interchangeable. Wilson wants to hold on to the notion of distinctions in status (in fact, a large portion of his treatment of jesting relies on it), but he also implicitly recognizes that such distinctions are constructed by rhetoric and language, and can be undone just as easily as they were created.

Wilson is not alone in undermining distinctions between orators or courtiers and buffoons. In his discussion of decorum, Puttenham often includes funny anecdotes in which orators and courtiers either display buffoonish behaviors or are outright objects of laughter. As we have seen, Sir Andrew Flamock, a courtier to Henry VIII, farts in his majesty's presence, an act that constitutes not only a bodily disruption but a disruption in the hierarchic relation that should exist between the king and his attendants. On another occasion (again as we have seen), Flamock sings, impromptu, obscene and scurrilous verses while on a barge with Henry; as a result, the king banishes him from his sight. Orators are a particularly favorite target of Puttenham, and they are featured in several jests and anecdotes he rehearses in order to illustrate boundaries between the decorous and indecorous, the seemly and the unseemly. In one jest, the emperor Antoninus becomes "greatly annoyed" by an orator who is speaking in a "small and shrill" voice. In order to make this orator "shorten his tale, " Antoninus says, "By thy beard thou shouldst be a man, but by thy voice a woman" (271–72). In another jest, king Antiochus compares Hermogenes, "the famous Orator of Greece," to "fowles in their moulting, when their feathers be sick, and be so loase [loose] in the flesh that at any little rowse they can easilie shake them off." In a similar fashion, says the king, "Hermogenes of all the men that ever I knew, [can] as easilie deliver from him his vaine and impertinent speeches and words" (272). In still another jest illustrating proprieties in speech, Puttenham tells of an orator who addresses king Cleomenes, saying much to him about the subjects of "fortitude and valiancie in the warres." While listening to this "great Oratour," Cleomenes begins to laugh, and the orator, puzzled by the king's response, asks, "Why laughest thou . . . since thou art king thy selfe, and one whom fortitude best becommeth?" To this the king replies, "Would it not make any body laugh, to heare the swallow who feeds onely upon flies, to boast of his great pray, and see the eagle stand by and say nothing?" (273). In all of these anecdotes, orators are presented breaching thresholds of decorum, and in doing so, they not only make themselves ridiculous but also create opportunities for others to crack jests at their expense—that is to laugh *at,* rather than *with,* them.

A similar confusion between orators or courtiers and buffoons can be found in the lives and representations of several historical figures in sixteenth-century England. John Skelton, poet laureate of Oxford and tutor to Prince Henry (later Henry VIII), was known for his wit though his satires, biographical accounts, and popular legend. Biographer John Bale says, in his *Scriptorum Illustrium Maioris Brytanniae* (1557), that Skelton "knew how to speak about various matters in a pleasant manner, so skillfully, pleasantly, deceitfully, albeit bitingly, that he seemed another Lucian or Democritus. . . . He saw many great evil deeds being carried out among the clergy, which he sometimes attacked with lively rhetoric and judicious sneers."[49] Although Bale offers this description in praise of Skelton, it nevertheless hints, with its qualification "albeit bitingly" and its mention of "sneers," that Skelton's wit veered toward the buffoonish. A similarly mixed appraisal of Skelton appears in William Webbe's *Discourse of English Poetry* (1586), where the author says that Skelton "was doubtles a pleasant conceyted fellowe, and of a very sharpe wytte, exceeding bolde, and would nyppe to the very quicke where he once sette holde."[50] Puttenham is decisively negative in his views on Skelton and even identifies him with the buffoon: "Skelton a sharpe Satirist, but with more rayling and scoffery then became a Poet Lawreat, such among the Greekes were called *Pantomimi,* with us Buffons, altogether applying their wits to Scurrillities and other ridiculous matters" (76). The popular imagination of the mid–sixteenth century was somewhat more favorable to Skelton, offering representations of him that both portray and celebrate him for his buffoonish antics. In 1567 *Merry Tales Made by Master Skelton* was published, and although the tales it includes seem "based on living popular legend" rather than on actual events, it does incorporate "such factual matters as Skelton's laureatship . . . and his rectorship at Diss."[51] In one tale, Skelton conceals a bit of butter in the cap of a Northern man and convinces him that he has the "sweating sickness"; in another, Skelton, while delivering a sermon, displays his naked and illegitimate child "to all the parish"; in still another he defecates on a "friar's belly and navel" who had passed out from drink.[52] These actions are remarkable not so much for their scurrility (similar actions are ubiquitous in jest books of the period), but for their being attributed to a man who styled himself *regius orator*—that is, the "king's orator."

A somewhat more complicated mixture of wit and scurrility can be found in the life, writings, and representations of Thomas More.[53] More was perhaps the most famous English humanist, and his epigrams reflect his classical learning. Most are Latin translations from *The Planudean Anthology,* but others have their sources (or at least analogues) in jest books of the period, including Poggio's *Facetiae.*[54] Beatus Rhenanus, who wrote the introduction to the first edition of More's epigrams, offers enthusiastic praise: "How pleasantly his poetry flows! How utterly unforced is his work! How adroit it all is! . . . He provokes laughter, but in every case without pain; he ridicules, but without abuse."[55] Thomas Wilson interrupts his discussion of jesting to deliver a brief encomium to More's wit: "Sir Thomas More with us here in England had an excellent gift not only in [the use of irony] . . . but also in all other pleasant delights, whose wit even at this hour is a wonder to all the world and shall be undoubtedly to the world's end" (175). Not all of More's jests were necessarily pleasant or delightful, and not everyone was amused by them. Peter Ackroyd lists several scathing scatological attacks More leveled against Luther in his *Responsio,* and Lipking examines several indecorous jests appearing in More's *Dyaloge* (1529) and *Confutacyon of Tyndales Answere* (1532, 1533).[56] Among those who disliked More's sense of humor and considered it buffoonish is William Tyndale who, in the index to his response to More's *Dyaloge,* supplies the following entry: "More. skilful. subtile. a jester. a mocker. A dissembler . . . [etc.]."[57] In the anonymous *Souper of the Lorde* (1533), which Tyndale probably wrote, More is called "Master Mocke."[58] Even Erasmus, who was a close friend of More and clearly enjoyed his company, suggests that More lacked an element of restraint in his jesting, saying that his countenance had "a little air of raillery" about it, and that his behavior might foster the impression of his being consumed by jesting.[59]

After his death, More took on multiple lives in the imaginations of many writers in the period and their audiences. Like Skelton, he became the subject of many stories and even a play which took his name as its title. Gabriel Harvey, who collected a handful of jests attributed to More, compares him with Cicero, saying that both "were borne with a jest in their mowth."[60] Francis Bacon includes several More-jests in his *Apophthegms New and Old,* and in his *Advancement of Learning,* Bacon praises More for his composure on the scaffold, recounting two jests as evidence of his "serenity of mind" in the face of death. In one, a barber visits More the day before his execution and asks, "Whether he would be pleased to be trimmed." More replies, "The King and I . . . have a suit for my head, and till the title be cleared I will do no cost upon it." The next day, as More places his head on the block, he "gently drew aside his beard, which was somewhat long, saying, 'this at least hath not offended the King'" (Bacon, 4:375). In his *Actes and Monuments,* John Foxe rehearses several other jests More supposedly delivered on the scaffold. But unlike Bacon, Foxe criticizes More's wit, saying that it was "so mingled . . . with taunts and mockery, that it seemed to them that best knew him, that he thought nothing to be well spoken, except he had ministered some mock in the communication." This characterization suggests that Foxe considered More a buffoon, a suggestion that is all but confirmed in the way Foxe ends his narration of More's execution. After recounting a variation on More's beard-on-the-block jest, Foxe concludes, "Thus with a mock he ended his life" (5:100).

John Harington, godson of the Queen, offers us an example of an Elizabethan courtier whose buffoonish wit (or witty buffoonery) at first won him recognition at court, but then (among other disgraces) frustrated his career.

In a description that seems to fit nicely with Wilson's characterization of the upwardly mobile man of wit, Lipking says that Harington "belonged to a large court, where recognition easily passed the minor courtier. . . . We do not know what Harington wanted, but he clearly did not want to be over-looked. His display of wit and his excesses must be seen against the back-ground of insecurity and personal ambition . . . of the courtly *realpolitik*."[61] His first two major literary efforts, a translation of Ariosto's *Orlando Furioso* and his epigrams, did win him the recognition he desired, but failed to secure him a position at court. As tradition has it, the first of these works was the offspring of prank and punishment. Harington translated a ribald story from Ariosto's work and circulated it at court. When the translation fell "into the hands of the Queen" and she heard that it came from the pen of her godson, she immediately sent for him and "severely reprimanded him for endangering the morals of her maids of honor by putting in their hands so indecorous a tale."[62] As punishment, Elizabeth banished Harington from court until he produced a translation of the poem in its entirety.[63] Harington soon completed this task, and when the first edition of Harington's *Orlando Furioso* appeared in 1591 (with a dedication to Elizabeth), it was a great suc-cess, winning him "favorable notice throughout his career."[64] His epigrams, which were published only after his death, were also immensely popular and "circulated widely . . . [in] multiple manuscript versions."[65] Harington hoped that these literary endeavors would serve as vehicles for promotion, but nothing more tangible than a reputation for wit materialized from them. He refers to his translation and epigrams as "thankelesse paines, and fruitless cost," and by 1594 he left the court for his country home in Kelston.[66]

Disappointed but not defeated, Harington continued to exercise his wit from his country estate. Noting that the Queen "loveth merrie tales," he says he will "send goode store of newes from the countrie, for hir Highnesse entertainmente," including a story about a local cuckold: "I shall not leave behinde my neighbour Cotton's horn, for a plentifull horn it is."[67] In addition to being a versifier and raconteur of "merrie tales," Harington was also a tin-ker of sorts, particularly fascinated with plumbing. During one of his retreats to the country, he "made a significant contribution to civilization in his invention of the water closet."[68] To commemorate this invention and rekindle his career at court, he composed, under the pseudonym *Misacmos* or "hater of shit," *A New Discourse of a Stale Subject; called the Metamorpho-sis of Ajax* (1596).[69] In a letter to Lady Russell (widow of Thomas Hoby), he describes his most recent work as being full of "skurrill and toying matter," yet he also expresses his hopes to gain something from it: "I was the willinger to wryte such a toye as this, because, I had layne me thought allmost buryed in the Contry these three or fowre yeere; and I thought this would give some occasion to have me thought of and talked of."[70] His *Metamorphosis of Ajax* did create a stir, but it was not the reaction for which he had hoped. His enemies wanted to bring him before the Star Chamber, and the Queen was reported to have said that "that merry poet, her godson, must not come to Greenwich, till he hath grown sober, and leveath the ladies sportes and frolics."[71] In an "Apologie" appended to *The Metamorphosis of Ajax,* Harington confesses that he played the court jester with the hope of receiving favor in return: "the time is so toying, that wholesome meates cannot be digested without wanton sauce, and that even at wise mens tables, fooles have most of the talke, therefor I came in with a bable [bauble] to have my tale heard."[72] The Queen eventually restored her favor to Harington, and in 1599, she sent him along with Essex on that ill-fated expedition to Ireland where Harington was placed in "commande of horsemen in consorte" and where he received an unauthorized knighthood from Essex.[73] In spite of his involvement with the Irish expedition and in spite of his many other indiscretions, Harington visited the court frequently. He speaks affectionately of his visits with the Queen in her last days and says he employed his "fancifulle braine" to cheer her in her illness.[74] After the succession, he was granted an interview with James I, who remarked upon Harington's "good report for merth and good conceit," although during this interview, Harington could "not refraine from a scurvey jeste . . . notwithstanding to whom it was said."[75] Harington's wit and antics both facilitated and frustrated his chances at court; it won him both recognition and disdain. But unlike Skelton and More for whom popular legend played a considerable role in transforming them into buffoonish characters, Harington picked up the jester's bauble himself.

Several characters from the stage also challenge the handbooks' characterizations of orators, courtiers, and buffoons. Writers of comedies in the late sixteenth and early seventeenth centuries repeatedly portray the socially ambitious man of wit as nothing more than a buffoon. Jonson's Sir Politic Would-be and Shakespeare's Malvolio come readily to mind. However, occasionally a writer will create a character who, if he does not break down the dichotomies between wit and buffoonery or laughing with and laughing at someone, at least makes the lines between them fuzzy. Shakespeare's Don

Armado in *Love's Labor's Lost* seems at times to confuse these categories. Armado hopes to advance socially by imitating the manners and speech of the court. However, his extravagant language and behavior—his buffoonish excesses—frustrate his efforts and often make him an object of laughter to King Ferdinand and his courtier, and even to Armado's own page, Mote. Ferdinand describes him as a "man in all the world's new fashion planted, / That hath a mint of phrases in his brain" (1.1.162–63). He is a "child of fancy" (1.1.168), a "man of fire-new words, fashion's own knight" (1.1.177). The effort he invests in fashioning his courtly identity is too strained and too visible to the other members at court who respond to it with laughter. Yet, when the gates of Navarre are to be closed, and the King and his courtiers are to begin their three-year long retreat cloistered from the outside world, Ferdinand has Armado stay with them (1.1.173–75). In part, his presence is required so that the supposedly true courtiers can reaffirm their own identities and have a constant reminder present of the differences between themselves and would-be courtiers. But, perhaps there is a certain pleasure in hearing Armado speak in his high-flown way, not the pleasure that derives from feelings of superiority, but from delighting in his exuberant and fantastical language. The King admits, almost as if divulging a secret pleasure, "I protest I love to hear him [Armado] lie" (1.1.174). Even Berowne, the court's supposedly true wit, finds delight in Armado. When Dull, the constable, brings a letter to the King penned by Armado, Berowne states, "How low soever the matter [of Armado's letter], I hope in God for high words" (1.1.90–91) and that "the style shall give us cause to climb in merriness" (1.1.197–98). Although the "magnificent Armado" is an object of fun, he is also a source of pleasure, someone the aristocrats want to keep around not only to laugh at, but also to delight in.

We could even say that Armado is, in a sense, identical to the king and his courtiers. Like Armado, these nobles fashion identities for themselves by playing language games, adopting stylized manners, and engaging in staged activities for rhetorical effect. Also the courtiers, and even the king, become objects of laughter in the course of the play, falling victim to a practical joke played by the Princess of France and her attendants. Despite their vow of celibacy, the king and his courtiers, disguised as Muscovites, come to woo the ladies. Catching wind of their pending arrival and fearing that a joke is being played on them, the ladies decide to launch a preemptive strike and in the end, make laughingstocks of their disguised suitors, rebuffing their amorous advances. When the king and his courtiers shed their disguises and return to the Princess's camp, the ladies expose the suitors and mock them even further. Their scoffs and jests knock Berowne off balance and he exclaims, "Your wit makes wise things foolish" (5.2.375), a remark suggesting just how far the ladies' prank has blurred the bounds between wit and folly. And it is precisely the overly stylized behaviors of the king and his courtiers—behaviors that supposedly display their difference from a buffoonish would-be—that offer the ladies an opportunity to turn them into fools.

But perhaps more than any other character in Elizabethan comedy, Sir John Falstaff blurs the distinctions the manuals are so hard bent to maintain. In one sense, he possesses all the attributes of a buffoon. His body seems to exceed its own bounds. He is called "Sir John Paunch," "fat guts," "this huge hill of flesh." Hal says he "lards the lean earth as he walks along" (2.2.99), suggesting that Falstaff's body is unbounded, open, porous. Falstaff himself describes what he believes to be his moral and physical dissolution in terms used by the manuals to characterize buffoons: "I live all out of order, out of all compass" (3.3.19–20). Even Falstaff's speech is excessive. He is the master of hyperbole, and his language, like his body, seems to exceed all measure. In Rabelaisian fashion, he spins out a list of epithets against Hal: "'Sblood, you starveling, you elf-skin, you dried neat's tongue, you bull's pizzle, you stockfish! O for breath to utter what is like thee! You tailor's yard, you sheath, you bowcase, you vile standing tuck" (2.4.242–46). Yet for all these excesses, maybe because of them, he eludes precise definition and confuses how the audience and the other characters in the play are to respond to him. One instance of this confusion appears in a line spoken by Hal, a remark that calls into question Falstaff's status as an object of laughter. At the end of the Gadshill scene, Hal says of Falstaff, "Were't not for laughing, I should pity him" (2.2.99). Like the handbooks, which insist that the wretched and the poor are inappropriate objects of laughter and more deserving of compassion than ridicule, Hal examines his own feelings about Falstaff and seems to wonder, if only for an instant, whether or not his joking at the expense of Falstaff is too severe and cruel.

The strongest argument against viewing Falstaff as exclusively an object of laughter, someone to laugh at rather than with, is Falstaff himself. Despite his corpulence, he radiates a certain vitality and agility. He is able to adapt, like a nimble-witted orator, to any and all circumstances. Even though his narration in the tavern about the Gadshill incident is a barefaced lie, "gross as a mountain, open, palpable" (2.4.224), the virtuosity he displays in adjusting and revising it extempore while Hal smugly pokes holes in it is admirable. At moments like this one, when Falstaff is at his most exuberant, the audience is invited to laugh neither exclusively at him nor exclusively with him, but to do both simultaneously. Toward the end of the play when Hal sees Falstaff lying on the battlefield and thinks that he is dead, Hal's words suggest that his feelings for Falstaff waver. As soon as he says something that betrays his affection for Falstaff, he qualifies that affection. He says over what he believes is Falstaff's lifeless body:

> O, I should have a heavy miss of thee
> If I were much in love with vanity!
> Death hath not struck so fat a deer today,
> Though many dearer, in this bloody fray.
>
> (5.5.105–8)

These lines suggest a movement not only in Hal's attitudes toward Falstaff but in the audience's as well, a perpetual oscillation between identifying with Falstaff and keeping him at a distance, laughing with and laughing at him. The manuals try to preserve these differences and pull them apart as far as possible. They are trying to create a place, or protect an already established one, for the orator and courtier in Elizabethan society. The buffoon must be excluded and vilified in the orator's and courtier's acts of constituting their identities. The comedies, however, are more hesitant about pulling them apart; they create characters that hover between or straddle these oppositions. The audience and other characters in the plays simultaneously pull back from them, yet betray a desire to embrace them.

4

Audience

THE
MANY-HEADED
MONSTER

While discussing the "entrance" or introduction of a speech, Wilson recounts an anecdote in which Demosthenes gains the attention of his audience with a jest. Demosthenes, "seeing at a time the fondness of [his listeners] . . . to be such that he could not obtain of them to hear him speak" about important matters of state, promised them that, if they would stay and listen to him, he would first tell them a funny story. The audience took the bait, "stayed and longed to know what that [story] should be." Demosthenes went on to tell of a man who bought an ass from another man. After the two men had completed their deal, they decided to travel together to the "next market town." It was a hot day, and the man who had just sold the ass kept himself cool by walking in its shadow. The new owner would have none of this and said that since he was the "owner and in full possession" of the ass, he should be the one who walks in its shadow. The old owner replied, "Nay, by Saint Mary, sir, you serve me not so; I sold you the ass, but I sold you not the shadow of the ass, and therefore pike you hence." Having "won [his listeners] . . . by this merry toy," Demosthenes then admonished them and "rebuked their folly that were so slack to hear good things, and so ready to hear a tale of the tub." Nevertheless, since he now had their attention, he was able to persuade "them to hear him in matters of great importance, the which otherwise he could never have done if he had not taken this way with them" (Wilson, 134–35).

This example is conflicted over what it says about mirth. On the one hand, it belittles jesting: Demosthenes' anecdote is a "merry toy" or "tale of the tub." Wilson himself adopts this attitude when he says the audience would "rather hear a foolish tale than wise and wholesome counsel" (134). On the other hand, Wilson praises Demosthenes' strategic use of jesting in this situation. Demosthenes is faced with an inattentive, and perhaps unruly, audience, yet he has to relate "an earnest cause concerning the wealth of his country" (135). He improvises a solution, offers his audience a funny story, and captures their attention long enough to deliver his speech. In effect, Demosthenes gains control over his listeners, who are initially unwilling to hear his "earnest cause," by bribing them with the pleasure the tale affords. So, although the "merry toy" is contrasted negatively with "wholesome counsel," it has strategic value because it allows Demosthenes to master the situation and accomplish his purpose.

In addition to revealing Wilson's conflicted attitude toward jesting, this example actually dramatizes a conflict—one between Demosthenes and his audience. We have already seen variations of just such a conflict in chapter 1 where we explored the issue of pulpit jesting and how several early modern writers, Wilson included, characterize the typical preaching situation as one in which the preacher must continually contend for the attention of his listeners. In the present instance, where Demosthenes serves as a representative of oratory in general, a similar dynamic is operating. Although Demosthenes successfully manages the situation in the end, Wilson acknowledges the possibility that the audience could resist Demosthenes' attempts to "obtain of them to hear him speak" and could even deny Demosthenes a hearing altogether. Demosthenes, says Wilson, could never have delivered his serious speech "if he had not taken this way with them." In order to avoid this possibility and win his audience over, Demosthenes has to submit to the tastes of his listeners and give them a "merry toy." But he does so grudgingly. His rebuking "their folly" and their readiness to hear a "tale of the tub" rather than "good things" points to his disdain for having to pander to their tastes.

This conflict between speaker and audience is central to Renaissance rhetoric in general. As Rebhorn argues, it is a defining characteristic of how rhetoricians of the period conceive of their art, a characteristic that distinguishes Renaissance rhetoric from the rhetorics of other periods. Roman rhetoricians typically construct the rhetorical exchange as a contest between two rival orators. Inscribed in this construction is a "particular political model, a republican one, in which orators all theoretically equals, engage in a free competition in the public arena, aiming for victory over their fellow orators."[1] Renaissance rhetoricians also inscribe a political model in their construction of rhetoric. However, it is not a republican model; rather, it is a hierarchical one. This model "does not pit the rhetor against his equals, but implicitly sets him above his auditors who are presented as inferiors and whom he aims to dominate by means of his art."[2] In other words, Renaissance rhetoricians viewed their art in monarchical terms and imaged the orator as a ruler or king and his audience as subjects: rhetoric in this period is thus conceived as the "very *paradigm of rule,* for if the rhetor's eloquence makes . . . [his audience] subjects, it necessarily makes him their ruler at the same time and in the same act, thereby bringing into existence the political hierarchy that connects them together."[3] In a sense, Renaissance rhetoricians conflate the roles of the audience and opponent. The orator does not fight an opponent; instead, he "fights and triumphs over his very listeners."[4]

A jesting exchange is a specific instance of this more general dynamic. Demosthenes, who at first could not "obtain" his listeners, used his rhetorical powers and eventually "won" them with a "merry toy." Having secured their attention, he talks down to them and rebukes them for their folly. This anecdote, however, also suggests a certain instability in the balance of power between speakers and their listeners, an instability that is also suggested in other early modern discussions of how jesting affects an audience and how speakers use it to manage the relationship between themselves and their hearers. The handbooks recognize that jesting has strategic value for refreshing, gaining the attention and good will of and—in short—controlling an audience. But they also suggest that in exchange for this power, a speaker must, paradoxically, become the servant of his audience, adapt his discourse to their needs, and feed them merry toys. In order to keep control of the situation, a speaker has to do a little song and dance to accommodate his listeners—he has to *please* them. As we shall see, this speaker-audience model of jesting becomes even more complicated when we consider the social ranks of members of the audience in relation to the speaker and the various effects of listeners ignoring or, even worse, withholding laughter from a speaker's jests.

A commonplace in both classical and early modern texts is how jesting rejuvenates listeners and makes them attentive and well disposed toward the speaker. As we have already seen, Cicero says in his defense of jesting that wit "wins goodwill for its author" and "relieves dullness" (2.58.236). The author of the *Ad Herennium* recommends using humor or "something that may provoke laughter" at the beginning of a speech, especially when "the hearers have been fatigued by listening" to previous speakers (1.6.10).[5] Early modern writers offer similar advice. Peacham, for instance, says the jesting figure of *asteismus* is useful because it provides "mirth to the hearer, wherby the time is pleasantly passed, and the dull and wearisome minds of men are much refreshed" (34). In his *Galateo,* Della Casa says, "And bycause Jestes do geve us some sport, and make us merry, and so consequently refreash our spirits: we love them that be pleasaunt, merry conceited, and full of solace" (67–68). Here the dynamics of jesting are expressed in terms of reciprocity: the listeners give their good will to a speaker in exchange for the pleasure and refreshment he supplies. For Wilson, jesting, and the pleasure it affords listeners, is a "structural element in . . . [an entire] oration."[6] Taking the suggestion offered in the *Ad Herennium* a step further, Wilson advises his orator to season his entire speech, and not just the beginning, with witty sayings and humorous tales, for not only may an audience be fatigued by a previous speaker, but they also may grow tired within the time it takes to hear a single speech. To avoid the possibility of listeners' becoming "wearied" during an oration, Wilson recommends that speakers include the occasional "pleasant" digression to rejuvenate listeners and keep them in an emotional state conducive to hearing more substantial matters (164). Without these delightful interludes, Wilson says elsewhere, "weightier matters will not be heard at all" (47).

Variations on this commonplace can also be found in the medical and ethical discourse that treats jesting and laughter. By examining how this commonplace is unpacked there, we will better see what is at stake when orators and courtiers follow its advice in rhetorical situations. Glending Olson traces several threads of this tradition from antiquity into the later Middle Ages, although he discusses it under the more general heading of literary pleasure or delight. He argues that medieval writers felt compelled to justify the pleasure afforded by literature: to defend it against accusations that it encourages idleness and sloth and to rescue it from its associations with classical (that is, pagan) culture. They did so on two grounds: what Olson calls the "hygienic justification" and the "recreational justification." First, medieval writers justified literary delight, of which humor is a species, by claiming it had "hygienic" or medical benefits: it "instills *gaudium* [gladness] in the reader or listener, which when appropriately moderated is the ideal emotional state, useful not only in preserving health but also in attaining the finest disposition of the mind and body."[7] Second, literary delight is a form of recreation, and as such, it is a necessary component of human life. Acknowledging this need is a Christian admission of our imperfect and fallen nature; it is "tied to man's frailty; it is a concession to corruption."[8] This need also has a secular source, Aristotle's *Nicomachean Ethics*, where Aristotle quotes and expands on Anacharis' motto: "Play in order that you may work. . . . For amusement is a form of rest; but we need rest because we are not able to go on working without a break, and therefore it is not an end, since we take it as a means to further activity" (10.6.6). Not only does amusement preserve bodily and emotional health, but it also ensures the continued productivity of the individual.

Both the "hygienic" and "recreational" commonplaces persist into the early modern period where they appear in a variety of texts. In his *Dialogue of Comfort against Tribulation,* Thomas More has one of his interlocutors, Vincent, say, "For a merry tale with a friend refresheth a man much, and without any harm lighteth his mind and amendeth his courage and his stomach" (85). Vincent goes on to cite St. Thomas Aquinas who, alluding to Aristotle, said that "proper pleasant talking . . . is a good virtue, serving to refresh the mind and make it quick and lusty to labor and study again, where continual fatigation would make it dull and deadly" (85). In the opening scene of *Love's Labor's Lost* (1594), just after swearing an oath to lead, along with the king and two other courtiers, a cloistered life devoted to study for three years, Berowne asks, "But is there no quick recreation granted?" (1.1.160). The king replies that Don Armado, that "child of fancy," will serve as "interim to our studies" (1.1.170), suggesting that Armado will relieve the tedium of their serious pursuits. Longaville, another courtier, adds that the clown Costard will also stay and "be our sport; / And so to study three years is but short" (1.1.178). In the epistle dedicatory of *The Wonderfull Yeare* (1603), a work composed when an outbreak of the plague had closed down London playhouses, Thomas Dekker says that he hopes his reader will "happilie laugh . . . because mirth is both *Phisicall,* and wholesome against the *Plaugue*" (3). Jest books of the period, not surprisingly, also make frequent use of the "hygienic" and "recreational" commonplaces in their front matter. In the preface to his *Apophthegmata,* Erasmus says, "Neither dooe I esteme it a thyng worthie blame ever now and the[n] with laughter to refreshe the mynde." The editor of *The Mirrour of Mirth* (1583) assures his readers that "mirth . . . cutteth off care, unburdeneth the mind of sorrow, healeth the grieved heart, and filleth both soul and body with inestimable comfort" (Zall, *Hundred Merry Tales,* 353). And in his prologue to *Scoggin's Jests* (1680), the editor gives special stress to the medical benefits of humor: "There is nothing, besides the goodness of God, that preserves health so much as honest mirth used at dinner and supper, and mirth towards bed" (Zall, *Nest of Ninnies,* 105). In all of these passages, jesting and laughter are presented as recipes for taking care of the self which, if properly and moderately administered, promise physical and emotional well-being. They are sources of comfort and relief from sorrows, burdens, and even disease.

Laurent Joubert's *Treatise on Laughter* (1579), an extremely detailed Renaissance work on the physiology of humor, is a virtual compendium of commonplaces about jesting and laughter, even if Joubert sometimes deploys them in strangely inventive ways. Joubert invokes the "hygienic" commonplace when he discusses the emotional constituents of laughter. According to him, laughter is beneficial to a person's health because it keeps that person's emotional condition on an even keel or in a state of equilibrium. In particular, because laughter as Joubert defines it is made up of two contrary emotions, "joy and sorrow," each of which offsets the other, it prevents a person from straying from the "middle way" and experiencing either joy or sorrow in their extreme forms, an experience that could "cause the loss of life."[9] Later, when Joubert addresses the question "Whether or not only man laughs and why," he invokes the "recreational" commonplace: "Now the virtue and power to laugh is fittingly conceded particularly to man so that he might have the means to refresh his mind from time to time, overworked and tired due to serious occupations. . . . For of all animals only man is born apt to study, contemplation, negotiation, and all sorts of affairs; which occupations make him a little gruff, severe, sad, difficult, brusque, angry, and depressed. And since it is fitting for a man to be a sociable, civil, and gracious animal, such that one might live and converse pleasantly and benignly with another, God has ordained, among man's enjoyments, laughter for his recreation in order to conveniently loosen the reins of his mind" (94–95). Again laughter is portrayed as a rejuvenating force that refreshes the mind and provides a temporary release from the daily grind of the workaday world. In this way, this passage echoes Anacharsis's motto, "Play in order that you may work." In addition, this passage from Joubert suggests something new: jesting and laughter help people "live and converse pleasantly and benignly" with one another. Jesting and laughter not only preserve the emotional and bodily health of a single individual, but also maintain civil relations *between* individuals.

So far, we have failed to address what has been implicit in the medical and ethical lore all along: the potential for expressing analogical relationships between the physiological body and the body politic, and the employment of such analogies for ideological and rhetorical purposes. The use of the body as a "metaphoric vehicle" for making sense out of complex and abstract systems beyond the body, such as a commonwealth, was pervasive in early modern England; it was a particularly convenient and powerful vehicle since the body was thought to be itself a "complete and finite system, highly complex but at the same time familiar and immediate."[10] The regimens prescribed in the medical treatises and the advice offered in the ethics manuals are recipes for regulating the mind, the body, and behavior. When these recipes are translated by way of metaphor and analogy onto the body politic, they take on a distinctly socially conservative character. In his *Dialogue between Reginald Pole and Thomas Lupset,* Thomas Starkey, chaplain and sometimes critic of Henry VIII, compares a strong and healthy body to an orderly and well-functioning commonwealth in which each part works in cooperation with all the other parts: "Like as we say then every man's body to be strong, when every part can execute quickly and well his office determined by the order of nature; as the heart then is strong when he, as fountain of all natural powers, ministreth them with due order to all other, and they then be strong when they be apt to receive their power of [the] heart, and can use it according to the order of nature, as, the eye to see, the ear to hear, the foot to go, and hand to hold and reach; and so likewise the rest. After such manner the strength of this politic body standeth in every part being able to do his office and duty. For this body has parts, which resemble also the parts of the body of man."[11] This analogy is meant to bolster the official ideology of an organic, highly stratified, and self-regulating society. It does so by mystifying the social order in terms of what Starkey calls the "order of nature," which is itself presented as a system of mutual, albeit unequal, responsibilities and obligations.

If forms of amusement preserve the physical and psychological well-being of the individual body, then by analogical extension they can preserve the well-being of the commonwealth. This extension is implicit in Joubert's comments that laughter will cause people to behave in a "sociable, civil, and gracious" manner and "live and converse pleasantly and benignly" with one another. With these comments, Joubert moves beyond the individual body into the realm of the social. It is also implicit in Anacharsis's motto, "Play in order that you may work." In effect, this adage implies a pattern that organizes everyday life and supplies a rationale for amusement that might appeal to subjects and rulers alike. The pattern suggested divides everyday life into a time of play and a time of work in such a way that the former is subordinate to the latter. As Aristotle says, amusement "is not an end, since we take it as a means to further activity." From the perspective of the subject, the adage simultaneously offers comfort and a strategy for getting through the day-to-day grind. It promises, even sanctions, a period of rest and relaxation from the toils of labor, and with this promise, the common drudge might find it easier to get out of bed (or roll off the pallet) each morning and start the day's tasks, knowing that a promised break from work lies in the near future. From the perspective of masters and employers, Anacharis's motto promises that the service or employment of the common drudge will be gainful, provided that he or she is allowed times of play. In *The Civile Conversation,* Guazzo's brother tells how he has seen "peasants of the countrie, who having laboured al the weeke, spende Sunday in daunsing out of al crie: in so much that . . . they stink of swet, and take more payne that day only, then they doe in all the worke dayes besides." Annibale is untroubled by this apparent imbalance in effort, for he says, "Albeit they exercise the body lesse in working then in daunsing, yet they doe the one with paine and griefe, and the other with so great pleasure, that it maketh them the next day after goe to their worke a great deale more lustily" (1:246). Masters also need the occasional break from their daily affairs. Annibale says that after a day of walking or riding great distances to see his patients, he enjoys an evening walk "out of towne" where he finds "great ease and refreshing" to his mind "that is weeried with the travel of the day" (1:247). Even rulers need a respite from the concerns of governing their kingdoms. The editor of *The Mirrour of Mirth,* while discussing the need for recreating and refreshing the mind, says that "many mighty and excellent Princes, whose heads are troubled with divers and sundry enormities, do . . . entertain and accept of such persons whose pleasant nature and disposition may move them to delight" (Zall, *Hundred Merry Tales,* 353).[12]

Anacharis's motto may appeal to rulers and princes for another reason: it also offers them a strategy for social control. In a passage near the beginning of Castiglione's discussion of jesting, the regimens of the body merge with the regimens of the body politic, and the physical and psychological functions of recreation merge with its rhetorical and ideological functions. This passage can be seen as a hybrid of voices and discourses ranging from medical, to philosophical, to ethical, to rhetorical, to historical, even to protoanthropological and protosociological. It opens with a variation of one of the commonplaces we have already seen: the mind "by nature is drawen to pleasantness and coveteth quietness and refreshing" (156). Having posited this as a human universal, Castiglione goes on to make a historical claim: in order to satisfy this inherent desire for pleasant things and refreshment, "menne [sometime in the distant past] invented many matters, as sportes, games and pastimes, and so many sortes of open showes" (156–57). Apparently, in the process of inventing and supplying these various forms of recreation, others began to realize that people "beare good will to suche as are the occasion of this recreation." With this statement Castiglione suggests the possibility of using recreation as a rhetorical strategy, as a way to secure the good will of an audience. This strategy of exchanging forms of recreation for good will was then, according to Castiglione, appropriated by ancient kings in order to secure the good will of all their subjects:

> And because we beare good will to suche as are the occasion of this recreation of oures, the manner was emonge the kinges of old time, . . . to get the good will of the people withall, and to feede the eyes and myndes of the multitude, to make great Theatres, and other publyque buildings, and there to showe new devices of pastimes, running of horses and Charettes, fightinges of men together, straunge beastes, Comedies, Tragidies, and daunses of Antique. Neither did grave Philosophers shonn these sightes, for manie tymes both in thys maner and at bankettes they refreshed their weerysome myndes, in those high discourses and divine imaginacions of theirs. The which in lykewyse all sortes of men are wyllinge to doe, for not onlye Plaughmen, Mariners, and all such as are inured wythe harde and boysterous exercises, with hande, but also holye religious men and prisoners that from hour to hour waite for death, goe about yet to seeke some remedy and medicine to refreshe themselves. Whatsoever therefore causeth laughter, the same maketh the minde jocunde and giveth pleasure, nor suffreth a man in that instant to minde the troublesome greefes that oure life is full of. (157)

Here recreation is characterized as a form of social control, a characterization that anticipates modern "safety-valve" theories used by sociologists and anthropologists to analyze the functions of ritual and festivity.[13] According to these theories, designated periods of release from the constraints of everyday life are sanctioned because they allow subjects to blow off steam, so to speak, and vent frustrations toward the powers that be. Having vented these emotions in a safe way, the reasoning goes, these subjects are less likely to revolt in earnest.

Although protoanthropological and protosociological, Castiglione's passage characterizes the mechanisms of this form of social control in rhetorical terms, as a motivated gesture to secure a particular effect. The construction of theaters and public buildings by the "kinges of old time" is motivated by a desire "to get the good will of the people withall, and to feed the eyes and myndes of the multitude." By doing so, the kings may secure the internal stability of their realms and perpetuate the power of their positions. And recreation seems a particularly effective means for achieving these ends because, according to Castiglione, it is desired by all levels of society and affects social types ranging from philosophers, clergymen, mariners, and ploughmen, down to prisoners. Moreover, as Castiglione describes it, recreation has an almost narcotic effect; it is "medicine" that causes all people, while under its spell, to forget "in that instant . . . the troublesome greefes that [their] life is full of." In effect, kings who supply recreation to their subjects are engaged in a rhetorical gesture writ large. In exchange for the "pleasantness" derived from recreation, they hope not only to win the good will of their subjects but also to secure their willing compliance.[14]

On a much smaller scale, orators and courtiers are to use funny stories and witty sayings to secure similar effects. According to Wilson, a speaker, when he sees that his listeners are "wearied either with the tediousness of the matter or heaviness of the report," is to invent some pleasant device "both to quicken them again and also to keep them from satiety" (164). In effect, the recipes in the medical and ethical lore concerning the psychological and physical benefits of jesting and laughter are to be used by speakers and applied so that they can better control both the minds and bodies of their listeners. We might even extrapolate from Wilson and rephrase Anacharis's motto: "Tell funny stories and use witty sayings in order that your audience may listen to more substantive matters." However, all of these recipes presuppose success—that jesting will work its magic unproblematically and that an audience will submit without resistance to the power of laughter. More important, they do not take into account that, by telling funny stories and using witty remarks, a speaker is surrendering some of his control over his listeners by accommodating their needs. If we take Castiglione's history of the origins of recreation at face value, then even the "kinges of old time" were, in a roundabout way, submitting to their subjects. These kings had to devote considerable money and manpower to the construction and mainte- nance of the "greate Theatres, and other publyque buildings" Castiglione mentions. They also had to hire (or devote energy toward enslaving) gladia- tors, trainers, actors, and dancers to perform in whatever form of entertain- ment they provided. And presumably, they had to do all of this on a periodic basis in order to keep the goodwill of their subjects once they had initially won it. In short, these kings are in the same predicament as Demosthenes: they must continually feed the multitude merry toys and tales of the tub.

This paradoxical and potentially conflictual relationship comes up again and again in Wilson who describes its dynamics on a more local level: that is, not between kings and their subjects, but between an orator and his immediate audience. Actually, Wilson offers a spectrum of possible repre- sentations of this relationship and how jesting is used to manage it, a spec- trum ranging from one extreme in which a speaker has complete control over the minds and bodies of his listeners to the other in which the speaker is totally in their power. In between these two extremes, Wilson offers a dialectical model of speaker-audience interaction in which the power of the speaker and the power of his audience are held in tension as opposing forces. Because Wilson supplies perhaps the most thorough description of the dynamics between joke teller and audience in the period and because these dynamics are a continual preoccupation of his throughout his manual, what follows will primarily focus on his remarks, although passages from other writers will be brought in to amplify or qualify what Wilson has to say.

At one end of the spectrum of possible representations is the ideal case in which the speaker, through jesting, assumes complete control over his audience, inspiring in them a sense of awe and even fear. The crucial passage expressing this ideal appears near the beginning of Wilson's treatment of jesting when he says, "The witty and learned have used [jesting] . . . ever among their weighty causes, considering that not only goodwill is got thereby . . . but also men wonder at such a head as hath men's hearts at his commandment, being able to make them merry when he list" (166). The possibilities for punning on the word "head" in this passage are tempting. In one sense it refers to the mind and intellect of the speaker; in another sense, though, it suggests the "head," or ruler, of the body politic, a ruler who commands "men's hearts" and instills in them a sense of wonder. In other words, the familiar and pervasive image of the orator as ruler, which we have seen before, appears again in this passage. The orator is a commander over his audience; the source of his power and the wonder it instills is his ability to move them to laughter whenever he wishes. But even though the instrument of his power, at least in this case, is jesting, the speaker's rule is not necessarily a benevolent one, for according to Wilson, the speaker can utterly demolish whomever he selects as the object of his jests: "we see that men are full oft abashed and put out of countenance by such taunting means, and those that have done so are compted to be fine men and pleasant fellows, such as few dare set foot with them" (166). As this passage suggests, the power of the speaker over his listeners is also fed by his ability to club his opponents with a jest. Why this verbal beating makes a speaker a "pleasant" fellow in the eyes of his audience and a source of fear to present and future opponents, "such as few dare set foot with," is a complex question.

Elias together with Freud provides one possible answer. From the late Middle Ages and into the early modern period, increasingly greater restrictions were imposed on individual conduct. Many of these restrictions limited violence and brutality and rechanneled the pleasure derived from aggression, the "pleasure in killing," into more socially acceptable forms. For example, sporting contests and games, such as jousting, bearbaiting, wrestling, and cock fights, provide special enclaves in which "belligerence and aggression find socially permitted expression."[15] In such enclaves, the "pleasure in killing" is primarily experienced vicariously, that is, in watching: "in the imaginary identification with a small number of combatants to whom moderate and precisely regulated scope is granted in the release of such affects."[16] Joking, at least as Freud describes it, is also a spectator sport in which sexual and aggressive impulses find socially accepted modes of expression. A sexual or aggressive joke requires, in addition to a speaker and an object of laughter over whom the speaker triumphs, one or more listeners who simultaneously validate the speaker's victory with their laughter and partake, by way of watching, in the pleasure associated with the speaker's expression of hostility. Freud says, "By making our enemy small, inferior, despicable or comic, we achieve in a roundabout way the enjoyment of overcoming him—to which the [audience] . . . bears witness by [their] laughter. . . . A joke will allow us to exploit something ridiculous in our enemy . . . [and will] *open sources of pleasure that have become inaccessible.*"[17] Wilson's witty speaker might also be said to "open sources of pleasure" for his audience who watch him verbally beat his opponents through jesting and who, in exchange for this pleasure, give their admiration to the speaker.[18]

As for the fear that jesting inspires in potential opponents, it is similar to the fear and shame associated with being physically beaten in front of others. Wilson says, "I have known some so hit of the thumbs [with a jest] that they could not tell in the world whether it were best to fight, chide, or go their way. And no marvel, for where the jest is aptly applied, the hearers laugh immediately, and who would be gladly laughed to scorn?" (164). The metaphor Wilson uses here to characterize what it feels like to be the target of another's jest is one of physical violence, of being "hit of the thumbs." The effect is something like shell shock. The target is so dazed that he does not know what the appropriate response is: should he fight, parry with a retort, or run away. That one of his options is fighting suggests how fuzzy Wilson sees the line between jesting and fighting to be. For Robson, some situations might demand that a speaker substitute a physical blow for a witty retort, especially when that speaker's attackers include "impudent and shamelesse persons" or others "knowen to be overwenyng fooles in their owne conceyte." If such a situation arises, then the speaker must be "as readie of courage to maintaine it *with his hand,* as of speeche to utter it with his tongue" (13, emphasis added). Those who cannot maintain it with either run the risk of public humiliation. Those who can do both and gain a reputation for doing both may be counted among those "such as few dare set foot with."

But jesting does not only command "men's hearts." It commands their bodies as well. We have already seen statements to this effect in the medical lore where jesting and laughter are said to ensure bodily health, to create and sustain a balance between physiological and emotional extremes. The manuals, however, offer another view on laughter's impact on the body, one which suggests that laughter causes disequilibrium, loss of balance, and—in short—loss of control. The source of this view is Cicero who, while excusing himself from not being able to offer a precise definition of laughter, nevertheless characterizes it as a form of power so strong that hearers lose control over their bodies: laughter "bursts out [*erumpat*] so unexpectedly that, strive as we may, we cannot restrain it, and . . . at the same instant it takes possession [*occupet*] of the lungs, voice, pulse, countenance and eyes" (*De oratore*, 2.58.235). According to Quintilian, laughter has an "imperious force [*vim imperiosissimam*]" which listeners cannot resist: laughter "breaks out [*erumpit*] against our will and extorts confession of its power, not merely from our face and voice, but convulses the whole body as well" (6.3.9). Similar images of bodily possession and eruption appear in early modern texts. Following Cicero closely, Castiglione says that laughter "taketh the veines, the eies, the mouth and the sides, so that whatever resistance we make, it is not possible to kepe it in" (157). And Wilson: "laughter . . . stirreth and occupieth the whole body . . . it altereth the countenance and suddenly brasteth out that we cannot keep it in" (165). In his *Galateo,* Della Casa offers a similar, but more tempered, characterization of the power of laughter, claiming that listeners, when they hear a good jest, "cannot forbeare their laughing, but laugh in spite of their teeth" (72). In all of these passages, laughter is described as violating the boundaries of the body: first, invading and occupying the body, and then, erupting and bursting forth with such force that the laugher cannot resist. These convulsions and outbursts are signs testifying to the power of the speaker who makes his audience laugh.[19]

Joubert also views laughter as having an irrepressible and irresistible impact on the bodies of those who laugh, but he goes even further than the rhetoric and courtesy manuals in detailing the nature of that impact. Laughter, says Joubert, "escapes so quickly that it seems to come without our knowing, almost sneaking out, and . . . letting ourselves be overcome with laughter, we cannot stop or suppress it" (120). It causes the diaphragm and chest to shake convulsively and the mouth of the laugher to gape open (Joubert, 47–48, 50–51). If experienced in extreme or prolonged forms, laughter can cause other bodily emissions as well. In his chapter titled "Whence it comes that one pisses, shits, and sweats by dint of laughter," Joubert offers a detailed description of how those muscles, which (under normal circumstances) allow a person to retain control over bodily excretions, can go out of control when laughing: "It is, then, likely that when these muscles press a long time and with much violence, soliciting the bowels and the bladder to give up their contents (as it happens in laughter), if there is a quantity of liquid matter, all escapes us indecorously. For the agitation and jouncing is so strong that the sphincters are unable to resist, especially when after a long duration they become loose and weak, like the rest of the body, losing all its strength" (60). By deforming the body, by distorting the face, and by "indecorously" violating the body's boundaries, laughter makes the listeners themselves ridiculous. That is, they become equivalent to what, as we have seen, the handbooks define as the subject matter of laughter—deformity. Gail Kern Paster draws a similar conclusion from the passage in Joubert cited above, and she goes on to argue that laughter has a leveling effect on members of an audience: "laughter operates indiscriminately but predictably on the body of the laugher, without regard for the social coordinates of age, rank, and especially gender by which hierarchical difference is constructed."[20] In this way, the speaker who makes his audience laugh displays his power not only in controlling the minds and bodies of his listeners, but also in turning them into an undifferentiated and grotesque mass. And if he, as several of the handbooks advise, refrains from laughing at his own jests, then the scene presented is one in which the speaker, while in complete control over his own emotions and body, towers above a group of convulsing and gaping laughers.[21]

This representation of the relationship between speaker and audience, in which the speaker has complete control over the minds and bodies of his listeners, is a fantasy of audience control. It ignores the possibility that listeners might resist a speaker's attempts to master them—that they might not listen to a speaker or might even wander off. Earlier in the *Art,* where Wilson discusses the three offices of an orator (to teach, delight, and persuade), he offers another representation of speaker-audience relations, one that constructs those relations as being dialectical. While discussing the second office of orator, to delight, Wilson mentions "moving laughter," and suggests that it is crucial to the success of any rhetorical exchange. Its importance derives primarily from Wilson's conception of the audience or, more generally, from his conception of human nature. With images and phrases that echo the language of the medical and ethical treatises, Wilson explains why audiences need to be delighted: "And assuredly nothing is more needful than to quicken these heavy-loaden wits of ours, and much to cherish these our lumpish and unwieldy natures, for except men find delight, they will not long abide: delight them, and win them, weary them, and you lose them forever" (47). The metaphors in this passage reveal the controlling hand of the speaker, yet also reveal forces that resist that control. The adjectives "heavy" and "loaden" suggest that we are, by nature, dull and that our "wits" are weighed down by something (perhaps fatigue, sin, or the body) that makes us unreceptive to an orator's message. The verbal, "to quicken," however, implies that the speaker who moves his audience to laughter will somehow counteract the pull of whatever is weighing us down. The nature of that counteraction varies according to the multiple meanings and connotations of "quicken." If we take the heavy load to mean sleepiness, then "to quicken" takes on the relatively neutral meaning of reviving, refreshing, and awakening. But "quicken" also has a religious meaning, as in "to quicken the spirit." In this case, the orator would be a preacher who uses jesting to stir the souls of his listeners, which are weighed down (perhaps) by sins of the flesh, in order to make them more receptive to some spiritual truth. Finally, in its intransitive sense, "quicken" has the medical meaning of a woman passing into that stage of pregnancy when the fetus begins to show signs of life. Here the heavy load could be interpreted as the heavy body of a pregnant woman, and the orator, either as God or inseminating male, brings what is lifeless to life. However we read the metaphor, the common denominator is that the orator is imaged as a force that lifts his audience out of some state, whether it be sleep, sin, or lifelessness, an act that the inherent sluggishness of an audience resists.

The second cluster of metaphors in the passage, "to cherish these our lumpish and unwieldy natures," invites another set of interpretive possibilities. Given that the context of this passage is concerned with delighting an audience, the primary sense of "cherish" would most likely be to "cheer" or "gladden." But to describe the hearers' natures as "lumpish and unwieldy" is to evoke another meaning for "cherish." The adjectives "lumpish" and "unwieldy" suggest that an audience is not only formless but also so massive as to be difficult to control. The semantic pressures of these adjectives thus force another meaning of "cherish," one that coheres with the physical qualities of the adjectives. One possibility would be to take "to cherish" as "to caress, fondle; to hug; to stroke or pat endearingly" (OED). Thus the speaker can be seen as stroking an audience into shape and circumscribing, as with a hug, their unwieldy bodies. So in addition to lifting his listeners up, he is also imaged as pulling them in.

Wilson's construction of the dynamics between speakers and listeners derives primarily from his very Protestant conception of human nature and from the fact that the rhetorical situation most frequently implied in Wilson's treatment of jesting is pulpit oratory. To say that our wits are "heavy loaden" and that our natures are "lumpish and unwieldy" is to suggest that humans are fallen and imperfect. Wilson also suggests humans' inherent imperfections in the following passage: "Considering the dullness of man's nature, that neither it can be attentive to hear, nor yet stirred to like or allow any tale long told except it be refreshed or find some sweet delight, the learned have by wit and labor devised much variety. Therefore, sometimes in telling a weighty matter, they bring in some heavy tale and move them to be right sorry, whereby the hearers are more attentive. But after, when they are wearied either by the tediousness of the matter or heaviness of the report, some pleasant matter is invented both to quicken them again and also to keep them from satiety" (164). Again we find images of the speaker shaping his audience—in particular, shaping the emotional responses of his listeners by moving them back and forth between pity and mirth. However, more to the point, because humans are, by nature, "heavy loaden," "lumpish," "unwieldy," and dull, they are born with an inherent need to be lifted out of their fallen and imperfect state. In fact, what necessitated rhetoric in general was, according to Wilson, the fall of Adam. According to Wilson's adaptation of Cicero's myth of the origins of eloquence, it was the "fall of our first father" that created the conditions necessitating God's "gift of utterance." With this gift, God's "appointed ministers" rescued humankind from a fallen world, "persuaded with reason all men to society," and "fram[ed] them . . . to all good order" (41). The operation of rhetoric in general is thus an act of simultaneously pulling an audience up out of some fallen state and gathering them together and framing them to "all good order."

Wilson's construction of the speaker-audience dynamics is also influenced by the pragmatic difficulties he sees facing preachers when delivering sermons. One of these difficulties involves keeping churchgoers attentive and awake. Because "our senses be such that in hearing a right wholesome matter we either fall asleep when we should most harken, or else are wearied with still hearing one thing without any change," preachers must mingle funny stories and witticisms "ever among their weighty causes" (166). Another difficulty involves the possibility that listeners will simply wander off out of earshot. We have already seen hints of this possibility in phrases such as "will not long abide" and "lose them forever." Wilson explicitly calls attention to it when he recommends that preachers move laughter during sermons, "or else they are like sometimes to preach to the bare walls, for though the spirit be apt and our will prone, yet our flesh is so heavy, and humors so overwhelm us, that we cannot without refreshing long abide to hear any one thing" (47). Wilson's conception of human nature thus has pragmatic consequences for a preacher. The inherent sluggishness of the mind and body are forces that continually work against a preacher and threaten to derail his professional and spiritual obligations to impart religious instruction. So like God's "appointed ministers" who redeemed the postlapsarian world, lifted fallen and wayward humans out of their sinful condition, and drew them in to live with others in society, a preacher must delight his listeners with the pleasure afforded by jesting and keep them from falling asleep or wandering off.

It would not be far-fetched to say that the listeners' inherent sluggishness, the possibility that they will wander off, and the need for a speaker to overcome that sluggishness and waywardness by jesting are Wilson's preoccupations. When he comes to discuss the rhetorical value of fables, another means for delighting an audience, the hearers and the difficulties they create become out and out sources of anxiety, for here Wilson explicitly constructs the relationship between speaker and audience as one in which the speaker lowers and submits himself to the tastes and learning of his listeners in order to persuade them:

> The feigned fables, such as are attributed to brute beasts, would not be forgotten at any hand. For not only they delight the rude and ignorant, but also they help much for persuasion. And because such as speak in open audience have ever more fools to hear them than wise men to give judgment, I would think it not amiss to speak much according to the nature and fancy of the ignorant, that the rather they might be won through fables to learn more weighty and grave matters, for all men cannot brook sage causes and ancient collations, but will like earnest matters the rather if something be spoken thereamong agreeing to their natures. The multitude, as Horace doth say, is a beast, or rather a monster that hath many heads, and therefore like unto the diversity of nature variety of invention must always be used. Talk together of most grave matters . . . or use the quiddities of Duns to set forth God's mysteries, and you shall see the ignorant, I warrant you, either fall asleep or else bid you farewell. The multitude must needs be made merry. (221–22)

Several of the key images appearing in earlier passages are reversed here. The compassion that is implicit in phrases we have already seen, such as "these heavy loaden wits of ours" and "our lumpish and unwieldy natures," is transformed here into blatant hostility toward the audience. That is, in these earlier passages, the pronoun "our" is inclusive and suggests that Wilson, the audience, and—in fact—all people are united and share the common feature of being imperfect and fallen. In the present passage, however, Wilson distances himself from and places himself above what he views as the typical audience, and he aggressively attacks them: they are a rude, ignorant, and foolish multitude. In this way, the tone Wilson uses here echoes that of Demosthenes when, after telling his listeners a "merry toy" to gain their attention, he chastises and talks down to them. The image of the speaker who shapes and elevates his audience is also reversed. Instead of a speaker's giving form to his "lumpish and unwieldy" hearers, the listeners shape the speech of the speaker so that it accords with their "nature and fancy," and in the process of doing so, they force the speaker to come down and talk to them on their level. Finally, no longer is the speaker a source of wonder and fear "such as few dare set foot with" him; rather, it is the listeners who become a powerful force to be reckoned with. Their power resides partially in their ability to withhold attention and even get up and leave. If a speaker talks only of "grave matters" and uses the "quiddities" of Duns Scotus without refreshing his listeners with the delight afforded by fables, then that speaker "shall see the ignorant . . . either fall asleep, or else bid [him] farewell." This danger is even more possible given the type of rhetorical situation that, according to Wilson, almost necessitates the use of fables: that is, in "open audience." In such a setting, the boundaries that physically demarcate the situation are more permeable than they are, say, within the walls of a church: more "fools" can come within earshot, and it is easier for others to wander off. The power of the hearers also resides in the sheer massiveness of their number, which makes them a source of fear to a speaker. Wilson describes them as a "beast" or a many-headed "monster" for whom a "variety of invention must always be used." Again, the rhetorical practice of the speaker is shaped by his audience; his invention of subject matters must fit the "nature" of his listeners. Moreover, by portraying the hearers as a many-headed monster, not only does Wilson disparage, degrade, and rebuke them for their ignorance and express disdain for pandering to their tastes, but he also constructs them as something to be feared—something, perhaps, that could gobble up the speaker.

The manuals see jesting as a strategy speakers can use to gain control over their listeners. The medical and ethical lore suggests what the nature of that control is and how jesting affects both the minds and bodies of an audience. Jesting has the somewhat innocuous, yet beneficial, effect of refreshing and rejuvenating listeners, making them better disposed to further activity, whether that activity be work or, in the case of listening to a speech, the hearing of more substantial matters. Once these recipes for emotional and bodily health are extended by analogy to the body politic, they take on a distinctly ideological character and can be made to serve, justify, even mystify the established order. Jesting also has the much more powerful effect of causing its listeners to surrender control over their own bodies: laughter convulses the body and makes it transgress its own boundaries. Both of these effects, the one relatively innocuous and the other more violent, demonstrate the power of speakers over their listeners. As we have seen, however, Wilson complicates this model of speaker-audience interaction and suggests that the relationship between speaker and audience can also be characterized by an inherent tension between the participants in a jesting exchange. While jesting may place "men's hearts at [a speaker's] commandment," it also requires the speaker to submit to the needs and tastes of his listeners: he must please them if he hopes to be heard at all.

Kenneth Burke captures this paradoxical relationship between speakers and listeners in his analysis of the relationship between the "artist-entertainer" and the audience for whom he performs. But he complicates it even further by also considering the hierarchical relationships already in place before any type of rhetorical exchange is initiated and how those relationships may continually invert themselves, topsy-turvy, once an exchange is under way. According to Burke, "the artist who relies upon smartness as a mark of 'urbanity' may be 'socially inferior' to the 'ideal public' he is courting."[22] Yet the artist, like the trained orator, is supposedly "professionally superior" to his audience. However, "as soon as you thus set him up, you must recall . . . that the artist-entertainer is the servant of the very despot-audience he seeks to fascinate (as the spellbinder can tyrannize over his audience only by letting his audience tyrannize over him, in rigidly circumscribing the range and nature of his remarks)."[23] In jesting exchanges, laughter offers orators immediately visible and audible evidence of whether or not they have succeeded or failed "to fascinate" their audiences. It is an index of the orator's control over his listeners. As Wilson suggests, however, an orator's need to make his listeners laugh evidences his dependence on them, and although their failure, even active refusal, to laugh at an orator's jest constitutes their power (their ability to withhold what the orator seeks), the impact of such a refusal varies according to the hierarchical relationship already in place prior to a jesting exchange.

In all the passages we have examined from Wilson, the implicit hierarchical relationship between speaker and audience has been one in which the speaker is already superior to his audience. Even in preaching situations where a preacher might address his social betters, the preacher still supposedly ranks higher in spiritual authority. If such a relationship obtains, then an orator's failure to make his audience laugh could simply be dismissed or written off as the audience's ignorance, their inability to get the jest. Or an orator can express hostility toward his listeners, similar to the attitude Demosthenes and Wilson adopt, and rebuke listeners for their ignorance. In a sense, a speaker's social or spiritual superiority to his audience offers a buffer against failure; it can always be invoked to rescue him in a situation gone bad. It might even encourage an audience of inferiors to laugh: that is, they may feel obliged to laugh whenever their social better cracks a jest even if they do not find that jest very funny. In his *Anatomy of Melancholy* (1621), Robert Burton says, "If the King laugh, all laugh."[24] By extension, if the king favors some courtier, even if he is "most ignorant," then others might feel compelled to laugh at that courtier's "boording and certein cartarlike jestes, that should [in other circumstances] rather move a manne to vomite, then to laughe" (Castiglione, 141).[25] Robson also recognizes that an inferior will likely feel obliged to laugh when his superior jests, but he recommends that the inferior respond in a more guarded manner. If a courtier's "better seeme to deride any for his beehavour," then that courtier should "appeare by a smiling countenance to be of the same opinion: but in woords [he should] . . . escuse it, if hee may, as the doings of him that is mocked shew simpliticie." Robson hopes the "smiling countenance" will satisfy the need to defer to one's superiors and show an appreciation of their jests. The verbal "escuse," which might seem at odds with this visible sign of appreciation and deference, is actually intended to insulate the courtier from being an object of derision himself, for "even some of the same defects which he seeth scoft at in an other, may be in himselfe" (9). In other words, if the courtier laughs at a jest targeting a defect that he himself possesses, then he makes himself vulnerable to similar attacks by others. By not laughing outright, the courtier avoids such vulnerability, but he risks, of course, having his "escuse" being interpreted as a departure from or even an oblique criticism of the "opinion" of his superior.

In the reciprocal case—when a speaker's hearer is a social superior—then both the dynamics and the stakes change. A speaker can still use jesting as a means of audience control. The jests of Flamock's "unmannerly act" and the master who called his servant "King of fooles" demonstrate that jesting is a particularly powerful means by which a social inferior can criticize a superior while, at the same time diminishing the risks of retaliation by that superior. In his *Apophthegms New and Old,* Bacon includes several anecdotes in which inferiors offer oblique (and sometimes not so oblique) criticisms of the Queen to her face. In one, Bishop Whitehead cracks a jest alluding to the controversial subject of the Queen's failure to marry. One day Elizabeth says, "I like thee better, Whitehead, because thou livest unmarried." Whitehead replies, "In troth Madam, I like you the worse for the same cause" (7:163). In another anecdote, a courtier's jesting response to the Queen seems to rebuff and embarrass her. Seeing Sir Edward Dyer in her garden, the Queen leans out her window and asks him in Italian, "What does a man think of when he thinks of nothing?" Dyer, "who had not had the effect of some of the Queen's grants so soon as he had hoped and desired," pauses and then replies in Italian, "Madam, he thinks of a woman's promise" (7:174). Whitehead's reply is rather blunt, and Bacon says nothing of the Queen's response to it. Perhaps the Queen was incensed by it, and perhaps Bacon omits her reaction because it reaffirms his (and many others') opinion regarding the Queen's failure to marry. Dyer's response, by contrast, comes with several distancing mechanisms. It is delivered in Italian, and the referent of the word "woman" is not specifically determined. Yet, by Bacon's account, it seems to have secured at least one of its desired effects. For after hearing Dyer's reply to her question, the Queen "shrunk in her head" from the window (7:174).

In addition to being a vehicle for indirect criticism, jesting can be an effective means of delighting a superior in exchange for which a speaker might win that superior's favor. In *A Comedy of Errors,* Antipholus of Syracuse, who chides his servant Dromio for what Antipholus mistakes as his ill-timed antics, also praises his servant for lightening his "melancholy" with "his merry jests" (1.2.21). John Harington was often in trouble for his wit, but it also won him the attention of both queen and king. Elizabeth referred to him as "that witty fellow, my godson," and a friend told Harington, "The King hath often enquired after you, and would readily see and converse again with the 'merry blade,' as he hath oft called you, since you was here."[26] Castiglione says that a speaker who delights his superiors with jests might even win some kind of reward: "It is not againste good maners sometimes to use Merrie Prankes with great men also. And I have heard of manie that have bine played to Duke Fredericke, to King Alphonsus of Aragon, to Queene Isabel of Spaine, and to manie other great Princis, and not onlie they tooke it not in ill part, but rewarded very largely them that plaid them those partes" (192). Social superiors, in addition to rewarding a merry prankster for the pleasure his prank affords, may also be delighted by being given the opportunity to boost their own ethos: to show their inferiors that they can be good sports and a take a joke too. The author of *The Schoolemaster* says the Emperor Augustus, who "delyted in jesting," actually made himself more marvelous to his subjects by bearing the brunt of others' jests: "Many marvayled more at the jestes and quippes which he [Augustus] bare, then those which he gave" (M4^v).

A social inferior can also use jesting to repair a situation gone bad and, for example, mitigate the anger of a superior. Castiglione tells an anecdote in which there was a certain cleric in charge of a nunnery in Padua who, "hauntinge much to the Nounrye verie familiarlie, and confessynge often the Sisters, beegat five of them with child, where there was not passinge five mo [nuns] in all." When the bishop found out, he was outraged and intended to punish the cleric severely. Before the bishop's punishment was carried out, a friend of the cleric came to speak on his behalf, appealing to the bishop to consider extenuating circumstances, human frailty, and so on. Still the bishop would not budge and said, "What answere shall I make to God at the day of judgement, whan he shall say unto me *Redde Rationem villicationis tue* [Give a reckoning of your stewardship]?" The cleric's friend immediately replied, "*Domine quinque talenta tradidisti mihi, ecce alia quinque superlatus sum* [Lord, you gave five talents to me, behold I have gained five more]." Having heard this response, the bishop could not "absteine laughing and he asswaged his anger and the punishmente that he had ordeined for the offender" (171–72). Puttenham recounts an anecdote in which the offender himself uses a jest to quiet the anger of his superior. John Heywood was a dinner guest of the Duke of Northumberland. Because the Duke had just pawned most of his tableware to pay off several debts he owed, he and his guests were drinking from several communal cups.[27] Unaware of the Duke's financial trouble and "being loth to call for his drinke so oft as he was dry," Heywood "turned his eye toward the cupbord" and said, "I find great misse of your graces standing cups." The Duke thought his guest's remark referred to the fact "that his plate was lately sold," and he "said somewhat sharpely, why Sir will not those cuppes serve as good a man as your selfe." Sensing that he had insulted the Duke but perhaps not knowing exactly how or why, Heywood quickly replied, "Yes if it please your grace, but I would have one of them stand still at myne elbow full of drinke that I might not be driven to trouble your men so often to call for it." This "pleasant and speedy revers of the former wordes [or, at least, the Duke's interpretation of them] holpe all the matter again, whereupon the Duke became very pleasaunt and dranke a bolle of wine to Heywood, and bid a cup should always be standing by him" (282).

Although a speaker can use jesting to criticize his superiors, impress them with his wit, and rescue a situation gone bad, he can never predict with certainty how his listeners will respond to a jest. Will they or will they not laugh? Even if they do laugh, there is still an indeterminancy about that laughter: are they laughing *with* the speaker or *at* him? Moreover, jesting situations in which speakers address their superiors are radically different from those in which they address their inferiors—in the former, there is virtually no buffer against failure. Although Flamock, after committing his "unmanerly act," recovers the situation with a witty response, others may not be so fortunate, especially in cases where they offend their betters. In an effort to rescue a situation, inferiors might appeal to previous gestures of allegiance and duty, but they cannot use their social status as something to fall back on because they are, in fact, inferiors. So even though Burke claims hierarchical relations between performer and audience "need not remain fixed" during a performance, the speaker who jests before social superiors is always at a disadvantage.

A tavern scene from *Henry IV, Part Two*, illustrates how inequalities in social status can be an insurmountable barrier in jesting exchanges. In this scene, Falstaff tries to assuage Prince Hal's anger with a jest, but Hal refuses to laugh. The Prince and Poins, disguised as drawers, eavesdrop on a conversation between Falstaff and Doll Tearsheet. In the course of this exchange, Falstaff, unaware of the Prince's presence, heaps abuse on him and calls him a "good shallow fellow" who "would have made a good pantler, 'a would of chipp'd bread well" (2.4.235–36). The Prince and Poins reveal themselves to Falstaff, and Poins, fearing that Falstaff will repair the situation with his jesting, warns the Prince not to be seduced by Falstaff's wit: "My Lord, he will drive you out of your revenge and turn all to merriment, if you take not the heat [and strike while the iron is hot]" (2.4.297–98). When the Prince demands that Falstaff confess his "willful abuse" of the heir, Falstaff tries to wriggle out of the situation with a jest, using a technique that resembles the one he used in his famous "coward on instinct" speech in *Henry IV, Part One* (2.4.264–74). He says to Poins and the Prince, "I disprais'd him [the Prince] before the wicked, that the wicked might not fall in love with thee [to Hal]; in which doing, I have done the part of a careful friend and a true subject, and thy father is to give me thanks for it" (2.4.318–22). This is a clever jest. Falstaff admits to the deed but redefines what is clearly an irreverent act as one of loyalty and respect, motivated by a desire to protect the Prince and deserving the gratitude of the king himself.

The Prince, however, does not laugh. Poins's warning not to let Falstaff "turn all to merriment" suggests that the Prince's withholding of laughter is a conscious gesture on his part. It is part of a larger process by which Hal gradually creates distance between himself and Falstaff. In the "coward on instinct" speech in *Part One,* Falstaff successfully jests his way out of a similar bind. Hal accuses him of being a coward, of running away from Hal and Poins, whom Falstaff thought were highway men, and of lying about the incident afterwards in the tavern. When Hal exposes Falstaff's story as a lie, Falstaff quickly recovers and explains that he ran away on instinct: "Should I turn upon the true Prince? Why, thou knowest I am as valiant as Hercules, but beware instinct. The lion will not touch the true prince. Instinct is a great matter; I was now a coward on instinct. I shall think the better of myself and thee during my life—I for a valiant lion, and thou for a true prince" (2.4.266–72). Although Falstaff's clowning is successful on this occasion, its success still depends on whether or not Hal lets Falstaff off the hook. In the scene from *Part Two,* Falstaff uses a similar technique of jesting, cleverly redefining the situation to his favor. In this latter instance, however, the Prince refuses to laugh, denies Falstaff what he seeks, and in this way anticipates his eventual banishment of his old companion.

As these two scenes suggest, the socially inferior speaker is clearly at a disadvantage when trying to make his superiors laugh. What would put him at an even greater disadvantage is an emergent attitude toward laughter in the early modern period, an attitude requiring gentlemen to regulate their laughter more strictly and, in some instances, to refrain from laughing altogether. Della Casa recommends that gentlemen only "laughe upon occasion, and not uppon custome," for those who laugh incessantly and without

restraint will appear "groase and uncomely" (115). Robson offers more specific advice, instructing his gentlemanly reader on how to laugh in the company of either social superiors or strangers. He says that if a gentleman "be
provoked to laughe in the presence of his betters, to do the same with as little noyse as may be: and likewise in the company of straungers, for too lowde
a laughter . . . doo make wisemen counted foolish" (34). These passages are
at odds with others we have seen where laughter is characterized as an
"imperious force" that bursts forth regardless of whatever resistance the
hearer might make: that is, they allow for the possibility of one's controlling
not only one's laughter but also one's body. A similar attitude is expressed by
Juan Luis Vives in the third book of his *De Anima et Vita* (1538), where he
says, "Laughter is always natural rather than willed, but it can be controlled
by habit and reason to prevent excessive outbursts that shake the entire
body" (53). While Vives agrees with other rhetoricians of the period in viewing laughter as a more or less involuntary action of the body, he departs from
them by saying that it can be harnessed through self-discipline and reason.
This departure places Vives' comments about laughter within a larger,
ongoing process by which the "new standards of bodily control and decorum" were being developed by members of the elite to differentiate themselves further from their inferiors.[28] Vives goes on to say that those who are
typically prone to "convulsions" of the body and who "loose their self-control
as they are overcome by laughter" include "the ignorant, the peasants, children, and women" (58). Unlike Wilson and others who suggest that laughter cuts across various kinds of boundaries and includes everyone within its
scope, Vives states that laughter and an ability to control it actually mark a
dividing line along several hierarchical axes, separating the well-educated
from the ignorant, the socially elevated from the base and ignoble, the
mature from the immature, and the manly from the womanly.

According to Castiglione's quasi-historical account, the "kinges of old time"
used recreation as a way to gain the good will of their subjects and, in doing
so, to secure the internal stability of their kingdoms. His account is remarkable not only because it assigns a socially conservative function to jesting,
but also because it suggests that jesting is somehow connected with political
power—that it could serve as a means of rule. Still, Castiglione is not alone
in viewing jesting in this way. Puttenham, for instance, offers many examples
of kings using jests to assert their own social superiority and put inferiors

back in their proper social place. While discussing upstarts and those who "brave it out like Gentlemen," Guazzo even allows laughter to stand in for a royal injunction regulating the apparel worn by subjects. But perhaps the most interesting example in which an early modern writer expresses a view similar to that of Castiglione is the passage from Wilson where he says that the "witty and learned" have always made use of the power of jesting because "men wonder at such a head, as hath men's hearts at his commandment, being able to make them merry when he lists." I have explored the possibilities for punning on the word "head," arguing that it stands not only for the intellect of the speaker but also for the "head," or ruler, of the body politic. In this way, the passage replays, although in a more condensed form, Castiglione's quasi-history, echoing its images of rule and the "wonder" they instill.

There is, however, a crucial difference. The people whom Wilson says wield this power are not the "kinges of old time," that is, the legitimate rulers. Instead, Wilson calls them the "witty and learned," names that do not locate these men in terms of social status, but in terms of ability. In a sense, these names suggest a certain autonomy, a certain independence, from the constraints and restrictions of the existing hierarchy. For if the power of jesting is as great as Wilsons says it is, then these "witty and learned" speakers could theoretically swagger into any situation, rifle off a few jokes, and take control of their listeners irrespective of their own social rank or the ranks of the other participants involved. The difference, then, between Castiglione's account of the origins of recreation and the passage just quoted from Wilson is that in the latter the power of jesting is dislodged from its legitimate seat and placed in the hands of anyone with the readiness and ability to master the techniques of jesting that Wilson is about to offer.

Wilson's remarks about these commanders of men's hearts help sum up one of the major arguments of this study. Jesting is something of a wildcard that can turn up anywhere and change the nature of the game. With a well-placed jest or quip, as the handbooks repeatedly suggest, an orator or courtier can snap a situation into a new configuration, realigning the ranks and allegiances of the persons involved. We have seen examples in which a witty saying or humorous anecdote captures the attention of a wayward or unruly congregation, shames boastful or irreverent courtiers, or even turns a king's anger into merriment. But we have also seen instances in which jesting goes beyond the control not only of the orators and courtiers who engage in laughing matters, but also of the men who wrote handbooks on rhetoric and courtly conduct during the period. Like Wilson's unfettered "witty and learned" speakers, a jest, once delivered, can dart off in unexpected directions, reveal more (or less) than the speaker had hoped, strike unforeseen targets, or even recoil upon the speaker, turning him into an object either of laughter or contempt. This elusiveness of jesting becomes all the more apparent when writers try to describe its operations, properties, and functions from the perspective of serious, prescriptive discourse. As Mulkay contends, efforts to understand humor in a serious mode (and then impart that understanding to others) will always fall short because humor "has a built-in semantic duality that persistently generates contradictions when approached from the perspective of the serious realm."[29] Throughout this study, we have seen the manuals repeatedly generate such "contradictions" in their serious treatments of jesting: for instance, the decorous jest is one that blurs distinctions between the seemly and unseemly, the fitting and unfitting; the "places" of jesting are not "places" at all, but vast, open territories with a potentially endless number of associations and meanings; the orator or courtier who jests gains control over his listeners by paradoxically knocking them out of control, causing them to lose command over their bodies. The many contradictions that we encountered in the handbooks' treatment of jesting suggest that any discourse on jesting and laughter (including this study) will always fall short, will always fail to fully grasp what it seeks to comprehend. But they also suggest the complexities and powers of this oftentimes puzzling rhetorical resource—how a single jest can have multiple meanings and secure conflicting ends while, at the same time, advancing the more general persuasive ends of the speaker, how it can simultaneously degrade and, as Freud says, "open sources of pleasure" normally kept in check, how it can utterly stupefy its target and cause a crowd of onlookers to burst forth with laughter.

Wilson's remark about his "witty and learned" speakers is also related to another major argument of this study. The supposed independence of these speakers from the constraints and restrictions of the existing social hierarchy points to the possibilities and dangers of social and geographic mobility that deeply informs not only the discourse on jesting in early modern England but also the discourse on rhetoric and courtly conduct in general. Unlike the Roman rhetorics where jesting encapsulates the more general dynamics of forensic and deliberative disputes—where two orators of the same status do battle in the "fighting-line" of the forum—the early modern texts are primarily concerned with encounters between people of divergent social origins and occupations, and because jests dramatize—or model—such encounters, they serve as particularly rich and powerful vehicles for thinking about and exploring liminal moments of exchange (and the anxieties, ambiguities, and contradictions that accompany them) when different kinds of people interact. Moreover, if the early modern discourse on jesting is ultimately about communication between different kinds of people, then it moves beyond the traditional, official arenas of rhetoric—the law courts and public assemblies—into unofficial territories. This discourse is still concerned with formal settings—with pulpit oratory, for instance, and interaction at court—but attention is also paid to informal settings and gatherings, suggesting that early modern rhetoric and courtesy manuals, more so than their classical sources, are interested in the operations of jesting in realms of experience other than, and in addition to, these official arenas.

The more expansive focus of the handbooks can partly be attributed to the extraordinarily public and communal nature of mirth and pastimes in sixteenth-century England. Laughter and festivity were an integral component of everyday life in early modern England, and (despite increasing pressures from Puritanism) church-ales, morris dances, Easter or "Hock" Tuesday, wassails, and May Day and Midsummer celebrations persisted throughout the period. By the time James I assumed the throne, however, the range of public mirth diminished considerably. In fact, James (and then later his son) felt compelled to launch a campaign to revive and protect public mirth, in the face of efforts that eventually succeeded in abolishing many forms of festivity and holiday play during the Puritan Interregnum.[30] The handbooks anticipate and reflect some of these changes. As we have seen, several of the handbooks on courtly conduct restrict the range of suitable targets of laughter, excluding deformity from the realm of the laughable. Several handbooks also forbid frequent and excessive outbursts of laughter, and Puritan divine William Perkins not only forbids preachers from jesting in the pulpit but also censures Christians for participating in or attending games, plays, and other pastimes, many of which took place in public spaces. Despite the increasingly greater restrictions imposed (at least in the handbooks) on mirth making, sixteenth-century England seems especially conducive to jesting and laughter. In an interesting analysis of the social and political scene in Tudor England, Robert Weimann characterizes the period as an "era of social compromise that achieved temporary stability and a cultural synthesis of old and new."[31] Economic growth, social and geographic mobility, New World exploration, emergent Protestantism, and the new Puritan morality weakened but did not displace completely "medieval structures of life."[32] As a result, "the old and the new confronted each other" at almost every level of experience: "Older conceptions of honor were confronted by the new pride of possession, hatred of usury by fervor for gold, the idea of service by the idea of profit, deeply rooted community consciousness by passionate individualism. Feudal family pride mingled with the bourgeois sense of family, pomp with thrift, frivolity with chastity, pessimism with optimism."[33] If social incongruity and contradiction are the ingredients of jesting, and if the period is distinguished by the confrontations and mixtures Weimann claims it was, then can we go so far as to say that early modern England was itself structured like a richly textured jest?

Notes

Introduction

1. Aristotle makes several references to the uses of wit in his *Rhetoric* (1419b 3–10, and 1412a–13b). He also treats the occurrence of jesting in everyday discourse and suggests what sort of impact it has on a speaker's ethos in his *Nicomachean Ethics* (4.8.1–12). The author of the *Ad Herennium* offers perhaps the first extant version of what is arguably the most durable rhetorical prescription concerning jesting: that is, to begin a speech with a jest or comic anecdote (1.6.10). Cicero devotes approximately one fifth of the second book of *De oratore,* nearly 85 sections, to the rhetoric of wit and humor and mentions it briefly in his *Orator* (26.87–90) and in his *De officiis* (1.29.103–4). Quintilian also devotes considerable space to the rhetoric of jesting, the entirety of the third chapter of the sixth book of his *Institutio oratoria.* In the later Middle Ages, jesting appears as part, though a small part, of the *ars praedicandi.* More common was its use in the actual practices of medieval preachers who often possessed collections of *exempla* many of which consisted of humorous tales and anecdotes. On this issue, see G. R. Owst, *Preaching in Medieval England,* 80–83. Since this is a study of the early modern rhetorical discourse on jesting, I'll move on to a brief consideration of subsequent developments. George Campbell's *Philosophy of Rhetoric* and Richard Whately's *Elements of Rhetoric* are two of the last canonical rhetorics in English to treat the uses of wit and humor. While Whately seriously, though briefly, considers the subject, Campbell's remarks suggest the shrinking role jesting is to play in rhetorical theory (humor and wit, of course, continue to be extremely important in rhetorical practices of all sorts). Campbell frames his discussion of "wit, humour, and ridicule" by saying they are "naturally suited to light and trivial matters" (150).

2. In his *Rhetoric in the Roman World,* George A. Kennedy does briefly mention Cicero's lengthy treatment of wit and humor in *De oratore.* However, Kennedy only speculates on its sources and presents a short synopsis of its content. In his important *Logic and Rhetoric in England,* Wilbur Samuel Howell has nothing

to say about jesting even though it is addressed (at times, to great length) by many of the writers he examines. There are, however, several important studies on ancient and early modern theories of the laughable, some of which appeared early in this century. A study that I have found invaluable is Joanna Brizdale Lipking's "Traditions of the *Facetiae.*" See also E. Arndt, "De Ridiculi Doctrina Rhetorica"; Ernst Walser, *Die Theorie des Witzes und der Novelle nach Jovianus Pontanus;* and Mary A. Grant, *The Ancient Theories of the Laughable.* E. R. Curtius's *European Literature and the Latin Middle Ages* also includes a relevant discussion of "jest and earnest" (417–35).

3. See *De oratore,* 2.54.216–18 and 2.56.227–29; Quintilian, 6.3.14–16; and Baldesar Castiglione, *Book of the Courtier,* 153. Subsequent references to these works will appear in the text.

4. There are at least two notable exceptions to this claim. Edward P. J. Corbett includes a brief discussion of wit in his *Classical Rhetoric for the Modern Student* (326–28). In their *New Rhetoric,* Chaim Perelman and L. Olbrechts-Tyteca include many humorous examples to illustrate (and caricature) types of argumentation, and although they claim that "humor is a very important factor in winning over the audience," they do not "believe that a study of humor in the art of oratory is directly pertinent to . . . [their overall] task" (188). I should also note that vestiges—and I mean only vestiges—of the rhetoric of jesting can be found in the many popular rhetorics of the "thousand-and-one-jokes-to-begin-a-speech-with" variety.

5. See, for instance, two recent essay collections on the subject of histories of rhetoric: *Rethinking the History of Rhetoric,* ed. Takis Poulakos; and *Writing Histories of Rhetoric,* ed. Victor Vitanza.

6. Jesting has fared better in literary and historical (broadly defined) studies of the Renaissance. In his *Lyric Wonder,* James Biester considers the subject of jesting and its relation to wonder and wit in poetry in early modern England. Daniel Javitch briefly treats Castiglione's discussion of jesting in his *Poetry and Courtliness* (34–37). For more sustained treatments of the subject, see Barbara C. Bowen, introduction to her *One Hundred Renaissance Jokes* (xiii–xx); Anne Lake Prescott, "Humanism and the Tudor Jestbook"; Keith Thomas, "Place of Laughter"; Raymond A. Anselment, *Betwixt Jest and Earnest;* and F. P. Wilson, "The English Jest-Books."

7. *Arte of English Poesie,* 272. Subsequent references to this work will appear in the text.

8. *Civile Conversation of M. Steeven Guazzo,* 1:158. Subsequent references will appear in the text, noted by citing the volume number then page number.

9. *Art of Rhetoric,* 164. Subsequent references to this work will appear in the text.

10. "Place of Laughter," 77.

11. *Preface to Shakespeare's Comedies,* 26.

12. "Place of Laughter," 77.

13. Ibid.

14. In his "Prose Jest-Books," Derek Brewer says, "There were of course jests in classical antiquity and in the Middle Ages, some of which survived for many centuries, but the first jest-book proper . . . is normally reckoned to be the *Facetiae*, the collection of jests made by Poggio Bracciolini, the great Humanist scholar (1380–1459)" (91). According to Lipking, "The isolation of the joke as a form and the development of a literature devoted exclusively to jokes occurred late in the fifteenth century, mainly in Italy and Germany" ("Traditions of the *Facetiae*," 18).

15. The rise of social and geographic mobility in the period has been amply documented. After Henry VIII's break with Rome and the dissolution of the monasteries, a tremendous amount of land (a chief index of social status) became available on the open market. This wide availability of land taken together with a number of other factors (including demographic growth, increased commercial activity, expansion of educational and professional opportunities, and, later on, New World exploration and settlement) contributed to a dramatic rise in social mobility, both upwards and downwards. Some of these same factors also encouraged increases in geographic mobility. Demographic growth, enclosure of open-field villages, unemployment or underemployment, and low wages caused many people, primarily the poor, to relocate (oftentimes on a seasonal basis) in order to make a living. However, geographic mobility was not limited to the poor. The sons of commoners and gentry alike flocked to the Universities and Inns of Court with hopes of receiving an education (and making connections) that would prepare them for a career in religion, law, or politics. Even among the gentry there was considerable migration. Lured by the attractions of London and by pressing legal and business demands, many nobles took up seasonal or semipermanent residences in the burgeoning metropolis. On these issues, see Lawrence Stone, *Crisis of the Aristocracy;* Frank Whigham, *Ambition and Privilege,* 1–31; A. L. Beier, *Masterless Men,* 29–48; and Peter Clark and David Souden, eds., *Migration and Society.*

16. Although there are different major theories of humor in modern studies of joking and laughter, it has become almost axiomatic that humor issues from the perception of some form of incongruity. The incongruity theory of humor, as it is now commonly called, is usually attributed to Kant, although it is implicit in Cicero's discussion of wit when he says that jokes "point out something unseemly in no unseemly manner" (*De oratore,* 2.58.236). Regardless of its origins, the incongruity theory of humor is the basis of many theories and analyses of humor offered by social scientists, philosophers, linguists, and literary critics. See, for instance, Arthur Koestler, *Act of Creation,* 35–36; Victor Raskin, *Semantic Mechanisms of Humor,* 81; Michael Mulkay, *On Humor,* 26–27; Neal R. Norrick, *Conversational Joking,* 8–9; and James F. English, *Comic Transactions,* 7–9.

17. See Owst, *Literature and the Pulpit,* 163–66.

18. "Language, Identity and Ethnic Jokes," 39–52.

19. This argument might be extended to representations of rhetoric in antiquity in general. In his *Emperor of Men's Minds,* Wayne A. Rebhorn argues that although social advancement through oratory was possible and did occur in ancient Greece and Rome, "only Tacitus among ancient writers directly addresses this aspect of the art" (113).

20. Ibid., 16.

21. Peter E. Medine, *Thomas Wilson,* chaps. 1 and 4.

22. Norbert Elias, *Civilizing Process,* 64.

23. Whigham, *Ambition and Privilege,* 5.

24. Ibid.

25. *Foundacion of Rhetorike,* Ai^v. Subsequent references to this work will appear in the text.

26. *English Secretary,* 4. Subsequent references to this work will appear in the text.

27. *Courte of Civill Courtesie.* Although Robson gives the impression that this work is a translation of an Italian treatise by Bengalasso del Monte, several modern scholars argue that Robson was indeed the author and not simply the translator, that the title page's claim "out of the Italian" was a ruse, perhaps in an effort to enhance the credibility of and lend authority to the English text. See F. P. Wilson, "English Jest-Books," 312 n.2. Subsequent references to Robson will appear in the text.

28. Much of the overall trajectory of this brief and tentative history is indebted to Lipking, "Traditions of the *Facetiae.*"

29. Ibid., 265.

30. Ibid., 165.

31. Quoted in Charles Speroni, *Wit and Wisdom,* 20.

32. In one of Poggio's tales, for instance, a man, thinking that his wife has two vaginas, is persuaded to donate one of them to the church, a gift which the local priest is happy to accept; in another, a stingy master, while snooping around the dinner table of his servants, accidentally takes a deep draught from a bowl of urine; in still another, a man approaches a woman and says, "The foreskin of the ass greets you," to which she replies, "Oh, is that so? Well, you do look like one of his envoys." The *facetiae* paraphrased here appear in *The Facetiae of Giovanni Francesco Poggio Bracciolini* (28–29, 73, and 69). For a more detailed discussion of Poggio's departures from classical standards of decorum, see Lipking, "Traditions of the *Facetiae,*" 88–93.

33. Quoted in Speroni, *Wit and Wisdom,* 4–5.

34. F. P. Wilson, "English Jest-Books," 287.

35. "Traditions of the *Facetiae,*" 66.

36. I'm quoting from a facsimile (New York: Da Capo Press, 1969) of Nicholas Udall's 1542 translation of the Erasmus's *Apophthegmata*. The "Preface of Erasmus" is not signed.

37. Wilson, "English Jest-Books," 289.

38. "Traditions of the *Facetiae*," 173.

39. "Humanism in the Tudor Jestbook," 6.

40. See "Biographical Notes" appended to Wilson, "English Jest-Books," 313–24.

41. Lipking, "Traditions of the *Facetiae*," 265. For more on Pontano and his *De Sermone*, see George Luck, "Vir Facetus," 107–21.

42. The relevant passage from Aristotle's *Ethics* appears at 10.6.6.

43. This paragraph is indebted to F. P. Wilson's discussion of the possible uses to which the jest books were put. See his "English Jest-Books," 308–12.

44. On More's use of jests in his epigrams, see Hoyt H. Hudson, *The Epigram in the English Renaissance*, 59; on Latimer, see Lipking, "Traditions of the *Facetiae*," 386–407.

45. On Harington's sources and ambitions, see Lipking, "Traditions of the *Facetiae*," 408–48.

46. *Essayes*, 47.

47. "English Jest-Books," 311.

48. See *Advancement of Learning*, where Bacon also discusses *apophthegms* (4:314).

49. *Emperor of Men's Minds*, 18–19.

50. *Rhetoric of Motives*, xiii.

51. "The Eighteenth Century," 114.

52. Mikhail Bakhtin, *Rabelais and His World*, 10.

53. Ibid., 19–20.

54. Ibid., 21.

55. Ibid.

56. Ibid., 26.

57. Ibid., 29.

58. Ibid., 38.

59. Others have also critiqued and questioned Bakhtin's characterization of medieval and Renaissance carnival, although for somewhat different reasons from mine. For a helpful survey of these critiques and questionings (at least, for those launched before 1986), see Peter Stallybrass and Allon White, *Politics and Poetics of Transgression,* chap. 1. For more recent challenges, see Walter Stephens, *Giants in Those Days,* 1–56; and Aaron Gurevich, "Bakhtin and His Theory of Carnival."

60. For a discussion of Castiglione's ideal of the courtly body, see Rebhorn, "Baldesar Castiglione," 241–74.

61. "Place of Laughter," 77.

1
Jesting Situations

1. "Study of Humor," 164.

2. Although Mary Douglas's study of the relationship between joking and social structure in her "Social Control of Cognition" is valuable for many reasons, it does illustrate this tendency. According to her, jokes are symbolic expressions of ambiguities and contradictions in the social structure: "a joke is seen and allowed when it offers a symbolic pattern of a social pattern occurring at the same time. As I see it, all jokes are expressive of the social situations in which they occur" (366). In other words, jokes reflect and mirror social patterns that exist prior to their expression in the form of jokes. If there are no ambiguities and contradictions in the social structure, no "joking can appear" (366). The social context is such a powerful force in determining and constraining all joking activity that it can, according to Douglas, actually call a joke into being: "a joke form in the social structure *calls imperatively* for an explicit joke to express it" (368, emphasis added). Persons who tell jokes, Douglas's model suggests, cannot use humor to manage or alter situations; instead, they are merely conduits through which ambiguities and contradictions are communicated. In his *On Humor,* Mulkay exhibits similar tendencies, though not to the extent as those found in Douglas. He argues that the degree of formality (or informality) of a situation conditions the joking practices of participants. Both Douglas's and Mulkay's models of joking—their strengths and weaknesses—will be discussed more fully in the next chapter.

3. Grant, *Theories of the Laughable,* 73.

4. In his *Jokes and Their Relation to the Unconscious,* Freud uses a similar, tripartite model of joking for his analysis of what he calls "tendentious," or sexual or hostile, jokes. However, Freud extends Cicero's version by presenting the various effects of jesting on the participants as a simultaneous and dynamic process. In other words, Cicero assigns particular effects to each participant separately: a joke enhances the ethos of a speaker, it wins the good will of an audience, etc. Freud, by contrast, sees the effects on the participants as part of the same process. According to him, "a tendentious joke calls for three people: in addition to the one who makes the joke, there must be a second who is taken as the object of the sexual or hostile aggressiveness, and a third in whom the joke's aim of producing pleasure is fulfilled" (118). That is, situations in which a sexual or hostile joke is delivered require a speaker, opponent, and audience. Freud then goes on to describe the operation of such jokes as a form of sublimated combat: "Since we have been obliged to renounce the expression of hostility by deeds . . . [we have] developed new techniques of aggression, which aim at enlisting . . . [an audience] against our enemy. By making our enemy small, inferior, despicable or comic, we achieve in a roundabout way the enjoyment of overcoming him—to which the [audience] . . .

bears witness by . . . [their] laughter" (122). A hostile or sexual joke allows a speaker to forge a new or strengthen an already existing alliance with his or her audience at the expense and exclusion of the speaker's opponent.

5. In effect, the functions Cicero assigns to jesting correspond to the three modes of artistic proof Aristotle sets forth in his *Rhetoric:* ethos, pathos, and logos (1356a). The correspondence with the first two modes is relatively clear: jests that show a speaker to be a man of "finish, accomplishment, and taste" also enhance the speaker's character and credibility; and jests that relive dullness and tone down austerity may be said, as most emotional appeals do, to place "the audience into a certain frame of mind" (*Rhetoric,* 1356a 3). However, the parallel with the third mode of proof, logos, may need further explanation. Logos primarily refers to rational appeals as they are expressed in the "speech itself" (*Rhetoric,* 1356a 19). According to a more general formulation, logos can also refer to the general substance or subject matter of a speech. In the case of humor, when a speaker aims a jest at his opponent, he makes that opponent the subject matter, or butt, of his joke, and the argument implicitly advanced is that this opponent is ridiculous or laughable.

6. Norman W. DeWitt, "Litigation in the Forum," 218.

7. *Literate Mode of Cicero's Legal Rhetoric,* 47.

8. Ibid., 48.

9. *Brutus,* 49.186.

10. Rebhorn, *Emperor of Men's Minds,* 34.

11. It is interesting to note that Cicero, in addition to using examples of wit in forensic settings, takes many of his examples from deliberative speeches or from conversations between the politically powerful (see, for instance, *De oratore,* 2.64.260, 2.65.267, 2.61.250, and 2.62.253). Quintilian, however, takes his examples almost exclusively from the courts (see especially 6.3.72–87). His doing so perhaps points to the orator's more limited role in society under the Empire. George Kennedy suggests that the eventual shrinking of the orator's sphere of influence is evident throughout Quintilian's treatise where "rather heavy emphasis is put on the orator's personal morality and technical competence, rather less on his political and intellectual leadership. His role in the law courts seems more evident than in the council chamber or before the people" (*Rhetoric in the Roman World,* 509).

12. Actually, Catulus does not snatch a word from Philippus, but he does turn the metaphor back against him by exploiting conventional associations people hold in regard to dogs—that is, dogs bark (or are supposed to bark) when they see an intruder.

13. The translators append the following note: "Although authority is scanty, it seems that, in certain criminal proceedings, the defendant had the right to propose a number of judges, limited by a sufficient right of challenge and exclusion on the part of the prosecution." It seems that Galba, as defendant, and Libo, as prosecu-

tor, were trying to exert these potentially conflicting rights, each trying to frustrate the other's exertion with a jest.

14. "Decorum," 152, 155.

15. Rebhorn, "Outlandish Fears." Hariman makes a similar point, claiming that decorum "embodied the ideology of the ruling elite" and was used by this elite in an effort to make the existing social order seem coincident with the natural order ("Decorum," 153).

16. In his *Rhetoric*, Aristotle characterizes youth as being "fond of fun and therefore witty" (1389b 10); of elderly men, he says they are not "disposed to jesting and laughter" (1390a 23). Also using age as a criterion for classifying forms of humor, Cicero says that irony is particularly appropriate to the *gravitas* of the mature statesman and lawyer (*De oratore*, 2.67.270). On the opposition between play and work (*otium* and *negotium*), see above in the text. As for how the categories of city and country figure in decorum and jesting, see Quintilian where he contrasts *urbanitas*, which befits the gentlemanly orator, with *rusticus*, that is, jests that smell of the country (6.3.17). Finally, the distinction (so common in classical rhetorical theory) between things and words is used by both Cicero and Quintilian to distinguish different categories of humor (*De oratore*, 2.59.240, and *Institutio*, 6.3.22).

17. These three social types correspond to the three locations on a spectrum Aristotle uses to define virtues in general—that is, a virtue is the mean between the extremes of some deficiency and some excess. The boor is deficient in wit, the buffoon excessive, and the witty man of tact is just right!

18. Grant considers all of these social types and the behaviors that identify them with the indecorous in her *Theories of the Laughable*, 88–96.

19. According to Grant, "*Scurra*, as used in its earliest meaning in Plautus, signified a fine gentleman of the city, or a fashionable idler. . . . In Cicero's time, however, the wit of the *scurra* became his most prominent characteristic; he had descended the social scale, and the word designated one in the suite of a rich man whose duty it was to amuse the guests at table" (*Theories of the Laughable*, 92).

20. For a survey of Cicero's references to Roscius, see Frederick Warren Wright, "Cicero and the Theater," 16–20.

21. Richard C. Beacham, *Roman Theatre*, 5. On the popularity of mimes, see Beacham, 128–40.

22. Ibid., 131.

23. Ibid.

24. Ibid., 130.

25. Ibid., 133.

26. Ibid., 131.

27. Ibid., 131. See also Wright, "Cicero and the Theater," 4–9.

28. *Letters to Atticus*, 14.3.

29. On the motives informing Quintilian's treatise and on how he wrote it in response to "what he saw going on around him," see Michael Winterbottom's classic article "Quintilian and the *Vir Bonus*," 90–97.

30. The translation here is from Wright ("Cicero and the Theater," 98) whose rendering of this passage seems more accurate to me than that of Hubbel who translates *mimicum* as "buffoonery." While the stage antics of mimes might be described as buffoonery or *scurrilis* (see, for instance, Quintilian, 6.3.29), the mime and the buffoon are relatively distinct social types. On these distinctions, see Grant, *Theories of the Laughable,* 88–96.

31. The phrase "hero of your tale" is a bit misleading—a liberty of translation, or perhaps the translator intends this phrase to be interpreted as irony. Whatever the case may be, the "hero of your tale" is no "hero" at all, but is an object of ridicule.

32. On fabricating portions of a funny story, see the passage immediately preceding the one quoted above.

33. Katherine A. Geffcken, *Comedy in the Pro Caelio,* 10.

34. Ibid.

35. Macrobius, *Saturnalia,* 166. Subsequent references to this work will appear in the text.

36. This model can also be found in several modern treatments of humor. It is implicit in Freud's analysis of the purposes of hostile jokes (see n. 5 above) and in many discussions of ethnic humor where jokes directed at minorities or foreigners simultaneously bolster solidarity within the dominate group and reinforce boundaries that separate and distinguish that group from outsiders. This model is also central to Susan Purdie's *Comedy* where she argues that the butt of a joke is "excluded from the Teller-Audience relationship and, in being so, reciprocally confirms the collusion of those positions as masterful jokers" (58).

37. Lipking, "Traditions of the *Facetiae*," 279.

38. On this shift in medieval rhetorical theory, see James J. Murphy, *Rhetoric in the Middle Ages.* On the increasing importance of pulpit oratory in the early modern period, see Debora K. Shuger, *Sacred Rhetoric.* As for poetry and drama's being available arenas for persuasion, see Javitch, *Poetry and Courtliness,* and Joel Altman, *Tudor Play of Mind.*

39. Horton Davies, *Worship and Theology in England,* 238.

40. *A Treatise wherein Dicing, Daunsing, Vaine Playes or Enterludes . . . are Reproved,* 44. Subsequent references to this work will appear in the text.

41. For discussions of the medieval versions of these debates, see Curtius, *European Literature,* 420–22; and Glending Olson, *Literature as Recreation.*

42. Here Wilson invokes a commonplace used in arguments defending rhetoric in general. For instance, Aristotle claims that one of the reasons rhetoric is useful is that truth, by itself, will not always secure conviction in an audience. In order

to secure that conviction, a speaker may often have to resort to rhetorical means (*Rhetoric,* 1355a 25–26). See also Augustine, *On Christian Doctrine,* 4.2.

43. See, for example, his *De oratore,* 2.27.115, and his *Orator,* 21.69. See also Quintilian, 12.10.58–59.

44. Robert of Basevorn's manual appears in James J. Murphy's anthology, *The Three Medieval Rhetorical Arts,* 212.

45. Ibid. See also Zall's introduction to his anthology *A Hundred Merry Tales,* 4–5.

46. On the competition between medieval preachers and other forms of entertainment, see G. R. Owst, *Preaching in Medieval England,* 82. For a discussion of the relationship between the church and drama in medieval England, see Robert Weimann, *Shakespeare and the Popular Tradition,* chap. 3.

47. Patrick Collinson, *Birthpangs of Protestant England,* 102ff.

48. *A Patterne for Pastors,* in *A Summons for Sleepers . . . Wherunto is annexed a Patterne for Pastors,* 45. Subsequent references to this work will appear in the text.

49. I will explore the subject of More's wit more fully in chapter 3.

50. Thomas More, *A Dialogue of Comfort against Tribulation,* 86. Subsequent references to this work will appear in the text.

51. All page citations are to the Basel edition (1539). All translations are by James Butrica whose translation of the entire *Ecclesiastae* will appear as part of the University of Toronto's Collected Works of Erasmus. Professor Butrica was kind enough to share with me portions of his working translation of this text.

52. Geneva Bible.

53. Quoted in J. W. Blench, *Preaching in England,* 306.

54. John Guy, *Tudor England,* 295.

55. Peter Clark, *English Alehouse,* 151–52.

56. Quoted in Guy, *Tudor England,* 296.

57. *Worship and Theology,* 232. See also Alan Fager Herr, *Elizabethan Sermon:* "The predilection of Elizabethan audiences for the amusing and the sensational is no mere assumption, for the most zealous of the preachers speak of it as one of their greatest problems and discouragements" (17).

58. Gerald Bray, ed., *Documents of the English Reformation,* 332.

59. Herr, *Elizabethan Sermon,* 18–19. As Herr explains, the sorry state of the clergy at this time can be attributed, at least in part, to the religious upheaval that occurred from Edward VI's reign through that of Mary to Elizabeth's assumption of the throne: "The number of lower clergy who fled from their posts at the time of the changing of religion or who were deprived of their office by the new regime is not known with any certainty, but it is certain that there was a great lack of men of the right calibre in the lower clergy and that replacements were difficult to make. The universities were not able to turn out enough men trained for the

priesthood even to begin to fill the vacancies, and so, pressed by the great need, the bishops filled the most crying gaps in the ranks with the next best men they could find, and left the less important vacancies unfilled or in the hands of lay readers" (19).

60. Ibid., 31–34.

61. Ibid., 34.

62. In his *Art of Rhetoric*, Wilson refers to this preacher as "our worthy Latimer" and goes on to paraphrase a jest Latimer delivered in his "Sermon of the Plough" (175).

63. "Traditions of the *Facetiae*," 390.

64. *Works*, 1:136. Subsequent references to this work will appear in the text.

65. "Traditions of the *Facetiae*," 394, 391.

66. *Elizabethan Sermon*, 24.

67. *Practis of Preaching*, 157. Subsequent references to this work will appear in the text.

68. *The Preacher*, 20.

69. *Arte of Prophecying*, 132 (original emphasis). Subsequent references to this work will appear in the text.

70. In the epistle dedicatory of his *Arte*, Perkins says that "prophecying" or preaching is the "most excellent gift of all." And according to Hyperius, preaching "is preferred before Baptisme or administration of the Sacraments: Like as also the hearing of the worde ought of necessitie to goe before the confession of faith" (3). On the primacy of preaching, see Horton Davies, *Worship and Theology in England*, 294–301.

71. *Birthpangs of Protestant England*, 99.

72. See also Castiglione, *Book of the Courtier*, 161; and Cicero, *De oratore*, 2.59.241.

73. *Ambition and Privilege*, 32.

74. Ibid., 34.

75. Ibid., 33. As Whigham is well aware, many men with "substantive powers," but without an aristocratic pedigree, were granted preferment under the Tudor and, especially, the Stuart regimes. What Whigham is characterizing here is the ideological campaign launched by the established gentry in order to defend "their exclusive right to power and privilege" (ibid., 32).

76. Ibid., 33 (original emphasis).

77. Ibid.

78. Ibid., 39.

79. Ibid., 36.

80. Ibid., 40.

81. Ibid.

82. For a modern discussion of jokes that come at the speaker's own expense, see Norrick, *Conversational Joking,* 45–47. I believe that Guazzo's claim about "taking" the jests of others is ahead of its time (or perhaps it's evidence of an emerging sensibility), for other early modern writers adamantly insist that the audience's laughter should always be *with* the speaker and never *at* him. In other words, being able to laugh at oneself counts as a virtue in, at least, contemporary American middle-class society. In early modern society, being laughed at was, for the most part, the equivalent of being shamed and humiliated.

83. *Poetry and Courtliness,* 34–36. Although I admire Javitch's analysis of jesting in *The Book of the Courtier* and have learned much from it, it is nevertheless flawed in two respects. First, he seems overly confident in the ability of listeners to inter-pret a jest with certainty (see below in the text). Second, he denies any political import to courtly jesting. In fact, he claims that the courtier's "functions are virtu-ally as apolitical as the setting in which he is defined" (26). As we have already seen and as we shall see again and again, all of the courtier's actions, including jesting, are deeply political.

84. Ibid., 31.

85. Ibid.

86. Ibid., 36, 35.

87. Ibid., 36.

88. *Works,* 7:133. Subsequent references to Bacon will appear in the text.

89. Ibid.

90. *Act of Creation,* 35.

91. *Lyric Wonder,* 75.

92. Castiglione is here following Cicero (*De oratore,* 2.54.219).

93. In fact, Castiglione goes on to devote a large portion of his treatment of jest-ing to what may be called an "art" of the spontaneous jest (168–89), thereby imply-ing that the true art of the spontaneous jest, as with *sprezzatura* in general, is to conceal all art with artlessness.

94. Castiglione, 174–81; Wilson, *Art of Rhetoric,* 174–75, 206, 209–10; Peacham, 33–39; Puttenham, 199–201; Day, 80.

95. Of course, not all distinguishings raise. In fact, Puttenham includes a set of figures he calls "vices" of speech, which should be avoided lest a speaker degrade himself. For further remarks on the "cultural implications of a rhetorical theory which equates true eloquence and hence true effectiveness with a system of stud-ied departures from the established patterns of everyday speech," see Howell where he equates aristocratic forms of speech with "those which originated in a repudiation of the speech of the lower classes" (*Logic and Rhetoric,* 117).

96. *Jokes,* 119.

97. *Outline of a Theory of Practice,* 11.

98. Mulkay, *On Humor,* 31.

2

The *Topoi,* or "Places," of Jesting
Official and Unofficial Territories

1. For more fully developed discussions of this distinction between "standard-ized" and "spontaneous" humor, see William F. Fry, *Sweet Madness,* 43ff. Also see Mulkay, *On Humor,* 57–66; and Norrick, *Conversational Joking,* 14–15.

2. This discussion of the indeterminacy of the meanings and effects of jests in specific situations is indebted to English, *Comic Transactions,* 10–14.

3. Ibid., 8.

4. Mary Douglas's article "Social Control of Cognition" is one of the earliest and most influential studies of joking that posits a congruence between social ambiguity and comic ambiguity. Thomas draws upon Douglas's work in his "Place of Laughter." Others have critiqued and further refined Douglas's model of joking. See, for instance, Mulkay, *On Humor,* 152; and English, *Comic Transactions,* 7–9.

5. *Schoolemaster,* M2ᵛ. Subsequent references to this work will appear in text.

6. Butler translates this passage as follows: "All forms of argument afford equal opportunity for jests." I altered his translation slightly so that I would avoid confusion: that is, *locis* is in the ablative not the nominative case.

7. *Jokes,* 207.

8. For the sake of simplicity, I will limit my discussion to the rhetorical, as opposed to the dialectical, topics. For a discussion of both kinds of topics, see Michael C. Leff, "The Topics," 23–44.

9. The doctrine of the rhetorical topics is indeed bewildering and confusing. Although Aristotle never explicitly defines the word *topos* in his *Rhetoric,* modern scholars typically translate it as "line of argument" or "strategy of argument." Aris-totle divides the *topoi* into two kinds: the special topics, which are the province of particular disciplines, such as physics and politics; and the common topics, which are applicable to all disciplines and subjects and which are thus more properly the province of rhetoric (*Rhetoric,* 1358a). Generally speaking, an Aristotelian *topos,* whether special or common, supplies an inferential link that allows a speaker to move from a premise to a conclusion (Leff, 26). For instance, the *topos* "what is rare is a greater good than what is plentiful" supplies an inferential link, allowing a speaker to move from the premise "Gold is rarer than iron" to the conclusion "Gold is a better thing than iron" (*Rhetoric,* 1364a 24). After Aristotle, *topos* takes on a number of different meanings. In Cicero's *De inventione,* Aristotle's distinc-tion between special and common topic (or *loci* and *loci communes* in Latin) becomes one between "arguments . . . [that] are related to the case that is being pleaded" and "arguments which can be transferred to many cases" (2.14.47, 2.15.48). In other words, both the special topics (*loci*) and the common topics (*loci*

communes) become, for Cicero, the sole province of rhetoric. More important, Cicero defines the *loci* not as inferential links, but as a collection or storehouse of "raw material for general use from which all arguments are drawn" (1.24.34). Here the emphasis is not on the formal relations between premise and conclusion, but on general subjects to be used in arguments (Leff, 26–30). The *loci communes* or "commonplaces" refer to general sentiments, general forms of reasoning, and even adages and maxims that would be commonly accepted by the orator's audience (2.15.48). They are to be introduced "when the audience is already convinced," that is, "when it is permissible to say something 'common'" (2.15.49). For the most part, Quintilian follows the doctrine of the topics as it is set forth in *De inventione*, but he adds another possible meaning to the *loci communes*: they can also refer to mini-speeches praising virtue or dispraising vice that an orator has composed and memorized in advance and that are general enough in application to be inserted in a longer speech as the occasion demands (2.4.22). Apparently, this additional meaning of *loci communes* comes from the *progymnasmata* or "elementary exercises" practiced by schoolboys in preparation for more advanced studies in rhetoric. One of these exercises was called a "commonplace" and was typically defined as set-speech amplifying good and evil. See Donald Lemen Clark, *Rhetoric in Greco-Roman Education,* 192–94; and Sister Joan Marie Lechner, *Concepts of the Commonplaces,* 17.

10. Cicero, *Topica,* 2.8; and Quintilian, 5.10.20.

11. *Rule of Reason,* 90.

12. *Collected Works,* 24:302. Subsequent references to this work will appear in the text.

13. And if the argumentative *topoi* are, as several of the rhetoricians claim, coincident with the jesting *topoi,* then practicing with either kind amounts to practicing with both. Lanham includes a concise discussion of the topics in his *Handlist of Rhetorical Terms* (152–53).

14. *Presence of the Word,* 82.

15. Ibid., 85. Ong frequently uses the word "commonplace" as a catchall term for all the diverse meanings and usages of the words *topos, locus,* and "place."

16. *Interfaces of the Word,* 163.

17. By way of digression (but interesting nevertheless), several modern humor theorists have made claims about or even proposed a method for joke production that echoes, albeit faintly, the method offered in ancient and early modern discussions of jesting. Discussing the theoretical limitations of the widely accepted distinction between "standardized" and "spontaneous" jokes, Neal R. Norrick claims that many supposedly "spontaneous" jokes have a "formulaic" character about them. As an example, he cites a joking remark a friend of his made when he heard of a recipe for tofu potato casserole. The friend said, "That's like the bland leading the bland." Using the familiar saying "the blind leading the blind" (the rhetoricians

would call this a *locus communis* or "commonplace"), Norrick's friend produces a joke that is simultaneously "formulaic" and "original [i.e., spontaneous] in its application" (14–15). Castiglione identifies a similar technique as one of the jesting *topoi:* "It is also a meerye devise to mingle together a verse or mo, takying it in an other meeninge then the Author doeth, or some other commune sayinge. Sometyme in the verye same meanynge, but alteringe a woorde" (170). Norrick's friend uses a "commune sayinge" and by "alteringe a woorde," produces a joke. In *What's So Funny,* Murray S. Davis, who subscribes to the incongruity theory of humor, is even closer to the rhetoricians when he says there is a "general technique comics use to explode phenomena into laughter." He calls this technique the "humorizer" (a cringe-producing coinage) and says comedians use it "to rub various things against their topic until they find one that can scratch off its attributes into incongruities or ambiguities or preferably both, generating the spark of laughter." Davis goes on to specify the nature of this process in a way that is not unlike running a subject or issue through the *topoi:* "The humorizer may produce humor by continually juxtaposing phenomena until a pair appears whose attributes are incongruous" (25). Although Norrick's and Davis's observations and claims about the creation of humor are not as systematic as topical invention, they suggest a view on joke production that is not altogether different from that found in ancient and early modern handbooks on oratory and courtly conduct: in their daily uses of humor, speakers resort to recurrent subjects and recurrent patterns of thought and language to produce a potentially infinite number of jests and witticisms.

18. Mulkay, *On Humor,* 26.

19. Davis, *What's So Funny,* 50–55.

20. My use of the word "uncooperative" is an intentional allusion to H. P. Grice's cooperative principle and his studies of conversational implicature. Although the handbooks never go so far as to articulate a theory about the normative forces of conversation, they at least make many obvious gestures in that direction. See Peter Burke, *Art of Conversation,* 91.

21. Fry, *Sweet Madness,* 138.

22. Leff, "The Topics," 29.

23. Mulkay, *On Humor,* 54. Mulkay's choice of the word "natural" is misleading and contradicts his definition of this type of humor, for it suggests that some forms of humor are created by nature independent of human fashioning, while his definition clearly asserts that this form of humor is a social construction.

24. Ibid.

25. See Cicero, *De oratore,* 2.65.261–63, 2.66.267–68, and 2.67.269–73; and Castiglione, 175–84.

26. The topics of genus, species, antecedents, and consequents appear in Cicero's *Topica,* a treatise on invention Cicero wrote toward the end of his life. His treatment of the *loci* in this work differs considerably from the one presented in

De inventione where the *loci* are primarily to be used to generate "raw material for general use" (*De inventione,* 1.24.34). In the *Topica,* by contrast, there is "greater emphasis on matters of logical relation" (Leff, 30).

27. Sister Miriam Joseph, *Shakespeare's Use of the Arts of Language,* 34.

28. When I say that calling attention to the lie of another may be "tactless," I am thinking of Erving Goffman's remarks on "protective practices" whereby conversational participants work "to save the definition of the situation projected by another" (*Presentation of Self,* 13–14). The impulse to engage in such "practices" was probably felt less strongly in early modern society where expressions of hostility, although increasingly censored, were relatively less inhibited. See Elias, *Civilizing Process,* 156–68.

29. *Rhetoric,* 226.

30. On changes in subjects of laughter across culture, see Christie Davies, "Ethnic Jokes," 383–403. On changes across time, see Freud, *Jokes,* 149–51; Thomas, "Place of Laughter," 77; and Douglas, "Social Control of Cognition," 365–66.

31. "Social Control of Cognition," 375.

32. Ibid., 365.

33. Ibid., 366

34. *On Humor,* 176.

35. My examination of stock characters and situations is by no means exhaustive. For a more complete catalog of stock characters of Tudor and Stuart jests, see Thomas, "Place of Laughter."

36. "Place of Laughter," 78.

37. Ibid. The full text of this jest can be found in Zall's anthology *A Hundred Merry Tales,* 247–48.

38. English, *Comic Transactions,* 8.

39. John Guy, *Tudor England,* 290.

40. H. Davies, *Worship and Theology in England,* 234–37.

41. A variation of this jest appears in *A Hundred Merry Tales,* and the editor supplies the following didactic tag: "By this tale a man may see that it is but folly to show or to teach virtue to them that have no pleasure nor mind thereto" (130). *A Hundred Merry Tales* was published in 1526—that is, before Henry's break with Rome—and anti-Catholic sentiments might not impinge as powerfully as they do in Wilson's variation.

42. "Language, Identity and Ethnic Jokes," 39.

43. Ibid., 42.

44. Ibid., 49.

45. For instance, Edward entered Wales in 1276 to crush the obstinate Llewelyn; two centuries later, Owen Glendower repeatedly eluded the grasp of Henry IV. In 1535, a year before the Act of Union, the preamble in the "Bill Concerning Councils in Wales" reads: "The people of Wales and Marches . . . have long time

continued and persevered in perpetration and commission of divers and manifold thefts, murders, rebellions etc. . . .which malefacts and scerelous deeds be so rooted and fixed in the same people, that they be not like to cease unless some sharp correction and punishment for redress and amputation of the premises be provided." This passage is quoted in J. Gwynfor Jones, *Wales and the Tudor State,* 7. Jones examines the rhetorical nature of this passage, observing that it was used to define the situation in Wales in such a way that it seemed to demand immediate attention (and intervention) by the English crown.

46. Susan Purdie, *Comedy,* 60–61.

47. Keith Wrightson discusses the possibility of early modern servants role-playing "out of a canny self-interest" in his *English Society* (60).

48. According to Whigham, master-servant relations in early modern England experienced a transformation from "unbounded service" to "contractual cash-nexus relations." The results of this transformation were far-reaching, and included decreases in "mutual comprehension" between masters and servants and increases in freedom to form other, oftentimes lateral allegiances and friendships (*Seizures of the Will,* 13–14).

3
Point out Something Unseemly in No Unseemly Manner
ORATORS, COURTIERS, AND BUFFOONS

1. *Taking Humour Seriously,* 147.

2. Ibid., 148–49.

3. Elias, *Civilizing Process,* 159.

4. Ibid., 165.

5. Ibid., 177.

6. Freud, *Jokes,* 121.

7. Ibid., 122.

8. Ibid., 123.

9. It is important to note that courtiers and nobles did still fight among themselves during Elizabeth's reign. In his *Crisis of the Aristocracy,* Lawrence Stone cites many instances of aristocrats' fighting with one another, especially over "prestige and property" (223). However, as Stone himself argues, the occurrence of such instances gradually decreased in late-sixteenth- and early-seventeenth-century England; ironically, one the factors contributing to this decline was the emergence of a "new ethical code [among the aristocracy]—the code of the duel" (243).

10. In his *Ethics,* Aristotle suggests that changes in stylistic and substantive predilections indicate advances in civilization. While enumerating the differences between the jesting of a buffoon and a witty gentleman, Aristotle compares each character type to Old and New Comedy, respectively: "The difference [between a

buffoon and a gentleman] may be seen by comparing the old and modern comedies; the earlier dramatists found their fun in obscenity, the modern prefer innuendo, which marks a great advance in decorum" (4.8.6). This comparison suggests
that smutty humor is less civilized than the more refined humor delivered through
innuendo.

11. Palmer discusses the boundary between the offensive and the funny in modern Western culture, and he also includes an interesting comparative analysis of
how this boundary is negotiated in a preindustrial culture (*Taking Humour Seriously,* 163ff.).

12. For another early modern imitation of this passage from Cicero, see Castiglione, *Book of the Courtier,* 158.

13. The third book of *The Courtier* is, of course, about the ideal female courtier
and treats, among other things, desirable character traits and virtues found in
women, as well as appropriate forms of interaction between men and women at
court. Guazzo also includes a relatively brief discussion of "conversation with
women" (1:232–45).

14. Implicit in jest books of the period is a rather different perspective, for their
compilers seem to have followed an "anything goes" policy in the case of women:
they are frequently the victims of obscene jests by men, but they are just as frequently portrayed as comic protagonists, cleverly outjesting and outthinking men.

15. Late in his treatment of jesting, Castiglione also raises the issue of women
and jesting both as a kind of afterthought to the present discussion and as a segue
into the next book, which concerns the ideal female courtier. According to him, a
courtier should never target a woman's "honesty" because "women are in the
number of selie soules and persons in miserye." In other words, Castiglione classifies women among the wretched who, as we saw above, are to be spared from an
orator's or courtier's jests. When explaining why they should be spared, Castiglione offers a reason similar to that of Robson: that is, "they have not weapon to
defende themselves" (190). This remark suggests not only that women are unworthy opponents, but also that jesting is a phallic prerogative of men.

16. "Place of Laughter," 80.

17. Ibid.

18. *Taking Humour Seriously,* 149.

19. Ibid.

20. *Ambition and Privilege,* 64.

21. This anecdote appears in a manuscript compiled by Nicholas Lestrange
which was eventually published in a collection edited by William J. Thomas,
Anecdotes and Traditions (15).

22. In some instances, however, an audience may respond favorably to an
incomprehensible jest, perhaps in the way that children delight in nonsense (Freud,
Jokes, 152–56). In *Twelfth Night,* the dim-witted Sir Andrew Aguecheek always

seems to miss the jokes told by the others in the play, but his failure to understand does not necessarily diminish the pleasure he derives from them. At one point, Sir Andrew inordinately praises Feste for his "gracious fooling last night." Sir Andrew, as he himself admits, was particularly struck by Feste's story of "Pigrogromitus, of the Vapians passing the quinoctial of Quebus" (2.3.23–24). Sir Andrew was so taken with this story, in fact, that he sent Feste a sixpence. When Sir Andrew asks Feste if he had received the money, Feste answers nonsensically, "I did impeticos thy gratility; for Malvolio's nose is no whipstock. My lady has a white hand, and the Myrmidons are no bottle-ale houses" (2.3.26–28). This gibberish impresses Sir Andrew even more than last night's gibberish about Pigrogromitus, and he says, "Excellent! Why this is the best fooling, when all is done" (2.3.29–30). Perhaps Sir Andrew believes that he is participating in a very erudite and witty conversation; he pretends to get the joke to show that he is privy to this secret language he thinks Feste is speaking. Or perhaps Sir Andrew's delight may simply issue from a pleasure similar to the pleasure children derive from nonsense: the enjoyment of playing with words, creating pleasurable rhythms and rhymes, and violating one of the most basic requirements and expectations of language—that it should make sense (Purdie, *Comedy,* 13; and Freud, *Jokes,* 153). Whatever the pleasure Sir Andrew gets from nonsense, Feste's response has the effect of mocking him, even if he doesn't realize he is being mocked. As Freud explains, the technique of many nonsense jokes "consists . . . in presenting something that is stupid and nonsensical, the sense of which lies in the revelation and demonstration of something else that is stupid and nonsensical" (67). In this case, the sense of Feste's nonsense, the "something else," is the stupidity of Sir Andrew who praises Feste's feigned and seeming erudition, his story of Pigrogromitus, thinking that it was real erudition. Our pleasure in watching this absurd exchange may partially reside in the sheer nonsense of Feste's remark which Freud would say temporarily releases us from the demands of logic and reason. In this way, part of our pleasure may be very similar to that of Sir Andrew who also may enjoy the nonsense in and of itself. However, the comic exchange may open up another source of pleasure, one that differentiates us from Sir Andrew, and that pleasure resides in the fact that Sir Andrew never figures out that he has been duped: he is excluded from the "revelation and demonstration" of his own stupidity.

23. On laughter as providing evaluative information, see Norrick, *Conversational Joking,* 23.

24. There are ways for speakers to distance themselves from the jokes they tell. Speakers might introduce jests with some variation of the phrase "I heard a good one." Humor theorists typically read such phrases as cuing or framing devices, ways to control the expectations of listeners and let them know that something humorous is on the way. But couldn't such phrases be used as distancing strategies as well: a way of saying, "This is not my own joke, but one that I heard someone

else tell before"? If the joke should fail, then the speaker could distance himself or herself from its failure.

25. This issue of performative failure in modern uses of humor and joking is explored by Palmer in *Taking Humour Seriously,* chap. 13.

26. *Sprezzatura* has antecedents in classical rhetoric, particularly in Cicero's expression *diligens neglegentia* or "careful negligence" where Cicero uses it to describe a desired feature of the plain or unadorned level of style (*Orator,* 23.78). In early modern courtesy theory, the scope of the similar concept *sprezzatura* expands to encompass all aspect of the courtier's everyday life.

27. This jest is adapted from one in Cicero, *De oratore,* 2.60.246.

28. Mulkay, *On Humor,* 22–30.

29. According to Freud, the "form" of a joke serves as a vehicle for the expression of some tendentious message while, at the same time, attracting the attention of listeners from that message (123). The distracting features of the joke "form" do not completely conceal the tendentious import of the joke; rather, it offers that message obliquely and through indirection. In a roundabout way, Freud's description of the purpose and operation of the joke "form" seems analogous to that of an enthymeme, if we define that term as a truncated syllogism with a missing premise. That is, just as listeners must reconstruct for themselves the tendentious import of a joke, so too must listeners, when hearing an enthymeme, supply the missing premise. If we push this analogy far enough, we could say that an enthymeme, like a joke, implies a rhetoric of distraction.

30. According to the manuals' classification of the practical risks of jesting, this rule would fall under inappropriate objects of laughter. That is, the "honestie" of a woman is an inappropriate topic of laughter.

31. *Comedy,* 129 (original emphasis).

32. Ibid., 137.

33. In "Outlandish Fears," Rebhorn explores the spatial imagery ancient and early modern rhetoricians often used to define decorum.

34. Ibid. For a detailed account of the social types who frequented alehouse during the period, see Peter Clark, *English Alehouse,* chap. 6.

35. *Advice to a Son,* ed. Louis B. Wright, 13.

36. Freud, *Jokes,* 119.

37. Later, while listing the "diverse effectes in jestes," Castiglione says there are jests that "bite sometime privily, otherwhile openlye" (189), but then he quickly adds the qualification that a courtier "be not *so* bitter and bitinge" in his jests (190, emphasis added).

38. This division of jests into "two kindes" has a long history in the rhetorical discourse on jesting. Grant finds it in early proverbial formulations about jesting by several of the pre-Socratics and then traces it through the writings of Aristotle

and Cicero. She uses the terms "liberal" and "illiberal" to denote each kind, terms which she borrows from Cicero who uses them in *De oratore, Orator,* and *De officiis.* However, she ignores their obvious class connotations: a *liberalis* is literally a "freeman" or "citizen," but it can also be taken to mean a "gentleman," while an *illiberalis* is a "slave," "noncitizen," or some one who is crude or ignoble.

39. Rebhorn, "Baldesar Castiglione," 242.

40. Ibid., 255–56. Although Rebhorn is right in claiming that courtiers and buffoons were both "denizens of the court," he seems to overestimate the social, spatial, and professional distance between Roman orators and comic performers, between the rostrum and the stage.

41. Ibid., 256.

42. *Popular Culture,* 280–81.

43. "Place of Laughter," 80.

44. This statement should be qualified. The emergence of a conscious rhetorical art in Roman culture was gradual and often met resistance, especially in the early years of the Roman Republic. Some of the factors that impeded this process included a cultural preference for deeds over words, a distaste for anything associated with the Greeks who were the principal bearers of rhetorical theory and teachings to the Romans, and a legal system that, in its earlier manifestations, was not conducive to speech making. Even so, an ability to speak well was listed among the traditional Roman virtues as early as the third century BCE, and by the time of Cicero, the orator's position as statesman, politician, and legal advocate was firmly established (Kennedy, *Roman Rhetoric,* chap. 1). After the fall of the Republic and under the emperors, the importance of the orator in society diminished, and he had little, if any, real political power, as Tacitus's *Dialogus de oratoribus* amply reveals (see especially the final speech of Maternus, 36–41).

45. Although this myth is commonly discussed as "Ciceronian," its earliest extant version appears in Isocrates' "Panegyricus" and again in his "Antidosis." Cicero's first, and most famous, version appears in his *De inventione* (2.2.2–3). Another rendition can be found in his *De oratore* (1.8.33–34). Early modern versions appear in Wilson's *Rhetoric* (41–43), Rainolde (A1ʳ–A2ᵛ), Peacham (iiiʳ–iiiᵛ), and Puttenham (22–24). For Puttenham, it is poetry (although a highly rhetorical poetry) that was the "cause and occasion of the first assemblies" of humans.

46. The title of Rainolde's treatise could be read as a pun. In one sense, his treatise is a "foundacion" because it offers instructions for and examples of the elementary exercise (i.e., the *progymnasmata*) which are the first stage, or foundation, for more advanced rhetorical training. In another sense, rhetoric, by Rainolde's account, is itself a "foundacion": it is the basis for an orderly and stable society.

47. Whigham discusses the threat a hierarchy based on intellect or ability poses to traditional hierarchies based on birth and landed wealth (*Ambition and Privilege,* 34).

48. These competing impulses (to preserve yet disrupt the existing social order) found in early modern representations of orators are explored by Rebhorn in great detail. See his *Emperor of Men's Minds,* esp. chaps. 1 and 2.

49. Quoted in Anthony S. G. Edwards, *Skelton,* 55.

50. Ibid., 60.

51. Zall, *Hundred Merry Tales,* 324.

52. Ibid., 328, 332–34, 335.

53. This paragraph and the one following it are indebted to the excellent analysis of More's wit in Lipking, "Traditions of the *Facetiae,*" 345–87.

54. On the sources of More's epigrams, see the introduction to volume 3 of his *Complete Works.*

55. Ibid., 75.

56. See Ackroyd, *Life of Thomas More,* 230; and Lipking, "Traditions of the *Facetiae,*" 368–75.

57. Quoted in Lipking, "Traditions of the *Facetiae,*" 363.

58. Quoted in Jackson Campbell Boswell, *Sir Thomas More,* 320. I owe Anne Lake Prescott thanks for directing me to Tyndale's name-calling and to Foxe's criticism of More's behavior on the scaffold (see below).

59. The relevant passages appear in a character sketch of More that Erasmus addressed to Ulrich von Hutton. They are quoted and translated by Lipking, "Traditions of the *Facetiae,*" 350–51. Although Erasmus repeatedly says that More's wit never went so far as buffoonery, the effort he invests in making this claim renders it equivocal at best.

60. *Gabriel Harvey's Marginalia,* ed. G. C. Moore Smith, 113–14.

61. "Traditions of the *Facetiae,*" 413.

62. *Nugae Antiquae,* 1:x.

63. On the reliability of this account of the origin of Harington's translation, see Townsend Rich, *Harington and Ariosto,* 23–29.

64. D. H. Craig, *Sir John Harington,* 12.

65. Ibid., 18.

66. *Letters and Epigrams,* ed. Norman Egbert McClure, 176.

67. *Nugae Antiquae,* 1:166.

68. Rich, *Harington and Ariosto,* 13.

69. The title is a multiple pun: "stale" can also mean "urine, etc."; and "a jacks" is an outhouse.

70. *Letters and Epigrams,* 65–66.

71. *Nugae Antiquae,* 1:240.

72. *Metamorphosis of Ajax,* 212.

73. *Nugae Antiquae,* 1:245.

74. *Letters and Epigrams,* 97.

75. Ibid., 110.

4

Audience

<small>The Many-Headed Monster</small>

1. Rebhorn, *Emperor of Men's Minds,* 34.

2. Ibid., 36

3. Ibid., 45

4. Ibid., 42.

5. For other ancient examples of how jesting refreshes an audience, see Aristotle, *Rhetoric,* 1415a; and Quintilian, 6.3.1.

6. Lipking, "Traditions of the *Facetiae,*" 318.

7. Olson, *Literature as Recreation,* 89.

8. Ibid., 99.

9. *Treatise on Laughter,* 44–45. Subsequent references to this work will appear in the text.

10. Leonard Barkan, *Nature's Work of Art,* 3.

11. Thomas Starkey, *Dialogue,* 57.

12. The irony in these last two instances, of course, is that, ultimately, it is the "swet" of peasants and servants that supply masters and rulers with periods of leisure.

13. See, for instance, Max Gluckman, *Custom and Conflict,* chap. 5; and Victor Turner, *Ritual Process,* chap. 5. Both writers discuss ritual inversions in primitive cultures and argue that rituals that may appear to challenge the social order actually preserve it. Gluckman says that "the lifting of normal taboos and restraints [during rituals] obviously serves to emphasize them." In *Popular Culture,* Peter Burke, using these two anthropologists as his point of departure, examines the relevance of their theories to early modern Europe (199–204). He argues that the ritual inversions that were part of popular festivals may not always serve the status quo. In fact, he examines several historical instances when ritual inversions offered the occasion for social revolt. For a more recent discussion of the social functions of ritual and festivity, see Linda Woodbridge and Edward Berry, introduction to *True Rites and Maimed Rites,* 1–43.

14. During the Stuart period, Castiglione's quasi-history of the origins of recreation actually plays itself out in James I's (and later his son's) repeated attempts to revive and protect "public mirth" not only for its associations with the Anglican church but also as an extension of his own political power. Instrumental in these attempts was James's *Basilikon Doron.* Although James composed this work before assuming the throne of England, it was reissued in 1603 and 1616, and it contains a statement that echoes Castiglione. James says that he knows of "no better meane . . . to rule" than to appoint,

> certaine dayes in the yeere . . . for delighting the people with publicke spectacles of all honest games, and exercises of armes: as also for conveening of

neighbours, for entertaining friendship and heartliness, by honest feasting
and merriness: For I cannot see what greater superstition can be in making playes and lawfull games in Maie, and good cheere at Christmas, then
in eating fish in Lent, and upon Fridays . . . so that alwayes the Sabboths
be kept holy, and no unlawfull pastime be used: And as this forme of con-
tenting the peoples mindes, hath beene used in all well governed Repub-
licks: so will it make you [James's son] to performe in your government
that olde good sentence,

    Omne tulit punctum, qui miscuit utile dulci. (27)

Leah Marcus documents James's and Charles's efforts to revive and restore "public mirth" (and the politics these efforts entailed) in *Politics of Mirth.*

15. Elias, *Civilizing Process,* 202.

16. Ibid.

17. Freud, *Jokes,* 122–23 (original emphasis).

18. By way of digression, we might note that the pleasure the downstairs
characters in *Twelfth Night* experience in shaming Malvolio is closely associated
with seeing and watching. Maria will write a letter by which she will make Malvolio suppose that Olivia is in love with him. She then plans to leave it in a place
where Malvolio will find and read it and where she and her companions can
"observe his construction of it" (2.3.174). Everything goes according to plan, the
letter planted, the companions hidden where they can watch. Malvolio enters, and
Maria says to her coconspirators, "Observe him, for the love of mockery" (2.5.18).
Following a suggestion in the letter, Malvolio dresses himself in yellow stockings
with cross-garters. That is, he turns himself into a spectacle—someone who is
visually ridiculous.

19. There is, of course, a paradox implicit in all of these passages: in exhibiting
his power over listeners by making them laugh irresistibly, the speaker actually
knocks them, if only temporarily, out of control. The manuals never confront this
possibility directly, but we need only turn to documents of the period detailing
instances in which revelers turned into rioters and threatened not only the peace
but also the equilibrium of the body politic. According to Peter Burke, festive rituals, which some modern scholars read as opportunities for the public to vent their
aggression in a relatively safe way, occasionally turned into riots: "in Europe
between 1500 and 1800 rituals of revolt did coexist with serious questioning of the
social, political and religious order. Protest was expressed in ritualised forms, but
the ritual was not always sufficient to contain the protest" (203). Thomas explores
this issue in late Tudor and Stuart England and arrives at an interesting conclusion. During the medieval period and through the first half of the sixteenth century, festive rituals and rites of inversion were generally tolerated, despite frequent
attacks by members of the clergy. Later, however, "the spread of religious and

political discord made mockery and affront appear a threat to the social order, rather than a means of symbolic reinforcement. . . . So long as the social hierarchy itself went unchallenged, the rites of inversion could be safely tolerated; their very levity reflected an underlying security. But once men had begun to question the principles of that hierarchy, then an annual ritual which emphasized its arbitrary nature came to seem positively dangerous" ("Place of Laughter," 79).

20. *Body Embarrassed,* 124.

21. On advice concerning speakers refraining from laughing at their own jests, see Cicero's discussion of irony, where he recommends that a speaker jest with a solemn expression and "with austerity" in order to enhance the effectiveness of the jest (*De oratore,* 2.67.269–71). Castiglione also suggests that some forms of jesting are more effective if delivered with a "certein gravitie" (184). The implication here, as in Cicero, is that the comic incongruity upon which a jest relies will be enhanced by an incongruous delivery—that is, delivering a jest in an earnest manner. Della Casa offers more explicit advice: a speaker should "not laughe at his owne gestes." His reasoning is that the listeners will think the speaker, by laughing at his own jests, is indirectly praising himself (115). In the context of the manuals' views on the bodily impact of laughing, there seems to be another motive for refraining from laughter: the nonlaughing speaker evidences his difference from, and power over, his laughing audience.

22. *Rhetoric,* 285–86.

23. Ibid., 286.

24. *Anatomy of Melancholy,* vol. 1: 53.

25. Biester offers a similar interpretation of the two passages just quoted from Burton and Castiglione (*Lyric Wonder,* 77).

26. The Queen's reference comes from *Letters and Epigrams* (90), and the remark attributed to James appears in *Nugae Antiquae* (1:391).

27. Although Puttenham does not explicitly say they were drinking from communal cups, I'm inferring that this is the case because it explains why Heywood had to "call for his drinke" so often. This inference also accounts for the Duke's mention of "those cuppes" later in the text.

28. Thomas, "Place of Laughter," 80.

29. *On Humour,* 64.

30. Marcus, *Politics of Mirth,* chap. 1.

31. *Shakespeare and the Popular Tradition,* 161.

32. Ibid., 161ff.

33. Ibid., 169.

Bibliography

Ackroyd, Peter. *The Life of Thomas More*. New York: Doubleday, 1998.

Altman, Joel. *Tudor Play of Mind: Rhetorical Inquiry and the Development of Elizabethan Drama*. Berkeley: University of California Press, 1978.

Anselment, Raymond A. *"Betwixt Jest and Earnest": Marprelate, Milton, Swift and the Decorum of Religious Ridicule*. Toronto: University of Toronto Press, 1979.

Aristotle. *Rhetoric*. Trans. Rhys Roberts. New York: Modern Library, 1954.

————. *Nicomachean Ethics*. Trans. H. Rackham. Cambridge: Harvard University Press, 1934.

Arndt, E. "De Ridiculi Doctrina Rhetorica." Ph.D. diss., University of Bonn, 1904.

Augustine. *On Christian Doctrine*. Trans. D. W. Robertson, Jr. New York: Macmillan, 1986.

Bacon, Francis. *Works*. 14 vols. Ed. James Spedding, Robert Leslie Ellis, and Douglas Denon. Heath, New York: Garret Press, 1968.

Bakhtin, Mikhail. *Rabelais and His World*. Trans. Helene Iswolsky. Bloomington: Indiana University Press, 1984.

Barkan, Leonard. *Nature's Work of Art: The Human Body as Image of the World*. New Haven: Yale University Press, 1975.

Beacham, Richard C. *The Roman Theatre and Its Audience*. Cambridge: Harvard University Press, 1991.

Beier, A. L. *Masterless Men: The Vagrancy Problem in England, 1560–1640*. London: Methuen, 1985.

Biester, James. *Lyric Wonder: Rhetoric and Wit in Renaissance English Poetry*. Ithaca: Cornell University Press, 1997.

Blench, J. W. *Preaching in England in the Late Fifteenth and Sixteenth Centuries*. New York: Barnes and Noble, 1964.

Boswell, Jackson Campbell. *Sir Thomas More in the English Renaissance: An Annotated Catalogue*. Binghamton, N.Y.: Medieval and Renaissance Texts and Studies, 1994.

Bourdieu, Pierre. *Outline of a Theory of Practice*. Trans. Richard Nice. Cambridge: Cambridge University Press, 1977.

Bray, Gerald, ed. *Documents of the English Reformation*. Minneapolis, Minn.: Fortress Press, 1994.

Brewer, Derek. "Prose Jest-Books in the Sixteenth and Seventeenth Centuries in England." In *A Cultural History of Humour: From Antiquity to the Present Day*, ed. Jan Bremmer and Herman Roodenberg, 90–111. Cambridge: Polity Press, 1997.

Burke, Kenneth. *A Rhetoric of Motives*. Berkeley: University of Californian Press, 1969.

Burke, Peter. *The Art of Conversation*. Ithaca: Cornell University Press, 1993.

———. *Popular Culture in Early Modern Europe*. London: Maurice Temple Smith, 1978.

Burton, Robert. *Anatomy of Melancholy*. 2 vols. Ed. Thomas C. Faulkner, Nicolas K. Kiessling, and Rhonda L. Blair. Oxford: Clarendon Press, 1989.

Castiglione, Baldesar. *The Book of the Courtier*. 1528. Trans. Sir Thomas Hoby. 1561. London: Tudor Translations, 1900.

Cicero. *De inventione*. Trans. H. M. Hubbell. Cambridge: Harvard University Press, 1949.

———. *De oratore*. 2 vols. Trans. E. W. Sutton and H. Rackham. Cambridge: Harvard University Press, 1942.

———. *De officiis*. Trans. Walter Miller. Cambridge: Harvard University Press, 1913.

———. *Brutus, orator*. Trans. G. L. Hendrickson and H. M. Hubbell. Cambridge: Harvard University Press, 1962.

———. *Letters to Atticus*. 3 vols. Trans. E. O. Winstedt. Cambridge: Harvard University Press, 1937.

———. *Topica*. Trans. H. M. Hubbell. Cambridge: Harvard University Press, 1949.

[Cicero]. *Ad Herennium*. Trans. H. Caplan. Cambridge: Harvard University Press, 1954.

Clark, Donald Lemen. *Rhetoric in Greco-Roman Education*. New York: Columbia University Press, 1957.

Clark, Peter. *The English Alehouse: A Social History, 1200–1830*. London: Longman, 1983.

Clark, Peter, and David Souden, eds. *Migration and Society in Early Modern England*. Totowa, N.J.: Barnes and Noble, 1987.

Collinson, Patrick. *The Birthpangs of Protestant England: Religious and Cultural Change in the Sixteenth and Seventeenth Centuries*. New York: St. Martin's Press, 1988.

Corbett, Edward P. J. *Classical Rhetoric for the Modern Student*. New York: Oxford University Press, 1971.

Craig, D. H. *Sir John Harington*. Boston: Twayne, 1985.

Crockett, Bryan. *The Play of Paradox: Stage and Sermon in Renaissance England.* Philadelphia: University of Pennsylvania Press, 1995.

Curtius, E. R. *European Literature and the Latin Middle Ages.* Trans. Willard R. Task. Princeton: Princeton University Press, 1953.

Davies, Christie. "Language, Identity, and Ethnic Jokes about Stupidity." *International Journal of the Sociology of Language* 65 (1987): 39–52.

———. "Ethnic Jokes, Moral Values and Social Boundaries." *British Journal of Sociology* 33 (1982): 383–403.

Davies, Horton. *Worship and Theology in England.* Vol. 1, *From Cranmer to Hooker, 1534–1603.* Princeton: Princeton University Press, 1970.

Davis, Murray S. *What's So Funny? The Comic Conception of Culture and Society.* Chicago: University of Chicago Press, 1993.

Day, Angel. *The English Secretary.* 1599. Intro. Robert O. Evans. Gainesville, Fla.: Scholars' Facsimiles and Reprints, 1967.

Dekker, Thomas. *Plague Pamphlets of Thomas Dekker.* Ed. F. P. Wilson. Oxford: Clarendon Press, 1925.

Della Casa, Giovanni. *Galateo.* 1558. Trans. Robert Peterson. 1576. Ed. Lewis Einstein. London: Grant Richards, 1914.

DeWitt, Norman W. "Litigation in the Forum in Cicero's Time." *Classical Philology* 21 (1926): 218–24.

Douglas, Mary. "The Social Control of Cognition: Some Factors in Joke Perception." *Man: The Journal of the Royal Anthropological Institute* 3 (1968): 361–76.

Edwards, Anthony S. G., ed. *Skelton: The Critical Heritage.* London: Routledge and Kegan Paul, 1981.

Elias, Norbert. *The Civilizing Process.* Trans. Edmund Jephcott. Oxford: Basil Blackwell, 1982.

English, James F. *Comic Transactions: Literature, Humor, and the Politics of Community in Twentieth-Century Britain.* Ithaca: Cornell University Press, 1994.

Enos, Richard Leo. *The Literate Mode of Cicero's Legal Rhetoric.* Carbondale: Southern Illinois University Press, 1988.

Erasmus. *Apophthegmes.* Trans. Nicholas Udall. 1531. Amsterdam: Da Capo Press, 1969.

———. *De Duplici Copia Verborum ac Rerum.* Ed. Craig R. Thompson. Toronto: University of Toronto Press, 1978.

———. *Ecclesiastae.* Basel, 1535.

Fine, Gary Alan. "Sociological Approaches to the Study of Humor." In *Handbook of Humor Research,* ed. Paul McGhee and Jeffrey Goldstein, 1: 159–81 New York: Springer-Verlag, 1983.

Foxe, John. *The Acts and Monuments.* 8 vols. New York: AMS Press, 1965.

Freud, Sigmund. *Jokes and Their Relation to the Unconscious.* 1905. Trans. and ed. James Strachey. New York: W. W. Norton, 1960.

Fry, William F. *Sweet Madness: A Study of Humor.* Palo Alto, Calif.: Pacific Books, 1963.

Geffcken, Katherine A. *Comedy in the Pro Caelio.* Leiden, Netherlands: E. J. Brill, 1973.

Gluckman, Max. *Custom and Conflict in Africa.* New York: Barnes and Noble, 1964.

Goffman, Erving. *The Presentation of Self in Everyday Life.* New York: Doubleday, 1965.

Golden, James L., and Edward P. J. Corbett, eds. *The Rhetoric of Blair, Campbell, and Whately.* Carbondale: Southern Illinois University Press, 1990.

Grant, Mary A. *The Ancient Theories of the Laughable: The Greek Rhetoricians and Cicero.* University of Wisconsin Studies in Language and Literature, no. 21. Madison: University of Wisconsin Press, 1924.

Guazzo, Stefano. *The Civile Conversation of M. Steeven Guazzo.* 2 vols. Trans. George Pettie (books 2–3, 1581) and Bartholomew Young (book 4, 1586). Tudor Translations. London: Constable, 1925.

Gurevich, Aaron. "Bakhtin and His Theory of Carnival." In *A Cultural History of Humour: From Antiquity to the Present Day,* ed. Jan Bremmer and Herman Roodenberg, 54–60. Cambridge: Polity Press, 1997.

Guy, John. *Tudor England.* Oxford: Oxford University Press, 1988.

Hariman, Robert. "Decorum, Power, and the Courtly Style." *Quarterly Journal of Speech* 78 (1992): 149–72.

Harington, Sir John. *Nugae Antiquae.* 2 vols. Ed. Henry Harington and Thomas Park. 1804. New York: AMS Press, 1966.

————. *The Letters and Epigrams of Sir John Harington.* Ed. Norman Egbert McClure. Philadelphia: University of Pennsylvania Press, 1930.

————. *A New Discourse of a Stale Subject, called the Metamorphosis of Ajax.* Ed. Elizabeth Story Donno. New York: Columbia University Press, 1962.

Harvey, Gabriel. *Gabriel Harvey's Marginalia.* Ed. G. C. Moore Smith. Stratford: Shakespeare Head Press, 1913.

Hemminsen, Niels. *The Preacher.* Trans. John Horsfall. 1574. Ed. R. C. Alston. Menston, England: Scolar Press, 1972.

Herr, Alan Fager. *The Elizabethan Sermon: A Survey and a Bibliography.* New York: Octagon Books, 1969.

Horner, Winifred Bryan, and Keri Morris Barton. "The Eighteenth Century." In *The Present State of Scholarship in Historical and Contemporary Rhetoric,* ed. Winifred Bryan Horner, 114–50. Columbia: University of Missouri Press, 1990.

Howell, Wilbur S. *Logic and Rhetoric in England, 1500–1700.* Princeton: Princeton University Press, 1956.

Hudson, Hoyt H. *The Epigram in the English Renaissance.* Princeton: Princeton University Press, 1947.

Hyperius, Andreas. *The Practis of Preaching*. Trans. John Ludham. London, 1577.

Isocrates. *Works*. 3 vols. Trans. George Norlin. Cambridge: Harvard University Press, 1929.

James I. *The Political Works of James I*. Intro. Charles Howard McIlwain. Cambridge: Harvard University Press, 1918.

Javitch, Daniel. *Poetry and Courtliness in Renaissance England*. Princeton: Princeton University Press, 1978.

Jones, J. Gwynfor. *Wales and the Tudor State: Government, Religious Change and the Social Order, 1534–1603*. Cardiff: University of Wales Press, 1989.

Joseph, Sister Miriam. *Shakespeare's Use of the Arts of Language*. New York: Columbia University Press, 1947.

Joubert, Laurent. *Treatise on Laughter*. 1579. Trans. Gregory David de Rocher. Tuscaloosa: University of Alabama Press, 1980.

Kennedy, George A. *The Art of Rhetoric in the Roman World*. Princeton: Princeton University Press, 1972.

Koestler, Arthur. *The Act of Creation*. New York: Macmillan, 1964.

Lanham, Richard. *Handlist of Rhetorical Terms*. 2d ed. Berkeley: University of California Press, 1991.

Latimer, Hugh. *Works*. 2 vols. Ed. George Elwes Corrie. Cambridge: Parker Society, 1844–45.

Lechner, Sister Joan Marie. *Renaissance Concepts of the Commonplaces*. New York: Pageant Press, 1962.

Leff, Michael. "The Topics of Argumentative Invention in Latin Rhetorical Theory from Cicero to Boethius." *Rhetorica* 1 (1983): 23–44.

Lipking, Joanna Brizdale. "Traditions of the *Facetiae* and Their Influence in Tudor England." Ph.D. diss., Columbia University, 1970.

Luck, George. "Vir Facetus: A Renaissance Ideal." *Studies in Philology* 55 (1958): 107–21.

Macrobius. *The Saturnalia*. Trans. Percival Vaughan Davies. New York: Columbia University Press, 1969.

Mangan, Michael. *A Preface to Shakespeare's Comedies*. London: Longman, 1996.

Marcus, Leah S. *The Politics of Mirth: Jonson, Herrick, Milton, Marvell, and the Defense of Old Holiday Pastimes*. Chicago: University of Chicago Press, 1986.

Medine, Peter E. *Thomas Wilson*. Boston: Twayne, 1986.

More, Thomas. *The Complete Works of St. Thomas More*. Vol. 3. Ed. Clarence H. Miller et al. New Haven: Yale University Press, 1984.

———. *A Dialogue of Comfort against Tribulation*. Ed. Frank Manley. New Haven: Yale University Press, 1977.

Morreal, John. *Taking Laughter Seriously*. Albany: State University of New York Press, 1983.

Mulkay, Michael. *On Humor: Its Nature and Place in Modern Society.* New York: Basil Blackwell, 1988.

Murphy, James J. *Rhetoric in the Middle Ages.* Berkeley: University of California Press, 1974.

———, ed. *The Three Medieval Rhetorical Arts.* Berkeley: University of California Press, 1971.

Norrick, Neal R. *Conversational Joking: Humor in Everyday Talk.* Bloomington: Indiana University Press, 1993.

Northbrooke, John. *A Treatise Wherein Dicing, Daunsing, Vaine Playes or Enterludes ... Are Reproved.* 1577. New York: Garland, 1974.

Olson, Glending. *Literature as Recreation in the Later Middle Ages.* Ithaca: Cornell University Press, 1982.

Ong, Walter. *Interfaces of the Word: Studies in the Evolution of Consciousness and Culture.* Ithaca: Cornell University Press, 1977.

———. *The Presence of the Word: Some Prolegomena for Cultural and Religious History.* New Haven: Yale University Press, 1967.

Owst, G. R. *Literature and the Pulpit in Medieval England.* New York: Barnes and Noble, 1961.

———. *Preaching in Medieval England.* Cambridge: Cambridge University Press, 1926.

Palmer, Jerry. *Taking Humour Seriously.* London: Routledge, 1994.

Paster, Gail Kern. *The Body Embarrassed: Drama and the Discipline of Shame in Early Modern England.* Ithaca: Cornell University Press, 1993.

Peacham, Henry. *The Garden of Eloquence.* 1593. Gainesville, Fla.: Scholars' Facsimiles and Reprints, 1954.

Perelman, Chaim, and L. Olbrechts-Tyteca. *The New Rhetoric: A Treatise on Argumentation.* Trans. John Wilkinson and Purcell Weaver. Notre Dame, Ind.: Notre Dame University Press, 1969.

Perkins, William. *Works.* 16 vols. Cambridge, 1609.

———. *The Arte of Prophecying.* London, 1607.

Poulakos, Takis, ed. *Rethinking the History of Rhetoric: Multidisciplinary Essays on the Rhetorical Tradition.* Boulder, Colo.: Westview Press, 1993

Prescott, Anne Lake. "Humanism in the Tudor Jestbook." *Moreana* 24 (Nov. 1987): 5–16.

Purdie, Susan. *Comedy: The Mastery of Discourse.* Toronto: University of Toronto Press, 1993.

Puttenham, George. *The Art of English Poesie.* 1589. Kent, Ohio: Kent State University Press, 1970.

Quintilian. *Institutio oratoria.* 4 vols. Trans. H. E. Butler. Cambridge: Harvard University Press, 1921.

Rainolde, Richard. *The Foundacion of Rhetorike.* 1563. New York: Da Capo Press, 1969.

Raskin, Victor. *Semantic Mechanisms of Humor.* Dordrecht, Netherlands: Reidel, 1985.

Rebhorn, Wayne A. *The Emperor of Men's Minds: Literature and the Renaissance Discourse of Rhetoric.* Ithaca: Cornell University Press, 1994.

————. "Baldesar Castiglione, Thomas Wilson, and the Courtly Body of Renaissance Rhetoric." *Rhetorica* 11 (1993): 241–74.

————. "Outlandish Fears: Defining Decorum in Ancient and Renaissance Rhetoric." Unpublished manuscript.

Rich, Townsend. *Harington and Ariosto: A Study in Elizabethan Verse Translation.* New Haven: Yale University Press, 1940.

Robert of Basevorn. "Form of Preaching." In *Three Medieval Rhetorical Arts,* ed. James J. Murphy, 109–215. Berkeley: University of California Press, 1971.

Robson, Simon. *The Courte of Civill Courtesie.* London, 1582.

The Schoolemaster or Teacher of Table Phylosophie. London, 1583.

Shakespeare, William. *The Complete Works of William Shakespeare.* Ed. David Bevington. 3d ed. London: Scott, Foresman, 1980.

Shuger, Debora K. *Sacred Rhetoric: The Christian Grand Style in the English Renaissance.* Princeton: Princeton University Press, 1988.

Sidney, Sir Philip. *An Apology for Poetry.* Ed. Forrest G. Robinson. Indianapolis: Bobbs-Merrill, 1970.

Stallybrass, Peter, and Allon White. *The Politics and Poetics of Transgression.* Ithaca: Cornell University Press, 1986.

Starkey, Thomas. *A Dialogue between Reginald Pole and Thomas Lupset.* 1536? Ed. Kathleen M. Burton. London: Chatto and Windus, 1948.

Stephens, Walter. *Giants in Those Days: Folklore, Ancient History, and Nationalism.* Lincoln: University of Nebraska Press, 1989.

Stone, Lawrence. *The Crisis of the Aristocracy, 1558–1641.* Oxford: Clarendon Press, 1965.

Tacitus. *Dialogus de oratoribus.* Trans. Sir W. Peterson and M. Winterbottom. Cambridge: Harvard University Press, 1981.

Thomas, Keith. "The Place of Laughter in Tudor and Stuart England." *Times Literary Supplement,* 21 Jan. 1977, 77–81.

Thomas, William J., ed. *Anecdotes and Traditions.* London: Camden Society, 1839.

Turner, Victor. *The Ritual Process: Structure and Anti-Structure.* Ithaca: Cornell University Press, 1977.

Vitanza, Victor, ed. *Writing Histories of Rhetoric.* Carbondale: Southern Illinois University Press, 1994.

Vives, Juan Luis. *The Passions of the Soul: The Third Book of De Anima et Vita.*

Intro. and trans. Carlos G. Norena. Lewiston, N.Y.: Edwin Mellen Press, 1990.

Walser, Ernst. *Die Theorie des Witzes und der Novelle nach Jovianus Pontanus*. Strasbourg, 1908.

Weimann, Robert. *Shakespeare and the Popular Tradition in the Theater: Studies in the Social Dimension of Dramatic Form and Function*. Ed. Robert Schwartz. Baltimore: Johns Hopkins University Press, 1978.

Whigham, Frank. *Ambition and Privilege: The Social Tropes of Elizabethan Courtesy Theory*. Berkeley: University of California Press, 1984.

———. *Seizures of the Will in Early Modern English Drama*. Cambridge: Cambridge University Press, 1996.

Wilson, F. P. "The English Jest-books of the Sixteenth and Early Seventeenth Centuries." In *Shakespearian and Other Studies by F. P. Wilson,* ed. Helen Gardner, 285–324. Oxford: Clarendon Press, 1969.

Wilson, Thomas. *The Art of Rhetoric*. 1560. Ed. Peter E. Medine. University Park: Pennsylvania State University Press, 1994.

———. *The Rule of Reason*. 1553. Ed. Richard S. Sprague. Northridge, Calif.: San Fernando State College, 1972.

Winterbottom, Michael. "Quintilian and the *Vir Bonus.*" *Journal of Roman Studies* 54 (1964): 90–97.

Woodbridge, Linda, and Edward Berry. Introduction to *True Rites and Maimed Rites: Ritual and Anti-Ritual in Shakespeare and His Age,* 1–43. Urbana: University of Illinois Press, 1992.

Wright, Frederick Warren. *Cicero and the Theater*. Special issue, *Smith College Classical Studies* 11 (March 1931).

Wright, Leonard. *A Patterne for Pastors*. In *A Summons for Sleepers . . . Herunto Is Annexed a Patterne for Pastors*. London, 1596.

Wright, Louis B., ed. *Advice to a Son: Precepts of Lord Burghley, Sir Walter Raleigh, and Francis Osborne*. New York: Cornell University Press, 1962.

Wrightson, Keith. *English Society, 1580–1680*. New Brunswick, N.J.: Rutgers University Press, 1982.

Zall, P. M. *A Hundred Merry Tales and Other English Jestbooks of the Fifteenth and Sixteenth Centuries*. Lincoln: University of Nebraska Press, 1963.

———. *A Nest of Ninnies and Other English Jestbooks of the Seventeenth Century*. Lincoln: University of Nebraska Press, 1970.

Index